THE FUTURE
OF THE
DEMOCRATIC
REVOLUTION

THE FUTURE
OF THE
DEMOCRATIC
REVOLUTION

Toward a More
Prophetic Politics

Neal Riemer

PRAEGER SPECIAL STUDIES • PRAEGER SCIENTIFIC

New York • Philadelphia • Eastbourne, UK
Toronto • Hong Kong • Tokyo • Sydney

Library of Congress Cataloging in Publication Data

Riemer, Neal, 1922-
  The future of the democratic revolution.

  Bibliography: p.
  Includes index.
  1. Democracy. 2. Political science. I. Title.
JC423.R488 1984   321.8   84-8254
ISBN 0-03-071997-6 (alk. paper)

Portions of Chapter 8 and 9 have been adapted from POLITICAL SCIENCE: An Introduction to Politics by Neal Riemer, copyright © 1983 by Harcourt Brace Jovanovich, Inc. Reprinted by permission of the publisher.

Published in 1984 by Praeger Publishers
CBS Educational and Professional Publishing
a Division of CBS Inc.
521 Fifth Avenue, New York, NY 10175 USA

© 1984 by Praeger Publishers

456789 052 987654321

Printed in the United States of America

on acid-free paper

To
My grandfather, Raphael Riemer
and
My future grandchildren

Acknowledgments

It is a pleasure to acknowledge those who helped me in the writing of this book. J. Mitchell Morse, Thomas C. Oden, Vukan Kuic, Mark H. Roelofs, and Clark E. Cochran read earlier drafts of the manuscript. Robert M. Rodes and Douglas W. Simon read, and gave me the benefit of their criticism of, Chapter 2. The National Endowment for the Humanities provided financial help one summer, which enabled me to do a penultimate draft. A number of students in my graduate seminars in political theory at Drew University worked through earlier drafts of the manuscript and offered helpful criticisms: Donald Chatfield, Daniel Heimbach, David Hinchen, James Annarelli, and Jeffrey Kolbo. I also want to express my appreciation to several editors at Praeger who have facilitated the publication of this book: Dorothy A. Breitbart, editor, who understood so well what I was trying to do; Patty G. Sullivan, project editor, who moved the manuscript along so intelligently and so expeditiously; and Susan Badger, copy editor, whose admirable skills helped to polish my prose and to achieve for this book a greater measure of stylistic consistency. Again, I am indebted to the reference staff of Drew University's library—and especially to Mary Davies Cole, Ruth M. Freedman, and William S. Brockman—for responding so kindly and efficiently to my many queries on bibliographic matters.

I especially want to acknowledge the constant encouragement and critical acumen of my wife Ruby, who had faith in my exploration of the challenge of prophetic politics and helped to sustain my own convictions about the value of this intellectual enterprise.

Contents

I : Introduction

1 : Search for a Guiding Model

INTRODUCTION

Is it really possible for humankind to move up to a new level of politics—one more compatible with civilized life, healthy growth, and creative fulfillment? What name shall we give to this pattern of politics? And what will be its character? Can those dedicated to this pattern successfully come to grips with rival patterns of contemporary politics by creatively avoiding their dangerous weaknesses while constructively incorporating their unquestionable strengths? Can this pattern of politics, if desirable in theory, be translated into practice without loss of its distinguishing characteristics? Must we adopt this pattern if we are to safeguard the future of the democratic revolution?

THE REVIVAL OF DEMOCRATIC THEORY AND BEYOND

These questions are the ambitious questions I propose to investigate in this book-length exploratory essay. To raise them, I know, will seem foolhardy to skeptics, futile to cynics, and naive to "realists." Moreover, to answer them will seem a bit mad to most contemporary political scientists. In this book I carry my answers beyond the position I advanced in an earlier study, *The*

1

Revival of Democratic Theory (1962)[1]—a position reinforced by my exploration in *James Madison* (1968)[2] of America's most creative political theorist; and strengthened, too, by my analysis in the *The Democratic Experiment* (1967)[3] of the brilliant generation of 1776–87. In *Revival* I first attempted to respond to key objections. I did so (1) by speaking to the pervasive fear of the sin of Procrustes—the dread of inhuman action based on arbitrary blueprints for people and society; (2) by addressing myself to the intimidation of Big Brother Science—the inhibiting consequences of the belief that only a scientific emphasis on precision of meaning, rigorous scientific theory, and empirical testing and verification will lead to a truer and more fruitful political science; (3) by seeking to analyze and respond to the debilitating effects of the unhappy democratic consciousness—our loss of faith in our humane and rational powers to shape a better world for all people; and, finally, (4) by facing up to the sterile atmosphere in the cloistered halls of academe—the failure of political scientists, particularly, to link the ethical, empirical, and prudential concerns of their discipline in fruitful synthesis in the real world of politics. This book, which in one sense is a sequel to *Revival,* rests upon my earlier responses and is strongly reinforced by my appreciation of the creative achievements of James Madison, Thomas Jefferson, and others of that remarkable generation of 1776–87 who engaged in the democratic experiment.

We must—I still maintain—clearly recognize that the sin of Procrustes is not the inevitable concomitant of the messianic tradition of Western political thought. A superior political theory may preserve the tension between what ought to be and what is without succumbing to totalitarianism. The development of a political theory to guide us does not mean that we must employ Procrustean techniques to make political reality fit an ideological bed. Respect for vital ingredients in the prescriptive tradition is not incompatible with a creative theoretical response often called for if men and women are to understand, change, and manage their evolving world.

Second, we must—I also still affirm—appreciate that Big Brother Science, however helpful he may be within his legitimate sphere, should not restrict us to his methods alone in the exploration of the truths—ethical and prudential as well as empirical—of politics. We must be particularly careful not to be so overawed by the demands of precise definition, grand scientific theory, and empirical verification as to abandon the search for vital truths in politics. These are the vital truths that advance our understanding of political life (in the *future,* as well as in the past and in the present); they enable us in practical politics to fulfill our purposes, balance conflicting equities, and civilize the enduring struggle for power more sanely. At our peril we neglect the search for life-sustaining ethical truths (old or new): ethical truths that have been subjected to the test of humane reason over time and that have been tested, too, in prescriptive institutions through the ages; and ethical truths that have not yet been fully articulated, let alone tested, in the laboratory of human evolution. At our peril we neglect the search for illuminating empirical truths that may be rationally perceived beyond the shifting patterns of contemporary political life or that may be today only unseen political potentialities or ill-understood intimations of the dominant future. At our peril, too, we neglect the *futuristic* search for feasible courses of action that are good because they are compatible with our thought-out values in a rapidly changing world, true because they are consonant with currently significant political actualities and *possibilities,* and prudent because they are better designed than other alternatives to advance our ends in the light of political reality—as it is and *can be in the future.*

Third, I still hold that all of life is a risk that demands a reasoned faith as a condition of existence, communication, sanity, and order. This is both an artistic and a scientific commandment. The nerve that manifests itself in the confidence we have in painting or experimenting is in fact not greatly different in character from the nerve we have in talking, working, and procreating. Such nerve is similar to the nerve that we need to affirm the possibility of a more rational, ethical order in the universe. We are bedeviled by the absurdity of our human condition only if we take a narrow and naive view of transcendent meaning.

Finally, there is growing evidence in academia—and in society—to underscore the existence of a prophetic challenge to the priestly mode. This challenge requires political scientists to integrate their ethical, empirical, and prudential concerns in a bold and fruitful way. We may still need Establishment priests, but we cannot do without societal prophets.

PROPHETIC POLITICS AND ITS REALISTIC AND IDEALISTIC COMPETITORS

But if this book rests upon my earlier responses, it carries the argument beyond *Revival*. It does so by looking beyond the liberal-democratic commitment toward the possibility of a more *prophetic politics*. Such a prophetic politics I shall try to distinguish (1) from *Machiavellian politics,* the "lion and fox" politics of the nation-state, the dominant politics of the dominant political community in today's world; (2) from *utopian politics,* the harmonious politics of salvation, a politics whose history runs from Plato to Marx and into the modern world; and (3) from *liberal democratic politics,* the conservative politics of pluralistic balance, a politics illustrated, for example, by the United States. I shall argue that prophetic politics is a superior democratic and constitutional politics because it endeavors to move beyond nationalistic idolatry, beyond utopian hubris, and beyond the complacency of the liberal democratic capitalist order.

In focusing on these four patterns, I do not mean to suggest that they exhaust all of the possibilities. Clearly, one could identify and analyze other patterns of politics—say Third World patterns, or democratic socialist patterns, or a variety of authoritarian patterns. My logical categories are not perfect or all-inclusive. Nonetheless, they permit me to juxtapose dominant and contending patterns—"realistic," "idealistic," and "idealistic-realistic"—and thus to illuminate the strengths and weaknesses of realistic (Machiavellian) politics, of idealistic (utopian) politics, and of the idealistic-realistic compromise in ordinary constitutional (liberal democratic) politics.

In this book, then, I will be exploring four patterns of politics. These patterns, I repeat, are not mutually exclusive. They may in fact overlap in certain respects. Yet, I believe, they constitute distinctive approaches to politics. Machiavellian politics, the realistic politics of the nation-state, is without question the *dominant* mode of politics in the modern world in all countries because, as we have noted, the nation-state is the dominant type of political community in the modern world. This pattern of politics is premised on the need for political leaders in the political community to protect the political community's vital interests (as the leaders perceive such vital interests) in the often beastly and deceitful struggle for power that politics often is. At the authoritarian extremes in the twentieth century, Stalin's Soviet Union and Hitler's Germany illustrate this pattern. Yet almost all—nay, all—countries illustrate this pattern to a greater or lesser degree, most notably in foreign affairs but also, although less prominently, in domestic affairs. To shrink from this unpleasant fact is to deny the real world of politics.

Utopian politics is a major adverse criticism of all existing patterns of politics, including the politics of the nation-state. A prominent variety of idealistic politics, it is characterized by a vision of overcoming the struggle for power, a vision that presupposes the ultimate possibility of a harmonious community marked by voluntary cooperation. Ironically, those addicted to utopian politics may, in attempting to achieve or maintain their theoretical objectives, succumb to the lion and fox politics they denounce when they are weak and in opposition. Or they may prove unable to govern if they retain their idealistic virginity.

Liberal democratic politics is the name I have given to the politics of the liberal democratic capitalist state. This pattern seeks to blend realism and idealism into a happy and judicious mixture. It is characterized by a commitment to constitutionalism and to democratic, pluralistic balance; and, historically, it is associated with a commitment to the value and sanctity of capitalist economic enterprise.

Prophetic politics constitutes a superior radical democratic and constitutional pattern of politics, one that seeks to get beyond nationalistic idolatry, utopian hubris, and liberal democratic complacency. Prophetic politics is committed to the fulfillment of prophetic values for all people, to fearless criticism of all political orders, to constitutional breakthroughs to a more prophetic order, and to continuous prophetic scrutiny and futuristic projection.

All nation-states illustrate Machiavellian politics to a large degree. No political community currently illustrates utopian politics, although Communist states—for example, the Soviet Union and China—are theoretically guided by an ultimately utopian Marxist theory, the theory of the classless Communist society. As I have indicated, the United States serves as an example of liberal democratic politics, although most nations of Western Europe, Japan, Australia, and some others would also be considered representative of this pattern. Liberal democratic politics dominates the First World, including those nations with strong, and sometimes governing, democratic socialist parties. No political community today illustrates prophetic politics. Although in some respects prophetic politics seems to resemble liberal democratic politics and perhaps even utopian politics, it is presented as a critical alternative to them, as well as to Machiavellian politics, and to all other existing patterns of politics. And even though prophetic politics may never be fully operational in any political system, there is value in pointing out how it may incorporate the strengths and avoid the weaknesses of the other models. In this fashion it may serve as a model to help us criticize existing, and competing, patterns. Beyond that, it may serve as a democratic model that we may seek to approximate in the twenty-first century.

THE MEANING AND CHALLENGES OF POLITICS

What, more explicitly, is my understanding of politics? Politics is an activity within or between political communities (1) whereby public values are articulated, debated, and prescribed; (2) whereby diverse political actors (individuals, interest groups, local or regional governments, nations) cooperate and struggle for power in order to satisfy their vital needs, protect their fundamental interests, and advance their perceived desires; and (3) whereby public policy judgments are made and authoritative actions on crucial public problems are taken. Every pattern of politics, therefore, illuminates ethical values, political phenomena, and public policy judgments. In my exploration of the four patterns of politics under study, I will, consequently, focus sharply on salient values, scientific understanding of political phenomena, and prudential judgment.

The theoretical and practical difficulties that confront those who would formulate prophetic politics are formidable, but they do not foredoom the attempt. Such a formulation involves the attempt to incorporate the strengths and to avoid the weaknesses of competing patterns. The weaknesses I have already outlined: nation-state idolatry, utopian hubris, and liberal democratic complacency. The strengths of the other patterns include: the protection of legitimate vital interests and a sagacious appreciation of the realities of the struggle for power; an openness to noble dreams and to the power of new possibilities; and sound rules for balancing liberty and authority and for achieving sensible accommodations among contending economic, social, and political interests.

I undertake this study because I am skeptical about the wise guidance currently provided by dominant patterns of politics or by utopian criticisms of status quo politics. I am worried about the future of the democratic revolution, that revolution concerned with universal fulfillment of popular rule and basic rights, that revolution dedicated to civilized life, healthy growth, and creative fulfillment for all peoples. The realistic, nationalistic, lion and fox perspective of Machiavellian politics is too narrow, too limited, too parochial—and, often, too brutal and deceitful—to permit us to deal with the problems of global war, systematic violations of human rights, worldwide economic depression and poverty, and ecological imbalance. The idealistic perspective of utopian politics, although broad enough, is premised (so I believe) on a false notion of earthly harmony and salvation, which, ironically, can lead to an intensification of battle lines between the Children of Light and the Children of Darkness, to costly authoritarian or totalitarian sacrifices to obtain or maintain utopia, or which, paradoxically, can lead to frustration, despair, and disengagement in politics. The realistic-idealistic perspective that is liberal democratic politics (in a host of ways an unquestionable advance in sensible and humane goverance that we cannot afford to jeopardize) is, alas, one that is not fully aware of the urgency—in developed capitalist countries or in poor developing countries or in international politics—of serious threats to civilized life, healthy growth, and creative fulfilment. And these are the threats that clearly jeopardize the future of the democratic revolution.

It is, of course, far easier to criticize Machiavellian, utopian, and liberal democratic politics than to make, and defend, the case for prophetic politics. The difficulty of that defense is underscored by the hard questions about prophetic politics that one must face. What conception of prophetic values can command the support of the diverse forces of the modern world—religious, philosophical, political, economic, social, scientific? How shall fearless criticism, in the prophetic tradition, go forward? Can a more prophetic politics be made constitutionally operational without itself becoming idolatrous, perfectionist, or complacent? Is a prophetic variety of futuristic scrutiny and projection really possible and genuinely fruitful? And, is it the paradoxical case that prophetic politics is ethically necessary but practically impossible, or, if possible, highly improbable?

To these difficult questions we will return in Chapter 10 after we have, in Chapters 2 through 9, set forth in more detail the cardinal characteristics of the four patterns under review. We shall start with Machiavellian politics.

II : Competing Patterns of Politics

2 : Machiavellian Politics: The "Lion and Fox" Politics of the Nation-State

INTRODUCTION

By *Machiavellian politics* I mean that pattern of politics whose *raison d'être* is the protection, by force and craft if necessary, of the vital interests of the nation-state in the (frequently) bestial struggle for power characteristic of all political communities. In giving the name *Machiavellian politics* to this pattern of politics, I am, of course, exercising artistic as well as scientific judgment. In this instance the particular aspects of nation-state politics that I have in mind have been described in the writings of Niccolo Machiavelli, who was himself attempting to cut through the complexity and diversity of political history to get at what he thought was the truth of politics.[1] Machiavelli was articulating a political philosophy that had, and still has, a grip on the rulers, or would-be rulers, of nation-states. It is this theory and practice that is my concern and not the historic Machiavelli and all of his personal political preferences. Hence, I will not here be concerned with whether Machiavelli, personally, was a virtuous republican patriot, a disinterested political scientist, or a cynical advocate of immoral politics. Moreover, although Machiavellian thought can help greatly in articulating this pattern of politics, we remain free to ask about the salient, fundamental, distinguishing characteristics of those political communities that, and those political leaders and political actors who, place the highest priority

11

on the supreme need to protect the vital interests of the nation-state. I should also emphasize that although Machiavellian politics is most prominent in international politics (that is, in relations between nation-states), it is by no means absent from domestic politics, either in civil wars or in normal, domestic politics. I grant that domestic national politics, particularly in liberal democratic countries, is usually characterized by a constitutional consensus on the decent rules of the political game—a consensus that normally rules out brutal force and treacherous deceit and that denies to political actors the "sovereign" power to engage in war to protect their vital interests. Yet we would be naive, indeed, about the morality of domestic national politics if we ignored the frequent reality of "dirty politics," of varied uses of force and craft by political actors to achieve success (the accomplishment of their "vital interests"). And most often, individual political actors will seek to cloak the protection of their selfish vital interests in the disarming garb of the national interest—the common good.[2]

The nation-state reflects certain values, illustrates certain behavior, and influences certain judgments by national leaders. Such values, behavior, and judgments are crucially related to the success of the nation-state. Because Machiavelli was among the first to articulate candidly this pattern of politics, I have chosen to call this pattern *Machiavellian politics*. To choose this term is not to say that ingredients of this pattern were not perceived before Machiavelli and would not be explored afterward. Obviously, Machiavelli was writing before the modern sovereign nation-state as we know it today had emerged. Yet, clearly, Machiavelli caught something of those political modes—especially *raison d'etat*, national patriotism, and "justice" as the interest of the stronger—that were to become the operational principles of the modern sovereign nation-state. So it is that, with Machiavelli's help, we can begin to understand better the lion and fox politics of the nation-state.

THE DISTINGUISHING CHARACTERISTICS OF MACHIAVELLIAN POLITICS
The Success of the Nation-State

Those committed to Machiavellian politics are committed to the independence, safety, security, freedom, order, dominion, prosperity, glory, and virtue—in a word, to the *success*—of the nation-state. These are its goals, its values, its vision. Above all, the vital interests of the nation-state must be protected.[3] To the protagonists of Machiavellian politics—as to Machiavelli himself—"country was"—and is—"a divinity, superior even to morality and law. . . . 'Reason of state' and 'public welfare' were the common banners by which this right of the fatherland was considered superior to all other rights. God had descended from heaven to earth and called himself the 'patria,' and he was no less terrible than before. The will and interest of fatherland were the 'supreme law.'"[4]

Those dedicated to Machiavellian politics, it would seem, are not dedicated to a prophetic paradigm (to peace, justice, freedom, love, prosperity for all humankind)—and not (necessarily) even to the domestic common good as seen by others than the existent rulers of the state. Such higher goals, it would appear, have been ruled out as indefensible, unrealistic, naive. Nationalism is and must remain ascendant. The values of nationalism ought to prevail—at all times. And most clearly and forcefully when a nation-state is on the make, and particularly in foreign policy, and especially during war. These values often translate into the power and prosperity of the dominant forces in charge of the nation-state.

Politics as a Struggle for Power

Those committed to Machiavellian politics see politics as a struggle for power, with power (primarily, but not exclusively, physical force) to be used to protect the vital interests of the state from internal and external enemies. Although there are—as we noted earlier—some crucial difference between domestic (constitutional) politics and international politics, it is still the case that all political actors (regardless of whether they are individuals or groups or political communities) seek to protect their own vital self-interest, seek to ensure their own success in the struggle for power. When their own vital interests are deeply engaged, they are usually not significantly moved by conflicting religious, philosophical, or humanitarian considerations. Conflicts —including civil war and international war—are inevitable because of incompatible interests. To protect their own interests in these conflicts, rulers (or would-be rulers) of nation-states must be able to muster and employ their own power, especially military power. Machiavelli, as usual, put the matter candidly and bluntly: "Only those defences are good, certain and durable which depend on yourself alone and your own ability." And: "A Prince should therefore have no other aim or thought nor take up any other things for his study, but war and its organization and discipline."[5] Force protects. Reliable force protects best.

Politics is not always a human activity, in the best sense of the word *humanity*; it is, in fact, often a beastly activity. In politics men do not usually behave in accord with a higher religious, philosophical, or humanitarian standard. They do often behave like lions and foxes. Consequently, those who confuse ideal and reality—what ought to be and what is—will lose out. And those who are not prepared to play the often beastly game of politics— to be both lions and foxes—will not be able to protect their vital interests. What ethical and religious purists see as the beastly, pathological, seamy, emergency side of politics is in fact the way things normally, or usually, are. To ignore such political behavior is disastrous. Brute strength and cunning duplicity are important facts of political life in the struggle for the protection of vital interests.

Those who practice Machiavellian politics accept it as fact that political actors have lowered their sights, have settled for less, are closed to higher standards. Political actors see political life realistically. They appreciate that "how we live is so far removed from how we ought to live, that he who abandons what is done for what ought to be done, will rather learn to bring about his own ruin than his preservation."[6]

Playing the Game of Lion and Fox

When we turn to the "prudential" characteristics of Machiavellian politics, we discover a great deal in the writings of

Machiavelli that is relevant and illustrative. These "prudential" characteristics—abundant in Machiavelli's writings—also illuminate subsidiary (but important) ethical and empirical characteristics. Here, let me note, I use *prudent* (that is, "practically wise") in a neutral sense. The authentic classical meaning of *prudence* might bar much of what follows as clever or shrewd but not genuinely prudent—that is, not practically wise in the sense of being both feasible *and* in accord with defensible higher ends.[7]

Practitioners of Machiavellian politics can protect the vital interests of the nation-state only if they will not be dissuaded by considerations of religion or morality or philosophy or humanitarianism when such considerations interfere with success in protecting the nation-state's vital interests. This means that they must not confuse (as we have already noted) what ought to be with what is. This is not only a scientific mistake; it is also a disastrous mistake of statesmanship. The statesman, or others who aspire to power in the state, must be prepared to engage, as a lion and a fox, in the beastly game that real politics often is. The nation-state cannot survive or prosper if statesmen know or play only the higher human game of religion, law, and morality. Nor can those who aspire to rule be successful if they ignore these insights. To engage successfully in the struggle for power, serious political actors must play the game of lion and fox.

> A prince [Machiavelli wrote] being thus obliged to know well how to act as a beast must imitate the fox and the lion, for the lion cannot protect himself from traps, and the fox cannot defend himself from wolves. One must therefore be a fox to recognize traps, and a lion to frighten wolves.[8]

Political actors will, of course, be justified in playing the game of lion and fox because "in the actions of men, and especially of princes . . . the end justifies [or, better, excuses] the means."[9]

> For [as Machiavelli wrote] where the very safety of the
> country depends upon the resolution to be taken, no
> considerations of justice or injustice, humanity or
> cruelty, nor of glory or of shame, should be allowed to
> prevail. But putting all other considerations aside, the
> only question should be, what course will save the life
> and liberty of the country?[10]

Consequently, when the occasion demands it (and the safety
of the nation-state will always demand it), force and craft must
be used boldly and shrewdly. On such occasions "good faith"
and "integrity" can be sacrificed. It is only necessary for the
Prince (as potential or actual ruler) "to be able to disguise this
character well, and to be a great feigner and dissembler."[11]

"Thus it is well to seem merciful, faithful, humane, sincere,
religious, and also to be so; but you must have the mind so
disposed that when it is needful to be otherwise you may be able
to change to the opposite qualities."[12] Hence, "in order to maintain the state," a Prince may be obliged "to act against faith,
against charity, against humanity, and against religion."[13] If he
is shrewd, the Prince will act

> to secure himself against enemies, to gain friends, to
> conquer by force or fraud, to make himself beloved and
> feared by the people [and] followed and reverenced
> by . . . [his] soldiers.[14]

And, in all his actions he must display Renaissance *virtu*—
that is, resolve and energy. With such resolve and energy he
must be prepared "to destroy those who can injure him."[15] He
must "maintain the friendship of kings and princes in such a way
that they are glad to benefit him and fear to injure him.[16] He
must win and keep widespread popular support. He must rely
upon a loyal citizen army. He must use muscle power and brain-
power, severity and kindness, with discrimination, with a shrewd
regard for his ends and for his power. Presumably, this "prudential" counsel holds for all serious political actors who seek to
triumph in the struggle for power.

THE STRENGTHS OF MACHIAVELLIAN POLITICS

The strengths of Machiavellian politics are considerable. They underscore its appeal and its staying power. It *is* ethically defensible to focus on protecting genuinely vital interests. It *is* accurate to see, as an important part of politics, the struggle for power. It *is* wise to avoid the confusion of what ought to be and what is in statesmanship.[17]

Certainly, a people gathered together in a political community are normally entitled to independence, safety, security, freedom, order, prosperity. These values are not necessarily in conflict with prophetic politics. Even dominion, understood as self-government, or as sovereignty over one's own legitimate interests, is defensible. Similarly, even glory in the state's excellence (understood as its integrity, honor, freedom, creative achievements, and so on) is acceptable as a desired quality. And virtue, understood as the energy to pursue one's legitimate vital interests, is to be commended.

Clearly understanding the actual behavior of political actors and political communities cannot, itself, be other than a strength. And politics is in fact, if not exclusively, a struggle for power among contending political actors who do, in reality, use force and craft, who do employ foul means (as well as fair means), who do seek to maximize their strength. Conflict, including war, is a reality of politics; and being equipped to deal successfully with conflicts, including war, is a condition of success in politics. Appeals beyond the nation-state (to God, natural law, the conscience of humanity, a nobler global morality, international law, philosophic reason) are not usually successful. Such appeals are not usually successful when the nation-state's vital interests are engaged and in conflict with the will of God (if it can be agreed upon); or with natural law (if we can identify it); or with the conscience of humanity (too often conveniently ignored or sacrificed by the mighty); or with a nobler global morality (deemed by the cynical an illusion of the righteous or a ploy to protect the weak against the powerful); or with philosophic reason (a quality notoriously absent from rulers of nation-states). These unhappy considerations are among the facts of life in politics up to the present. The political scientist cannot confidently predict that the future will be different. If those who rule, or aspire to rule, must face the truth of political behavior, however distasteful it may be, then the portrayal of the actual behavior of political actors and political communities can only be a strength.

The creative use by statesmen of power to protect the vital interests of the state links ethics, science, and public policy. And such creativity is the essence of the genuinely prudential response in politics. To avoid the confusion of what ought to be and what is constitutes the premise of all creative statesmanship and mandates the adoption of the strategy of political realism. Statesmen are not required to accept the edicts of fate passively. Virtuous, knowledgeable, and prudent political actors—political actors of ambition, wit, energy, resolve—can to some extent shape their own destiny and that of nation-states. Leading political actors are artists who can mold, within limits, the nation-state and its policies.

A knowledge of the Children of Darkness is essential to the Children of Light. Frederick the Great perceived this even as he attacked Machiavelli:

> If one is to ascribe any probity or good sense to the entangled thoughts of Machiavelli it can perhaps be done only in the following manner. The world is like a game of cards in which some of the players are honest but others are cheaters. Therefore, a prince who wants to play in such a game, if he does not wish to be taken, ought to be well acquainted with all of the tricks of the game, not in order to practice them himself, but to avoid becoming a dupe of the others.[18]

It is, then, a great source of strength to have a clearheaded recognition of the vital interests of a political community that need to be protected, of the real character of the struggle for power that may jeopardize those interests, and of the bold and yet prudent policies that must be employed in the real world of politics to protect those vital interests.

THE WEAKNESSES OF MACHIAVELLIAN POLITICS

If there are elements of strength in Machiavellian politics, the weaknesses of this pattern are also apparent. They are the weaknesses in the ethical, empirical, and prudential outlook of that pattern that we have subtitled "the politics of the nation-state."

Protecting the vital interests of the nation-state (instead, let us say, of the vital interests of humankind in a prophetic order) can become the idolatrous worship of the nation-state and its sometimes indefensible interests. We may be tempted to lower our political vision and accept what is (or *seems to be*) realistic or feasible—at too high a cost to our common humanity and to prophetic standards.

Moreover, preoccupation with the struggle for power as an empirical reality may lead us away from the investigation (or reality) of more civilizing efforts to work out more humane patterns of accommodation among conflicting interests. Such more humane patterns would be more in tune with religious and moral commandments, with philosophical imperatives, and with the dictates of international law.[19]

Finally, the lion and fox strategy of Machiavellian politics too easily leads to the brutal use of force or to the worst excesses of craft in the interest of success for the nation-state in its often beastly battles in the name of independence, freedom, safety, security, prosperity, dominion, prestige, glory, and virtue.[20]

These weaknesses become most visible in the thought and action of narrow-minded nationalists who do not even possess an appreciation of the true, vital, and legitimate interests of the nation-state; who lack a more complex understanding of the ambiguities of power; who misread shrewdness for prudence; who are unable to distinguish between a rational and an irrational means to achieve a good end; who confuse good intentions and good deeds; and who know not the virtues of magnanimity or compassion.

A host of disturbing questions emerge here. What, indeed, are the legitimately vital interests of the nation-state? Who determines them? Are clashes (including war) inevitable because of differences in viewpoint on such interests? Are conflicts inescapable in international politics because each nation-state has the sovereign power to determine its own interest? In one nation-state, are all vital interests compatible with these same vital interests in another nation-state? Is one nation's independence, freedom, and so on, another nation's disaster? Comparable questions could be set forth about conflicting conceptions of vital interests in domestic politics.

Independence pushed too far makes larger, more efficient political communities impossible and can nourish sovereign pride and political madness. Freedom, safety, security, dominion, and prosperity for a strong country or clique may mean oppression, wipeout, fear, domination, and exploitation for a weaker neighbor or less powerful inhabitants. Prestige and glory for one nation-state may be acquired at the price of humiliation and defeat of another. And always, civil war or international war—as the last resorts, respectively, of domestic rebels or of the sovereign nation-state—threatens to disrupt civilization.

The brutal struggle for power, the demonic will to dominate—these are facts of political life. But they are not the only facts of life. As Reinhold Niebuhr (himself a political realist) emphasized in *The Children of Light and the Children of Darkness* (1944), there is a will to live truly as well as a will to dominate in politics.[21] Moreover, civilized disagreements—approached in the spirit of our better political intuitions—can lead to sensible and humane accommodations based on a more enlightened consensus than that emanating from narrow self-interest. What is more, the broadening of our conception of self-interest is demonstrable. There are possibilities of breakthroughs in the future (reinforced by breakthroughs in the past) that can elevate and civilize the struggle for power. Indeed, the very protection of the vital interests of the nation-state may require a perspective wider, and a realism truer, than that of the nation-state.

Clearly, one can raise disturbing questions about the survival value of the beastly strategy of lion and fox. Brutal force and cunning duplicity may be counterproductive. Ironically, by lowering their sights, the practitioners of Machiavellian politics run the risk of jeopardizing the very vital interests they seek to safeguard. This adverse criticism leads us to investigate a newer realism as being more in accord with civilized survival in the modern age.

Those committed to Machiavellian politics as the "truth" of politics are too willing to settle for less, namely, the beastly politics of lion and fox. The consequence is a dangerous tendency to idolatry—the worship of the power and glory of the political community—which in today's world means the worship of the nation-state. The danger is a closure to higher standards and to the creative political breakthroughs that devotion to higher standards makes possible. The danger is a fascination with the world of lion and fox, the world of brute strength and cunning duplicity, a world with nations possessed of weapons of universal destruction, a world in which the safety of the state justifies or excuses any means used, a world in which it becomes so easy to sacrifice respect for life and law on the altar of national success.

CONCLUSION

Can one enjoy the strengths of Machiavellian politics without suffering its weaknesses? Or are the weaknesses of Machiavellian politics so interwoven with its strengths that the latter cannot be preserved without preserving the former? And is the central flaw of Machiavellian politics its tendency to worship power, and particularly the power of the nation-state? These questions require us to reassess the ethical, empirical, and prudential components of Machiavellian politics.

Ethically, we must ask some key questions about the vital interests of the nation-state and about the means used to safeguard these interests. What is to be safeguarded? The life, growth, and fulfillment of the nation-state or of the people in the political community? And, assuming for the sake of argument that it is the latter, should nation-states (and specifically their rulers) be the sovereign judges of such life, growth, and fulfillment? And how are the legitimate ends of politics to be advanced? Through the exercise of Machiavellian power or through the constitutional pursuit of the common good? Here Jacques Maritain's criticism is very much to the point. Maritain argues that the practitioners of Machiavellian politics have a wrongheaded view of the ends and means of politics. Maritain holds that the end is *not* the protection of the vital interests of the nation-state through the conquest and maintenance of power; rather, that it *is* the common good, which may include most of these interests *but* excludes their protection at the price of injustice to others.[22]

The argument above underscores the contention that the vision of Machiavellian politics is too limited. Because its vision is too parochial, this pattern of politics is unable to protect legitimate national interests in a larger political world of competing national interests except at great cost. This difficulty seems to be built into the very character of Machiavellian politics because this pattern requires national success—not justice or the common good—to be the standard to be employed in the interpretation, and national power to be the weapon to be used in the protection, of legitimate self-interest.

So it is that the limited vision of Machiavellian politics affects its empirical understanding of politics. Those who practice Machiavellian politics may fail to protect the vital interests of the nation-state. As Maritain emphasizes, short-run success may be noted, but this is the "illusion of *immediate success*." Maritain concedes that in "order to gain battles or immediate political successes, it is not necessary to be just"; indeed, "it may occasionally be more advantageous to be unjust." But, "as a rule Machiavellianism and political injustice, if they gain immediate success, lead states and nations to misfortune or catastrophe in the long run."[23]

A central empirical difficulty—and one intimately related to empirical success— is the frequent failure of many practitioners of Machiavellian politics to appreciate that there is more *to* power (certainly more than raw physical power) in politics than they see and that there is more *than* power in politics. G. P. Gooch correctly observes that the "will to power is not the sole key to human nature."[24] The best practitioners of Machiavellian politics, of course, recognize craft as well as force and recognize political, economic, psychological, scientific, even religious, power as well as sheer military and physical power. But it is still the case that most practitioners of Machiavellian politics are almost obsessed with the proposition that the unarmed prophet fares ill. It is not accidental that the art of war occupies a central, a predominant, place in the theory and practice of Machiavellian politics.[25]

The empirical understanding of Machiavellian politics can thus be severely critizised on two scores. First, the lessons of history as they inform us of the central role of power in the behavior of nation-states are incomplete and can lead to disaster. These lessons are faulted because, as Gooch has pointed out, the "professed realist" sees only "a limited portion of the vast field of experience."[26] And the lack of a more catholic vision is disastrous. Second, those committed to Machiavellian politics (even if they are right about past and present) shut themselves off from the future by ignoring the possibility of political-reality-in-the-making. They shut themselves off from new uses of power and from organizations of the political community different than those of the nation-state. By closing themselves off from significantly new political experiments—from creative breakthroughs in politics—they close themselves off from future empirical possibilities.[27]

The faulty ethical vision and empirical understanding of Machiavellian politics must therefore inevitably cloud sound judgment in politics—the true prudential sense of judgment. What Gooch says of the maxims of *The Prince* holds true, generally, for most practitioners of Machiavellian politics: "The application of the maxims of *The Prince* may achieve a temporary triumph, but they provide no foundation for the enduring happiness, prosperity, or security of the state.''[28] Here one calls into question the feasibility of Machiavellian politics—one of its supposed strong points—its alleged practicality. As our earlier doubts about the ethical and empirical outlook of Machiavellian politics should have made clear, these doubts corrode genuinely prudent (as opposed to shrewd or clever) judgment in politics.

Ethical and empirical weaknesses combine to render difficult, if not impossible, that very good and strong government designed to protect the vital interests of the nation-state. The practitioners of Machiavellian politics are open to Pasquale Villari's thrust about Machiavelli:

> He never puts himself the question: whether the excessive immorality of the means employed, may not, even while momentarily grasping the desired end, sap the very foundations of society, and render in the long run all good and strong government an impossibility.[29]

Several things are needed to enable us to rescue the strengths of Machiavellian politics, strengths that include a concern for the legitimate interests of political actors and political communities, a keen appreciation of the struggle for power, and (at best) a prudential effort to relate means and ends. What is needed is a more generous (a less parochial) goal than the vital interests of the nation-state. We need a broader sense of power and of becoming. This would include the power of such ideas as justice and the common good and would involve new possibilities in politics. We need, too, the prudential boldness to undertake new experiments in the very interest of such vital interests as life, growth, and fulfillment for all people. Within the framework of such a more encompassing outlook the strengths of Machiavellian politics may find a place.

Machiavellian politics is neither amoral nor totally immoral. Rather, its morality is limited. In one respect it is (surprisingly) utopian—in holding as a fulfillable goal the protection of the vital interests of the nation-states in a world of nation-states that (and by the admission of its own devotees) is imperfect.

Machiavellian politics is also limited as a science. In adopting a supposedly realistic attitude toward power and the use of power to protect the nation-state's vital interests, in refusing to confuse ought and is in politics, the emphasis is seemingly shifted from preachment to behavior. But the scientific price paid for this shift is attention to a narrow range of behavior only. Further, these limitations affect practical decision making insofar as certain options (involving, for example, a greater role for justice) are foreclosed, and the willingness to act on behalf of new, emergent, future possibilities is deterred.

The realism of Machiavellian politics does not come off well in this assessment. Our assessment suggests the need to reconsider seriously one of the key virtues of Machiavellian politics—its realism. But what might such a reconsideration involve?

Is it possible that the acceptance of the outlook of Machiavellian politics can lead (despite itself) to toleration and constitutional liberalism and a climate more receptive to the humane society? And might it be argued that this development is its saving grace? In this way might its strengths be maintained and its vices happily turned into virtues? Its virtues would be the ones I have already identified. Its central vice would be its very commitment to the proposition that the protection of the vital interests of the nation-state is the supreme standard in politics. Let me turn to the argument of Isaiah Berlin for help in answering these questions.[30]

Berlin argues that Machiavelli constituted such a threat to thinkers in the Western tradition because he challenged their Christian view that there is only one truth and standard for politics. By rejecting the standards for politics of Christian religion and by positing a pagan philosophy (what I have called the protection of the vital interests of the state), Machiavelli required those who accepted the Christian tradition to consider the possibility that there might be alternatives to a single, undisputed standard for life and politics or at least no certain way of knowing the true standard. Given the possibility of several standards and truths for politics, and given, too, the actuality of different political communities differing on the one, acceptable standard, the way is open for a grudging acceptance of several competing standards and truths for politics, for freedom to argue about which standard and truth (if any one) should prevail. The way is thus open for pluralism; for toleration of a number of different, and competing, views; for constitutional liberalism to ensure that no single orthodoxy is imposed by force; for an open society wherein competing truths seek, in a humane way, to gain acceptance.[31]

Berlin suggests that

> Machiavelli's cardinal achievement is his uncovering of an insoluble dilemma, the planting of a permanent question mark in the path of posterity. It stems from his *de facto* recognition that ends equally ultimate, equally sacred, may contradict each other, that entire systems of value may come into collision without possibility of rational arbitration, and that not merely in exceptional circumstances, as a result of abnormality or accident or error—the clash of Antigone and Creon or in the story of Tristan—but (this was surely new) as part of the normal human situation.[32]

> If what Machiavelli believed was true, this undermines one major assumption of Western thought: namely, that somewhere in the past or the future, in this world or the next, in the church or the laboratory, in the speculations of the metaphysician or the findings of the social scientist or in the uncorrupted heart of the simple good man, there is to be found the final solution of the question of how men should live.[33]

> If there is only one solution to the puzzle, then the only problems are first how to find it, then how to realize it, and finally how to convert others to the solution by persuasion or force. But if this is not so . . . then the path is open to empiricism, pluralism, toleration, compromise. Toleration is historically the product of the

realization of the irreconcilability of equally dogmatic faiths, and the practical improbability of complete victory of one over the other. Those who wished to survive realized that they had to tolerate error. They gradually came to see merits in diversity, and so became skeptical about definitive solutions in human affairs.[34]

These consequences, Berlin notes, were "wholly unintended" by Machiavelli. "Yet he is, in spite of himself, one of the makers of pluralism, and of its—to him—perilous acceptance of toleration."[35]

Berlin makes his argument about the historic Machiavelli and his writings. I am suggesting that a comparable argument could be made on behalf of Machiavellian politics—the politics of the nation-state. Nation-states, recognizing that there is no agreement on the standard or truth of any particular nation-state, and recognizing also the conflict of standards and truths (nation-state, religious, philosophic, ideological) might, as a prudential response to the best way to protect their own vital interests, opt for peace and constitutional and humane coexistence in a global open society. In this way, it could be argued, nation-states could protect their modestly conceived and truly vital interests; the struggle for power could then proceed realistically but within the limits of safeguarding these truly vital interests; and practical decisions in politics would be prudent, modest, sensible—a consummation devoutly to be wished!

But, alas, the argument assumes what is by no means established: namely, that nation-states can indeed put sensible reins on their power; can indeed avoid the arrogance of power; can indeed work out a pattern of peaceful and constitutional and humane accommodation. To do so, they would have to give up the old worship of the sovereign nation-state. They would have to accept a community of global interest on some crucial matters of ultimate concern. They would, sooner or later, have to ask deeper questions about the sense of life, growth, and development—and the relationship of these objectives to justice and the common good. They would have to ask fundamental questions about the national and international constitutional order that they themselves, in their own interest, are building. In doing these things, it seems to me, they would be abandoning Machiavellian politics on key points and moving toward a more genuinely national and international constitutional order.

Moreover, the kind of tolerance foreshadowed above may still be open to objection. The tolerance of intolerance and other evils may be perfectly compatible with protecting certain legitimate vital interests of the nation-state. And yet such tolerance may not be compatible with the need for a prophetic politics to be intolerant of intolerance and designated evils. A philosophy of tolerance may not be compatible with the need to be intolerant of those evils that do not perhaps threaten the nation-state but that *do* threaten a genuinely civilizing order. For example, leaders of nation-states may find it possible to avoid the big wars that threaten their survival; but they may still be tempted to fight nasty little wars, particularly in far-off places, which do not seem to interfere seriously with the well-being of the citizens of their nation-states. Powerful, affluent, healthy, educated nation-states will be remarkably tolerant of weakness, poverty, disease, and ignorance in other nation-states. Rich and mighty nation-states may find it easy to work out a pattern of peaceful accommodation, domestically or internationally, but often at the price of the perpetuation of the plight of the poor and the weak.

Ultimately, then, Machiavellian politics, even as modified in the scenario above, must come to grief because nation-states cannot easily abandon their sovereign power on matters of vital interest or of national selfishness. And such relinquishment (under appropriate safeguards) may, paradoxically, be necessary for the preservation of the vital interests of the inhabitants of the nation-state. A central conclusion is irresistible: Machiavellian politics is, at best, inadequate; at worst, disastrous.

By lowering their sights, the practitioners of Machiavellian politics run the risk of jeopardizing the very vital interests they seek to safeguard. To a pattern of politics—utopian politics—that seeks to raise people's sights, and to move beyond adequacy to salvation, we can now turn.

3 : Utopian Politics: The Harmonious Politics of Earthly Salvation

INTRODUCTION

But is it possible to raise one's sights? Can one move beyond inadequacy and beyond disaster to harmony and salvation? And is it possible to do this without making things worse? Is utopian politics—the politics of the good place that is currently nowhere—the proper response to Machiavellian politics? Are the optimistic alarmists right in arguing that our fate is "utopia or oblivion"? Or are utopia's adverse critics right in holding that the quest for the earthly paradise is a "perennial heresy" that will lead, inevitably, to the earthly hell?[1]

And which utopian model of the many that contend for our attention are we to follow? Should we follow the philosophic model of Plato—the Plato of *The Republic*—whom one keen student of utopian thought has called "the greatest of all utopians"?[2] Or do we turn to Marx for "the most widely known of all" modern utopias?[3] What help can we get from the religious imagination of Fyodor Dostoevski's Grand Inquisitor, a very strange utopian indeed?[4] Or from the scientific-psychological imagination of B. F. Skinner?[5]

Clearly, there are difficulties in articulating an ideal type of utopian politics that will do justice to the richness of utopian literature. Moreover, in view of politics as the art of the possible, and doubts about the achievement of a harmonious polity, one may wonder if utopian politics is not a contradiction in terms.

Yet Marxism as proletarian communism or democratic socialism has had an enormous impact on modern politics.[6] Even though Marx's vision has not (at least not yet) been fulfilled in Communist Russia or Communist China, or in any democratic socialist regime, it has unquestionably influenced the revolutions and regimes in the Soviet Union and in China—and in Yugoslavia and Cuba—as well as social democratic parties all over the world. It has also influenced thought and practice in capitalist as well as socialist lands. Elements of Marxism, albeit twisted and distorted, were woven into the design of fascism and nazism. In direct and indirect ways, Marxism has played a role in shaping some aspects of the liberal democratic welfare state. And, most certainly, Marxism has profoundly influenced modern social science—and thus our understanding of economics, society, and politics.

There are, of course, risks in focusing on the utopian ingredients in Marx. We may be tempted to throw out the soundly utopian ingredients in Marx along with the flawed utopian ingredients. That would be a serious mistake. On the other hand, without a clear-sighted perception of Marx's utopian weaknesses, it may not be possible to rescue his utopian strengths.

Moreover, one must approach Marx with a clearheaded recognition that he and his orthodox followers have consistently rejected utopian socialism.[7] Yet, as Paul Tillich has noted, "Marxism has never, despite its animosity to Utopia, been able to clear itself of a hidden belief in Utopia."[8] It should be possible, however, to recognize the intimate connection between Marx's utopian prophecy of a better Communist world and his realistic analysis of social forces, based upon his materialist conception of history, a radical critique of the bourgeois capitalist order, and a tough-minded strategy of revolutionary action. It should be possible to recognize this connection while still arguing that it is possible to preserve in Marx only his sound ethical prescriptions, his sound social scientific analysis, and his sound revolutionary judgments without endorsing all of his ethical norms, all of his social science, or all of his revolutionary recommendations. We must, then, at least momentarily, hold open the question of whether Marxism can be saved.

Our treatment of other utopian models in this chapter is warranted for several reasons. *Not* because the utopian models of a Plato, a Grand Inquisitor, or a B. F. Skinner have had a significant historical impact on practical politics! *But* because these models underscore common features of all utopian models— notably the quest for harmony. *And* because these models help us to see problems, patterns, and "solutions" that persist in politics. The Grand Inquisitor illuminates the logic and appeal of the authoritarian and totalitarian Right—particularly the appeal of the "escape from freedom" in a regime of "miracle, mystery, and authority." Skinner illuminates the persistence of the belief in a Scientific Savior—in a scientific solution for all serious human ills. Plato illuminates the continuing hold of the belief in a philosophical elite capable of uniting wisdom and power in the interest of earthly justice. In treating these other utopian models, I will be particularly interested in the light they throw on the strengths and weaknesses of utopian politics in general and of Marx in particular.

THE DISTINGUISHING CHARACTERISTICS OF UTOPIAN POLITICS

The distinguishing characteristics that will be identified will not hold in every case for every political projection deemed utopian. The main points, however, will hold for most utopias; and the correspondence will be greater for modern utopias.

The Dream of Universal Earthly Salvation

Utopian politics is a pattern of politics characterized by the dream of earthly salvation—salvation from the ills that afflict the human race: the ills of war, injustice, tyranny, inequality, enmity, disease, poverty, retardation, inferiority, misery, disintegration, sterility. Its devotees dream of harmony on earth—harmony within the self, harmony among individuals, harmony among groups, harmony within and among political communities. The vision of salvation, harmony, and perfection calls for the achievement of cherished and sought-after goals: peace, justice, freedom, equality, fraternity, health, prosperity, fulfillment, excellence, happiness, wholeness, creativity—to put its ideals positively. Those who share this vision see politics in terms of the elimination of conflict, the overcoming of the struggle for power, and the establishment of a political order that is true and good. They see men and women and children, groups, communities, working together cooperatively. Agonizing tension, divisive struggle, and destructive conflict will be overcome, abolished. The wondrous life will have come to pass.[9]

George Kateb, in his penetrating study *Utopia and Its Enemies,* supports my characterization. The "heart of utopianism," he writes, involves a "vision of perfection."[10]

> The imperfection [that is adversely criticized when people have lost their "original perfection"] is defined by the presence of authority and constraint, hierarchy and class, slavery and war, property and scarcity, labor and pain, disease and mutation. There is inequality of power, possessions, prestige, and liberty; there is an insufficiency of pleasure and tranquillity.[11]

The "perfect life" we would prefer, Kateb continues, would be "a life of brotherhood, equality, joy, leisure, plenty, peace, health, and a life of permanent, unrelieved, universal satisfaction."[12] According to Kateb, perfection in the utopian tradition involves "a world permanently without strife, poverty, constraint, stultifying labor, irrational authority, sensual deprivation." Kateb argues that we are entitled "to speak of utopianism as that system of values which places harmony" at its center.[13] His picture of modern utopianism emphasizes the harmony and perfection of peace, abundance, and virtue. In such a utopian society "all conflicts of conscience and conflicts of interest" are abolished, and all "obstacles to a decent life" are removed; it is a society "in which peace, abundance, and virtue [are] permanently and universally obtained."[14]

The utopian vision of earthly salvation, harmony, perfection can be illustrated by my four utopian candidates.

Marx's vision of the Communist society illustrates, at least superficially, the best impulses of the messianic tradition, secularized and partaking of the generous rational, democratic, and scientific spirit of the Enlightenment. The interrelated values that are to characterize the Communist society are the values of freedom; of integration, harmony, and peace; of authentic humanity and community; and of rich human development.[15] Emancipation, for Marx, must be total: economic, social, and political. Worker control of production will be the key to total emancipation. With workers in control of the economic system, communism would overcome the estrangement of the worker from his product, from joyous work activity, from his humanity or species being, and from other people.[16] Communism is characterized by a classless, harmonious society, "an association in which the free development of each is the condition for the free development of all." Neither individuals, nor classes, nor nations would exploit one another. Beyond egotism, alienation, and illusion, people could respond to genuinely human needs and become truly human in a truly human community. Communism makes possible the goal of human development: the fulfillment of human richness in a genuinely human, social, and productive community. The fulfillment of the Communist motto—from each according to his ability, to each according to his needs—rests upon "the all-around development of the individual" and upon abundant cooperative wealth.[17] Rich and diverse human development also rests upon a democratic society and government in which arbitrary social and political inequalities would have disappeared, in which governmental representatives would be truly responsible and government open and responsive.[18]

Plato, too, despite significant differences with Marx, is drawn to the ideal of the harmonious community. The supremely good political life for Plato, in *The Republic,* is the harmonious life: with each class (philosophers, soldiers, artisans/farmers) doing what it is best equipped by nature and training to do: philosophers ruling, soldiers defending, and artisans and farmers producing the necessities of life in the polis. This harmonious life is justice. Conflict is thus overcome. Life has been organized in accord with a higher truth and it is good.[19]

Fyodor Dostoevski's Grand Inquisitor also seeks harmony on earth. Indeed, this is the reason he has jailed Christ: Christ's message is disturbing, unsettling, subversive. The Grand Inquisitor would "correct" Christ's "work." With us, declares the Grand Inquisitor, "all will be happy and will not more rebel nor destroy one another." Thus, the Grand Inquisitor—along with Marx and Plato—emphasizes the theme of earthly salvation. Pursuant to the Grand Inquisitor's truth of miracle, mystery, and authority, universal earthly salvation for humanity is possible as well as desirable. The "universal happiness of man" can be planned. "Universal unity," the "universal state," "universal peace," the harmonious "reign of peace and happiness," can be achieved. The people will be fed and cared for and their dreadful burdens lifted from their shoulders.[20]

B. F. Skinner also puts before humankind the vision of earthly salvation. Skinner has characterized Walden Two as a community in which people were "living a Good Life." In an essay, significantly entitled "Utopia and Human Behavior," Skinner summarizes the "Good Life" of Walden Two.

> They enjoyed a pleasant rural setting. They worked only a few hours a day—and without being compelled to do so. Their children were cared for and educated by specialists with due regard for the lives they were going to lead. Food was good and sanitation and medical care was excellent. There was plenty of leisure and many ways of enjoying it. Art, music, and literature flourished, and scientific research was encouraged.

And . . . life in Walden Two was not only good but feasible—within the reach of intelligent men of good-will who would apply principles then emerging from the scientific study of human behavior.[21]

In Skinner's community, he says, "people are truly happy, secure, productive, creative, and forward looking."[22] The harmonious life, pursuant to scientific principles of human behavior, will prevail.[23]

Thus, we see that the dream of universal earthly salvation comes in many varieties. The quest for harmony, however, seems to be central to the dream.

The "Scientific" Foundation for the Harmonious Community

Those committed to utopian politics believe that there is a truth about political life that, if grasped and implemented, will produce the harmonious political community. This truth illuminates the past, charts the present, and predicts the future. It illuminates, in particular, a definite cooperative pattern of politics. The pattern may vary from one utopian theorist to another, but certain common features, in addition to a guiding truth, will be found in all patterns. The harmonious society will be brought about by an elite that is able to grasp the truth, organize the harmonious society in accord with the truth, and thus end dangerous conflict. Another important feature of the utopian outlook is a positive conviction about social change. Via education, indoctrination, "miracle, mystery, and authority," or behavioral modification, human beings can be changed, and society can be altered. Human will can through revolution and socialization accomplish earthly salvation. The character of the truth, the elite, and the theory of social change will differ from one variant of utopian politics to another, but these common features are apparent in each. Similarly, the specific ideals of these utopian variations will be different—sometimes sharply different—but the assumption is always that these particular ideals are the ones that embody the true reality and that are necessary to achieve the harmonious community, our earthly salvation. The truth involved permits the utopian to criticize existing society in a radical fashion and to sketch the scenario of the harmonious politics of earthly salvation.[24]

For Marx the truth about the political world is the truth of the historic movement toward communism. This movement is rooted in the reality of how people earn a livelihood and is in accord with the development of economic forces. This historical movement has produced capitalism and a proletariat. Weaknesses in the capitalist economic system, in conjunction with the growing strength of the proletariat, will—in turn—lead to the revolutionary overthrow of the capitalist, bourgeois order and, after a preliminary democratic dictatorship of the proletariat, the advent of communism. Marx sees history in terms of class conflict that will lead, ultimately, to a classless society. Marxists, members of the Communist Party, and conscious and educated workers will lead the revolution. In the end—after the revolution that will destroy the power of the bourgeoisie; after the "democratic" dictatorship of the proletariat, which permits the consolidation of the revolution and the economic, social, and political transformation of the defeated capitalist order; and with the achievement of communism—the state as an instrument of coercion will wither away. Cooperation will replace conflict in the affairs of human beings. These ideas illuminate the struggle and eventual triumph of the proletariat. They make clear how and why the old bourgeois capitalist order will be uprooted. They illuminate how and why the new Communist order will emerge and be built, via proletarian action and education, on the basis of worker control of the economic system.[25]

Marx's scientific understanding rests upon his materialist conception of history. This understanding leads to a devastating criticism of the bourgeois capitalist order and the bourgeois superstructure. And it points toward the inevitable Communist revolution. Life, material production, civil society, state, and the rest of the superstructure—this was the pattern Marx saw in history.[26] This pattern involved change in history. Changes in material productive forces would lead to changes in the relations of production and, therefore, to changes in civil society and, therefore, to changes in the state, in law, in religion, in philosophy, and in ethics. In brief, changes in the economic structure would lead to social, political, religious, philosophical, and ethical changes.[27]

Marx believed that he had uncovered the secret of the exploitation of the worker by the capitalist. Under capitalism, he argued, "the wage-worker has permission to work for his own subsistence, that is, *to live,* only in so far as he works for a certain time gratis for the capitalist."[28] Those extra hours—and the value they produced—were appropriated by the capitalist. The key formula for exploitation Marx put as follows:

$$[\text{T}]\text{he ratio} \ \frac{\text{surplus working time}}{\text{necessary work time}} \ \text{determines the}$$

rate of surplus value.[29]

In more lurid language, Marx argued that capital, "vampire-like, only lives by sucking living labor, and lives the more, the more labor it sucks."[30] Marx thus saw the worker making slavelike contributions through his surplus labor to the production of commodities over which he has no control. The worker was also separated from joyous work activity; he was subjected to dreadful, most unfavorable work conditions; and the long hours of surplus labor only intensified his lack of freedom. The worker was also divorced from his own humanity; and this divorce was underscored by the oppressive, dehumanizing conditions under which he worked. The worker was also estranged from his fellow workers, an estrangement that was intensified by the competition that pits worker against worker for jobs and subsistence wages and inures the worker to his exploited life.

The exploitation of the proletariat would lead workers to organize to overcome their oppression. Other key factors—competition among capitalists, overproduction, commercial crises—would weaken the capitalists and assist the workers in their revolutionary conquest. The revolution would be the outcome of the "natural laws of capitalist production," of those "tendencies working with iron necessity toward inevitable results."[31] So it is, then, that capitalism produces the proletariat, weakens itself economically, is unable to overcome the contradictions between socialized production and anarchy in other aspects of civil society, "is incompetent to assure an existence to its slave within his slavery," provides allies for the proletariat, and in other ways sets the stage for its own demise.[32]

Marx was also mordantly critical of the bourgeois superstructure. The key ideas of bourgeois society—property, family, religion, order—sustained capitalism, the liberal state, bourgeois law, the exploitative bourgeois institutions of marriage and family, and a religious orientation that dulled the radical, person-oriented consciousness of the worker by focusing on the false consciousness of another life. Bourgeois morality was a sham. The "physician, the lawyer, the priest, the poet, the man of science," were the "paid-wage-labourers" of the bourgeoisie.[33] Even "ideas of religious liberty and freedom of conscience" were bourgeois ideas that "merely gave expression to the sway of free competition within the domain of knowledge."[34] If the bourgeoisie, in a crisis, had to choose between the preservation of private property and liberal freedom, it would sacrifice freedom.[35]

These views reinforced Marx's conviction of the necessity of a fundamental revolution; "patchwork reforms" of the bourgeois order would not do.[36] Marx's ethics and his social science were in harmony: both pointed to the Communist revolutionary transformation of society.

What truths do the other utopians see as ensuring the triumph of their utopias?

In Plato's *Republic,* the truth is the concept of the Good (based on Plato's theory of ideas) that the philosopher-king (Plato's elite) seeks to grasp. Political life organized in accordance with the Good produces the harmoniously functional state that is justice. In such a harmonious state there can be no discord. Philosopher-kings are the elite and they rule. Soldiers defend the polis. Farmers and artisans produce the food and clothes and other necessities of a civilized life. Since not all are able to grasp the truth that leads to justice in the polis, the myth of the Royal Lie provides a legendary belief system to rationalize the acceptance of roles. The philosopher-kings are mixed with silver and hence designed to guard the polis. Farmers and artisans are mixed with bronze and hence intended only for menial work. Men and women in the political community can, therefore, be influenced to accept their proper role; and this contributes significantly to the elimination of conflict. Philosophers are shaped, via education, to rule; soldiers, via training, to fight; and farmers and artisans, via myth, to carry on the necessary menial work of the polis. Each group does what it best can do. The proper union of wisdom, courage, and temperance leads to the just, and harmonious, community.[37]

The Grand Inquisitor, too, believes that he has grasped the truth about how to make people happy: how to achieve universal salvation for humanity. The truth—this strange utopian argues—does not lie in freedom, love of God, and the quest for immortality. Rather, the truth lies in miracle, mystery, and authority. People in this world want bread, security, direction. The elite who have perceived this are the Devil's disciples. They will weave the myth of miracle, mystery, and authority that will lift the burden of dreadful freedom from man's shoulders. They will feed and clothe people. They will attend to his earthly needs. They will make him happy on earth. They will remove the specter of confusion and cannibalism. They will ensure a universal triumph.[38]

For Skinner, the truth is that of behavioral engineering— operant conditioning, behavior modification. The behavioral psychologists can put their principles into practice in communities such as Walden Two. Stimulus, response, consequences—and, in particular, positive reinforcement—these are the key ideas of the science of human behavior that can be put to work by the Skinnerian elite, the behavioral psychologists, to modify and condition behavior and thus to achieve the good and harmonious society. Old-fashioned and unscientific notions of "freedom and dignity" will be jettisoned and replaced by the new truth (which its critics would argue is a new myth). Skinner—like Plato, Marx, and the Grand Inquisitor—believes that society can be transformed. Human beings are malleable. They can be educated or, better, conditioned by the new scientists to behave in those ways that will produce the good society. Through the scientific control of our environment, we can successfully deal with the terrifying problems that threaten our survival: nuclear holocaust, world famine, the population explosion, pollution, disintegrating cities. "A scientific view of man offers exciting possibilities. We have not [writes Skinner] yet seen what man can make of man."[39]

In reflecting on the perceptions of reality of our four utopian candidates, we are struck by the fact that they are strongly allergic to human unhappiness rooted in human conflict. They all claim to be able to look beyond discord to the more genuine reality of the harmonious community. And all stress that earthly salvation calls for a theory of social change rooted in a truth perceived by a prescient elite. We can now turn to examine the character of the judgments called for to achieve change and to sustain the harmonious community.

The Decline of Judgment in the Conflictless Society

Here it is important to distinguish between the exercise of judgment in the preutopian stage and in the utopian stage. In the preutopian stage conflict still persists and, consequently, difficult judgments must be made. The wisdom of these judgments—especially as they relate to the calculus of costs—may remain controversial, but the reality and imperative of judgment are unmistakable. However, once the harmonious society has been achieved, the need for difficult judgments declines. Indeed, the very problem of making hard judgments—which many consider to be the very heart of politics—seems to disappear. So we find a sharp contrast in judgmental behavior between the preutopian and the utopian stages. In order to attain utopia, hard judgments—often involving the sacrifice of the traditional values, institutions, and behavior patterns of the existing order—have to be made. Later, presumably because of the absence of serious conflict in the achieved utopian society, little or no judgment is required. Apparently, all works out well in utopian politics because rules and roles are accepted voluntarily. Traditional politics, rooted in serious conflict and statesmanlike accommodation, atrophies.

This distinction is particularly helpful in our examination of the role of judgment in Marx's theory of politics. It enables us to do justice to Marx's often penetrating analysis of the capitalist society of his day, and to Marx's tough-minded revolutionary theory, while not forgetting—as is so often done—to ask about the exercise of judgment in the fulfilled Communist society. Moreover, in dealing with Marx's judgments, it will be helpful to distinguish four periods that call for judgment: under capitalism, at the time of the Communist revolution, during the period of the "democratic" dictatorship of the proletariat, and under communism. Although there is some overlap between the first and second, and between the second and third, of these periods, this categorization may serve to clarify Marx's conception of wise judgment in the several crucial stages of his theory. This approach also permits us to do justice (in Marx's spirit) to the relationship between judgment and action, theory and practice, understanding and change. For we must remember that it was Marx who wrote: "The philosophers have only *interpreted* the world, in various ways; the point, however, is to *change* it."[40] But what judgments do we bring to changing the world?

Clearly, Marx recognizes that important strategic judgments have to be made to guide the revolutionary cause under capitalism. Under capitalism, Marx argued, the workers must get ready and get set before they can go. They would get ready by understanding the march of history—from feudalism to capitalism to communism; by understanding the nature of class struggle under capitalism, particularly the exploitation of the worker; by understanding the operation and weaknesses of capitalism; by understanding the weapons that capitalism places in the hands of workers. They would get set by organizing, by unionizing, by working with progressive and democratic forces, by adopting an independent and militant stance on Communist revolution. They must avoid being deceived by utopian socialists, by bourgeois or socialist reformers. They must never lose sight of the need to overthrow capitalism by forcible means. Strategy would, of course, vary with circumstances, with the character of the bourgeois regime in question, and with the stage of capitalist development in which workers found themselves. Although Marx's judgments on correct strategy were not entirely consistent, they usually reflected a willingness to face changing circumstances. Thus, for example, in his later life he conceded that in certain advanced capitalist countries socialism might be accomplished peacefully. He did insist that overthrow would take place when the revolutionary situation was ripe and that the revolution involved a fundamental transformation of the economic order.[41]

Revolution, according to the model of the Paris Commune, meant the armed seizure of power, destruction of the repressive organs of the old bourgeois order, and building of new democratic forces. The proletariat must be raised "to the position of the ruling class," he had argued in the *Manifesto*. They would use their power to "wrest" "all capital from the bourgeoisie." The revolution would expropriate the expropriators. The revolution would transform "the means of production, land and capital" from "means of enslaving and exploiting labour" into "instruments of free and associated labour."[42]

The revolution would not stop with the seizure of power by the workers and their allies. That was why a "revolutionary dictatorship of the proletariat" was necessary to complete the process of transforming the old capitalist into the new Communist society.[43] Economic, social, and political life had to be transformed. The democratic majority of workers would make these changes. Repressive bourgeois organs of state power—"standing army, police, bureaucracy, clergy, judicature"—would be destroyed or transformed. Legitimate governmental functions would be "restored to the responsible agents of society."

Government, based on universal suffrage, would be democratic and responsible. Workers would not hesitate to use coercive, despotic power—state power—to achieve the fundamental transformation to communism. The Commune suggested the example: a communism of "co-operative production" under worker control; of "united co-operative societies" able "to regulate national production upon a common plan," and to "end . . . the constant anarchy and periodical convulsions . . . of Capitalist production."[44] In the interim stage of the revolution, between capitalism and communism, the democratic dictatorship of the proletariat would function to increase productive forces significantly.[45] In this interim period only socialist equality—not full Communist satisfaction of needs—would prevail.[46] However, although key judgments called for in the period of the democratic dictatorship of the proletariat are revealed, we still remain in the dark about the fuller range of judgments— economic, political, social—required in this period.[47] And, as we shall now see, even more darkness obscures Marx's views on judgments to be made under mature communism.

We know very little about mature communism and even less about the judgments that will have to be made in such a society. Our ignorance derives in part from Marx's hostility to a "ready-made solution," to "ready-made utopias," to utopian blueprints, to dogmatic efforts to "prefigure" "the new world." Very early in his life, Marx argued that one could only find the new world "through criticism of the old." And, presumably, judgments about what to do in the Communist world could only be made as that world emerged from the democratic dictatorship of the proletariat and in the light of the circumstances at that time.[48]

What we do know about mature communism suggests, despite Marx's hostility to the utopian socialists, a rather idyllic Communist society. It will be characterized by the absence of oppressive economic, social, and political power. It will be a classless society. It will be an association "in which the free development of each is the condition for the free development of all."[49] In such a society the "enslaving subordination of the individual to the division of labor" will have "vanished." The "springs of co-operative wealth" will "flow more abundantly." The Communist motto can then prevail: "from each according to his ability, to each according to his needs."[50] The individual can "do one thing today and another tomorrow . . . hunt in the morning, fish in the afternoon, rear cattle in the evening, criticize after dinner . . . without ever becoming hunter, fisherman, shepherd or critic."[51]

We are, nonetheless, curious about the Communist variety of the harmonious politics of earthly salvation. Do no judgments have to be made about cooperation and accommodation—if not rule—in the Communist society? What judgments have to be made about the operation of the Communist economic system? Will there be no serious conflict between some workers and other workers? Between economic interests? Between decision makers and decision followers—if not between managers and workers? Between those making legitimate rules and those obligated to abide by such rules? Between those executing legitimate government functions and those affected by such functions? Between those at the center and those at the circumference of power? These questions take on additional urgency because of previously unanswered questions about the democratic character of the dictatorship of the proletariat. Will the coercive, despotic use of state power by the workers be directed only at formerly repressive capitalist forces? Is even a democratic dictatorship of the proletariat compatible with universal suffrage, responsible government, an open society? Will the dictatorship of the proletariat really wither away? Unfortunately, Marx does not tell us how Marxists will handle these difficult questions. We must conclude that Marx's recognition of the need for judgment—serious and difficult judgment—declines as the revolution proceeds. And by the time the state has withered away, and communism has emerged, Marx's capacity to make judgments—or to see the need for judgments—on these crucial matters has also withered away.

What now of the role of judgment in our other utopian theorists? Here our treatment will be briefer. As we shall see, however, a comparable conclusion about the atrophy of judgment in their utopian communities emerges.

Plato argues that in order to bring his republic, his just political community, into being it will be necessary to start from scratch with fresh and impressionable youngsters. All of those over ten years of age will be banished from Plato's polis. Special, rigorous education and training will be required for potential philosopher-kings—and queens. Monogamy and private property are ruled out for the class of philosopher-rulers. Presumably, the military class—more accurately, perhaps, the class of civil servant soldiers—will also lead a fairly spartan life. Presumably, farmers and artisans will remain isolated from affairs of state. It seems clear that once the new political community has been achieved—and given the acceptance of the new status quo and, theoretically, the absence of conflict—there will be little need for difficult practical judgment because society will be functioning harmoniously. Seemingly, serious political judgment—involving the clash of values, interests, power, appetites—will not be required, even on the part of the class of ruling philosopher-kings.[52]

The Grand Inquisitor admits a long and hard struggle on the part of his spiritual and political mentors—going back to the advent of Christ—to grapple with and eventually reject Christ in favor of the Devil. That judgment, he argues, was an extremely difficult judgment; but it was necessary to ensure human happiness, even at the expense of human freedom. The "sinful," "rebellious," "vicious," "vile," "base," "worthless," "feeble," "foolish" nature of man left the Grand Inquisitor and his colleagues no alternative. The judgment on behalf of miracle, mystery, and authority—given the dreadful consequences of the exercise of freedom by weak humanity—was unavoidable. The Grand Inquisitor concedes a long, hard struggle—full of sacrifice—to achieve universal earthly salvation. "Oh, the work is only beginning, but it has begun. It has long to await completion and the earth has yet much to suffer, but we shall triumph and shall be Caesars, and then we shall plan the universal happiness of man." The "hundred thousand" who rule on behalf of the Grand Inquisitor's miracle, mystery, and authority will be unhappy with "the curse of the knowledge of good and evil," but "thousands of millions" of people will be happy because they have no hard decisions to make. "And they will be glad to believe our answer, for it will save them from the great anxiety and terrible agony they endure at present in making a free decision for themselves." Thus, by the time universal dominion has been won for the Grand Inquisitor's reign, hard, practical decisions will have ceased to exist for the bulk of humankind.[53]

Skinner does not see serious problems confronting those who seek to make a success of Walden Two. The big decisions involve the shaping of the environment of Walden Two. If the scientific principles of behavioral engineering are followed, the right environment can be created and all major problems solved. Once this environment is functioning properly, Skinner holds, most of the hard decisions that plague us today will be unnecessary. Once Walden Two is a going operation, all will proceed smoothly. Under the Skinnerian "Plan," major decisions are made by experts without difficulty. This includes political decisions. As Frazier, the father and cardinal planner of Walden Two, puts the point for Skinner:

> In Walden Two no one worries about the government except the few to whom that worry is assigned. To suggest that everyone should take an interest would seem as fantastic as to suggest that everyone should become familiar with Diesel engines. Even the constitutional rights of the members are seldom thought about, I'm sure. The only thing that matters is one's day-to-day happiness and a secure future.[54]

Dissidents and malcontents can easily be handled through psychological counseling. And, in rare cases, they simply opt out of Walden Two. How such rare cases would be handled in a universal Walden Two is not treated by Skinner. Nor does he treat the larger pattern of politics in communities larger than Walden Two. The need for democratic citizenship, democratic politics, and democratic decision making has disappeared in Walden Two. The need for judgment has disappeared along with the reality of conflict.

It can thus be seen that difficult judgments cease to be necessary in the harmonious politics of earthly salvation. Such judgments may be required to reach the utopian community, but once it has been achieved, judgment loses its traditional importance in politics.

But how do we assess the strengths and weaknesses of utopian politics? Let me attempt to examine these strengths and weaknesses, in turn, by noting what critical students of utopian thought have said and by focusing on the ethical values, scientific understanding, and prudential judgments of our four utopian candidates.

THE STRENGTHS OF UTOPIAN POLITICS

To what extent does utopian thought illuminate what is ethically desirable, what is really true, and what wisely can be done? The great strength of utopian politics—and we make a great mistake if we ignore this point—lies in the fact that, at its best, utopian politics inspires dreams of a better world, a world struggling to be born, a world that intelligence and action can bring into being: a world saved from the catastrophic ills that threaten civilized survival, healthy growth, and creative fulfillment. This world would be harmonious, and peaceful, and it would satisfy human needs. Utopian politics, at its best, inspires us to refuse to accept as inevitable the ugly aspects of the world as it is: a world of brutal power, of varying forms of slavery, of injustice, of exploitation, of poverty, of barbarism, of needless suffering, of unhappiness. It sees new possibilities for human behavior. It emphasizes what people can do to reshape their world in a more rational and humane way. At its best, it can—as Fred Polak has indicated—provide us with a helpful (indeed, an indispensable) image of the future that can enlighten the past, orient the present, and forecast the future.[55] It opens up imaginative courses of action for those distressed with a miserable status quo. By holding out new and challenging possibilities for men and women, it stimulates those who hunger for peace and justice, freedom and fraternity, prosperity and excellence. Its challenge is to intolerable established ways and to tolerated evils. It forces men and women to contemplate new models and new beginnings.

At its best—as Paul Tillich has perceptively observed—it is truthful, fruitful, and powerful. Utopia is truthful because it expresses the aim of man's existence in his fulfillment in a fulfilled society. It is fruitful because it "opens up possibilities which would have remained lost if not seen by utopian anticipation."[56] "The fruitfulness of utopia is its discovery of possibilities which can be realized only by pushing forward into the unlimitedness of possibility."[57]

> Every utopia is an anticipation of human fulfillment, and many things anticipated in utopias have been shown to be real possibilities. Without this anticipatory inventiveness countless possibilities would have remained unrealized. Where no anticipating utopia opens up possibilities we find a stagnant, sterile present—we find a situation in which not only individual but also cultural realization of human possibilities is inhibited and cannot win through to fulfillment. The present, for men who have no utopia, is inevitably constricting; and, similarly, cultures which have no utopia remain imprisoned in the present and quickly fall back into the past, for the present can be fully alive only in tension between past and future. This is the fruitfulness of utopia—its ability to open up possibilities."[58]

Finally, Tillich argues, utopia is powerful because it "is able to transform the given." The "power of utopia is *the power of man in his wholeness*—the power of man to push out of the ground of discontent, his ontological discontent, in all directions of being."[59]

Eloquent—and encouraging—words. But how do our four utopian candidates illustrate these strengths as identified in the critical literature of utopian studies?

In many respects, Marx—our most influential utopian theorist—certainly illustrates these strengths. Marx's great dream of freedom, integration, a humane community, and rich individual development is, unquestionably, an inspiring dream. Marxism does indeed look forward to man's "fulfillment in a fulfilled society,"[60] toward the transformation of the given, toward the opening up of possibilities for human realization. Marx saw more clearly than perhaps any other figure of the nineteenth century the emergence of the working man to a position of greater power in economic, social, and political life. He underscored key weaknesses of nineteenth century capitalism. He revealed powerful connections between economics and society, economics and politics, economics and culture. He not only set forth the idea of a new Communist society, but he also articulated a theory of social change that indicated how the transition would take place. The hold of Marxism on the minds of so many humane and intelligent people is a tribute to its great power.

Strengths in our other utopians—strange or odd or perverse as they may seem in perspective—can also be noted. The Platonic quest for the just political community—ruled by wise rulers—is an attractive objective. The Platonic insistence upon distinguishing between knowledge and opinion (*doxa*) requires us ever to penetrate and repudiate mere appearances. The Platonic demand that political action be based on a higher order of truth—ultimately the Good—dictates faithfulness to a higher constitution and forces us, theoretically, to distinguish between genuinely prudent and simply clever judgments. The Grand Inquisitor may not seem to be the utopian at his best, yet his concern for human happiness (however distorted the Grand Inquisitor's ideology) cannot entirely be dismissed. Moreover, his recognition of the burden of freedom (however flawed) does point to a reality that, especially in the light of the "escape from freedom" by so many Germans under Hitler, we cannot lightly ignore.[61] We may not endorse his choices, but we are dramatically confronted with the need for hard choices by his argument. Similarly, we may not be powerfully attracted to the society of Walden Two, but we are challenged by Skinner's scenario. We may challenge his understanding of science, but we can endorse the value of positive reinforcements of the right kind. Skinner may not have invented the idea of the right kind of socialization, but we can all profit from the right kind of education.

This halfhearted endorsement of some of the ideas in Plato, the Grand Inquisitor, Skinner, points toward a more critical look at the weaknesses of utopian politics, including the weaknesses in Marx, who has, in this section, escaped a more trenchant adverse criticism.

THE WEAKNESSES OF UTOPIAN POLITICS

Some very serious ethical, scientific, and prudential weaknesses characterize utopian politics. These interrelated weaknesses include (1) a defective vision—a maddening pride, a tendency to hubris; (2) a sometimes frightening divorce from reality—a loss of sense of the existent, of power, of the possible; and (3) a loss of prudent judgment—a failure to calculate the costs of achieving and maintaining utopia and a failure to perceive the need for a democratic and constitutional order in utopia.

Superficially, our four utopian candidates seem to illustrate these weaknesses. Violence will—or may?—be required to achieve the Communist revolution; the democratic despotism of the dictatorship of the proletariat will be required to usher in the mature Communist society; and, apparently, no comprehensive democratic and constitutional theory will be required in the mature Communist society. A rigid caste system will have to be accepted to achieve the harmonious polis, from which trouble-making poets will be banned. Miracle, mystery, and authority of a questionable kind will be necessary to achieve human happiness and overcome the dreadful burden of freedom. The gospel of operant conditioning, as practiced by a Scientific Savior, will become the prerequisite for the Garden of Eden "beyond freedom and dignity." Here we begin to see the link between salvation and hubris. Between utopian dedication and dreadful but "necessary" sacrifices. Between profound disillusionment with the status quo and fundamental repudiation of democratic and constitutional politics.

But let us look at these weaknesses more fully. And do our four utopian candidates *really* illustrate these weaknesses?

Adverse critics of utopian politics argue that the utopian vision is fundamentally defective. The belief in earthly salvation, harmony, and perfection is bound to lead to hubris. Hubris involves the sin of pride. In secular terms it involves the efforts of human beings to exceed their limits. In religious terms it involves the efforts of human beings to play—or deny—God. In attempting the unobtainable, utopian politicians run the risk of committing the sin of Procrustes, the sin of attempting to force people into a predetermined mold—and at the expense of their freedom.[62] (Recall that Procrustes was the Greek who stretched small visitors to fit his bed and cut off the limbs of larger visitors until they, too, would conform.) The utopian politician is prone to commit similar brutal acts of violence—either intellectual or physical—against those who do not fit his ideological bed. Sought-for harmony may thus be purchased at the price of agreement on the "party line." And the party line may be determined by Marx and his followers. By Plato and his philosopher-kings. By the Grand Inquisitor and his fellow priests. And by Skinner and the Fraziers of Walden Two.

Of course, our four utopians argue that the correct line will be freely accepted because it is in accord with the truth. But, of course, wrongheaded, counterrevolutionary capitalists may have to be coerced after the revolution, as before the revolution. And trouble-making poets will be banned from the polis. And dissidents in Walden Two will get appropriate psychological counseling.

But such arguments are not persuasive, especially in the absence of a fuller understanding of people and politics. We miss in our utopians a recognition that dissenters will exist, even among the faithful; a recognition, too, of the need for constitutional machinery to deal with ongoing conflicts. In the absence of such constitutional mechanisms, we have reason to be fearful that the price for agreement on the new utopian order will be authoritarianism, of one kind or another, and, in the worst cases, totalitarianism—and certainly dogmatism, thoughtless conformity, and violence and terror in extreme cases. The defective vision of earthly salvation leads the utopian to forget his human limitations—his fallibility, his weakness, his mortality. "The untruth of utopia," writes Paul Tillich, "is that it forgets the finitude and estrangement of man."[63] Utopia raises a false hope about the ability of human beings to overcome their finitude and radical estrangement. As Reinhold Niebuhr has convincingly argued, even the will to live truly can lead to trouble, to disaster.[64] Good intentions are no safeguard against the abuse of power.

We may thus begin to have serious doubts about the very desirability of the utopian vision of harmony, salvation, and perfection, especially if we insist upon exploring the potentially troublesome or, indeed, disastrous consequences that might flow from this vision. Hence, we may begin to doubt the very desirability in Marx's Communist society of completely overcoming alienation, of achieving universal human emancipation, of fulfilling the dream of the *"total redemption of humanity."*[65] There may, then, be something wrong with the dream itself, whether it be Marx's dream of the classless Communist society, Plato's dream of the just state, the Grand Inquisitor's dream of universal happiness, or Skinner's dream of the society made good by operant conditioning.

When Marx's utopian vision is placed in what some critics consider to be its falsely messianic, millenarian setting, it becomes frightening, the more so if this vision is related to modern totalitarianism. A. J. Talmon's criticism is sobering. Talmon sees striking similarities between the "Jacobin and Marxist conceptions of . . . Utopia." Both Jacobin and Marxist saw their utopia "as a complete harmony of interests, sustained without any resort to force, although brought about by force—

the provisional dictatorship."[66] Talmon notes "the human urge which calls totalitarian democracy into existence, namely the longing for a final resolution of all contradictions and conflicts in a state of total harmony."[67] "The totalitarian democratic school . . . is based upon the assumption of a sole and exclusive truth in politics. It may be called political Messianism in the sense that it postulates a preordained, harmonious and perfect scheme of things, to which men are irresistibly driven, and at which they are bound to arrive."[68] Talmon sees Marx as illustrating yet another nineteenth century scheme for "universal regeneration," a scheme "purporting to offer a coherent, complete and final solution to the problem of social evil."[69]

The defective utopian vision is rooted, Norman Cohn argues, in the pursuit of the millennium. Cohn notes that the concept of salvation is central to the understanding of the idea of the millennium. And millenarian movements, he writes, "picture salvation" as "terrestrial." Salvation "is to be realized on this earth and not in some other-worldly heaven." Salvation "is to be enjoyed by the faithful as a collectivity." It is "to come both soon and suddenly." And it is to be "total." It "is utterly to transform life on earth." The "new dispensation will be no mere improvement on the present but perfection itself."[70] Cohn saw similarities between millenarian movements and modern totalitarian movements. In both he saw "an inherent purpose which is preordained to be realised on this earth in a single, final consummation."[71] A number of these millenarian features, if not all, characterize the utopian philosophy and community of a Plato, a Grand Inquisitor, or a Skinner: Salvation will be earthly, collective, total.

The alleged science of our utopians calls attention to a second major weakness. A lack of a sense of reality can lead utopian politicians to describe "impossibilities as real possibilities." This, for Tillich, is utopia's unfruitfulness. Utopia "succumbs to pure wishful thinking," to "self-defeating unrealism," to the "fool's paradise," to "fantastic utopias."[72] The adverse critics of utopian politics argue that a conflictless world is an impossibility, a contradiction in terms. To function in such a world is to attempt to function in a cuckoo land. The outcome is bound to be futility: the futility of vain preachment; the futility of vain beliefs in, and action on behalf of, the radical transformation of people and society. Such a naive, unreal view of man and society, of harmony, of power, of social change, of human malleability, can only bring grief and tragedy in its wake. The suicides and murders at Jonestown in Guyana in 1978 illustrate the macabre consequences of one utopian sect's loss of reality. Sooner or later, the utopian myth is punctured. Neither the dream of the brave new world nor the dream of the brave new world's utopian elite can be sustained in a universe of sober realistic analysis. The "scientific" foundation for the harmonious community turns out to be an unscientific illusion.[73]

Cohn sees "a chronically impaired sense of reality" in the millenarians and their modern totalitarian counterparts.[74] To identify Marx with Stalin, or the Grand Inquisitor with Hitler, would be a serious mistake. Yet we would be blind if we did not see some connections between Marx and what subsequently developed as Marxism-Leninism-Stalinism, and between the Grand Inquisitor's regime of "miracle, mystery, and authority" and the escape from freedom under Nazism. According to Cohn, among the "unmistakable" "symptoms" of "paranoia" —to be found in the "phantasies" of medieval millenarian and modern totalitarian—are a "megalomaniac view of oneself as the Elect, wholly good, abominably persecuted yet assured of ultimate triumph"; a "refusal to accept the ineluctable limitations and imperfections of human existence, such as transience, dissention, conflict, fallibility"; and "the obsession with inerrable prophecies."[75]

Cohn may overstate his case, but the parallelism he draws between millenarian and totalitarian, if not fully convincing, forces us to heed his conclusion that "these ancient [millenarian] imaginings are with us still." Cohn contended: "Beneath the pseudo-scientific terminology [of national socialism and Marxism-Leninism] one can in each case recognize a phantasy of which almost every element is to be found in phantasies which were already current in medieval Europe. The final, decisive

Putnam's, 1900–10), 6:85. See also chap. 6, "The Anti-Republican Danger and Democratic Politics," in Neal Riemer, *James Madison* (New York: Washington Square Press, 1968; New York: Twayne, 1970).

5. See George Orwell, *1984* (1949) (New York: New American Library, 1983); Aldous Huxley, *Brave New World* (Garden City, N.Y.: Doubleday, 1932). See also Irving Howe, ed., *1984 Revisited: Totalitarianism in Our Century* (New York: Harper & Row, 1983); and Aldous Huxley, *Brave New World Revisited* (New York: Harper, 1958).

6. My own conviction about the probability of the possibility of a more prophetic politics—rooted in a superior ethical vision, a more generous and yet more realistic understanding of political reality, and a bolder and more far-sighted sense of political becoming—has been reinforced by the words and deeds of a number of twentieth century figures. Here I single out a few of these figures. Thus, among religious writers and leaders: Abraham J. Heschel, Paul Tillich, Pope John XXIII, and Martin Luther King; among philosophers and psychologists: John Dewey, Eric Fromm, and Abraham Maslow; among social scientists: Kenneth Boulding, Gunnar Myrdal, Fred Polak, and Richard A. Falk; and among physical and biological scientists: Albert Einstein, Rene Dubos, and Harrison Brown.

battle of the Elect (be they the 'Aryan race' or the 'proletariat' against the hosts of evil (be they the Jews or the 'bourgeoisie'); a dispensation in which the Elect are to be most amply compensated for all their sufferings by the joys of total domination or of total community or of both together; a world purified of all evil and in which history is to find its consummation. . . ."[76]

Certainly Marx does not fully fit Cohn's psychic portrait of the modern totalitarian. Yet he certainly saw the capitalist as responsible for the worker's abasement, enslavement, exploitation, alienation, misery, and dehumanization. He certainly saw the world purified of these evils, and of serious conflict, after the inevitable triumph of communism. Marx certainly seems unwilling to abandon a belief in the possibility of overcoming human estrangement. He certainly persisted in believing that under communism we could overcome the stultifying aspects of the division of labor and the disastrous effects of other divisions— between workers, between civil society and politics, between private and public, between the egoistic individual and the social community, and between nations. Marx's great admiration for the productive capabilities of capitalism, his recognition of some reforms under capitalism (particularly the ten-hour working day), and his appreciation of the possibility in advanced capitalist countries of a peaceful evolution to socialism did not convince him that real freedom might be achieved under a reformed capitalism. Modern Marxist analysis cannot survive as serious social science unless it is willing to abandon certain of Marx's fantasies about capitalism and about the democratic and constitutional welfare state in a mixed economy.

We must also ask embarrassing questions about our other utopians and their sense of science and reality. Can we accept, as good science, Plato's philosophical realism (the belief that ideas are the real reality)? And even if we do, does his just polis emerge as the only conclusion based on his epistemological premises? Is his harmonious political community in accord not with his understanding of knowledge but with his normative prescriptions? And is his system for selecting who shall be philosopher-kings, who soldiers, and who farmers and artisans grounded in science? (What of those who "bloom" late?) And, indeed, will Plato's "functional" community—with each class doing what it best can do—really produce justice? Is the Grand Inquisitor's view of man and society, at best, one-sided and, at worst, hopelessly distorted? Does he miss the reality of many groups and institutions—between the isolated individual and the monolithic state—that enables the individual to bear the burden of freedom? Does he miss the redeeming features of human nature by focusing only on man's worst qualities? Does Skinner, too, blithely ignore the more complex reality of human existence, of politics, of the historical setting for human existence, of politics, of the historical setting for human action, of the economic as well as the political struggle for power, of the interaction of political communities? I raise these questions because the consequences of their science can be seen in arenas beyond the academy. The aristocratic belief in the philosopher-king able to rule wisely in an orderly society, with each class in its place, lingers on. The dreadful burden of freedom still tempts Grand Inquisitors of the Left or the Right to overcome the burden even at the price of freedom. And we still seek a scientific-technological fix for major problems—whether of war and peace; or of resources, energy, and population; or of poverty; or of crime—in the modern world.

Having raised critical questions about the ethical and empirical outlook of utopian politics, let us now turn to the prudential perspective of the utopians. Here we discover that difficulties involving prudent judgments are abundant in utopian politics. My previous analysis of the ethical and scientific weaknesses of utopian politics has called many of these difficulties to our attention. Utopians, its adverse critics insist, are not clear on the prudent means to achieve, and on the prudent judgments to sustain, utopian politics.[77] This is a fatal weakness, they maintain, because it leaves unresolved the crucial question of accommodation of actors and interests in the utopian community. Can the gap be bridged? Can it be done wisely? How will disagreements among contending forces be handled? What are the costs of ushering in, and sustaining, the utopian society? In the absence of a prudential calculus of costs, rational decision is impossible. Too much is demanded on faith. And when the stakes are so high—involving as they do a radical restructuring of human life—such faith must be challenged. The need for challenge is underscored by the absence of any guarantee that utopian ideals will be fulfilled. The performance of even the most democratic dictatorship must be questioned, especially if it sanctions despotic, coercive powers. So must the performance of benevolent philosopher-kings, of authoritarian Grand Inquisitors, of behavioral psychologists with a messianic complex. Our suspicions are especially warranted in the absence of a full-fledged democratic and constitutional theory that might enhance wise decision making, in the light of real conflicts, in the best utopian society.

It is no accident, I believe, that our utopians are hostile to the democratic and constitutional politics of the existing orders they criticize. Liberalism tolerates intolerable evils. Greek democracy convicted Socrates on false charges and sentenced him to drink the hemlock. Freedom leads to confusion, cannibalism, and disaster. Old-fashioned notions of freedom and dignity obstruct the scientific way to salvation in Walden Two. This kind of politics exploits the masses. It is unjust. It leads to massive unhappiness. It permits a wide range of evils. It perpetuates a false consciousness, discord, human agony, societal hypocrisy. Hence, it is no accident, either, that our utopians move away from democratic and constitutional politics in their utopian communities or, as in Marx's case, neglect to develop a democratic, constitutional Communist politics.

But perhaps the best explanation of the failure of the utopians to do justice to democratic and constitutional politics lies in their hostility to conflict and their conviction that the advent of the harmonious society makes such politics unnecessary. Marx failed to develop a democratic and constitutional theory for his Communist society because his thinking about the Communist society was governed by certain millennial/utopian ideas that assumed that struggles for power, conflicts of interest, would disappear in the Communist society. And, hence, a democratic and constitutional theory to regulate the struggle for power, to achieve accommodation among conflicting interests, was unnecessary. Why should there not be conflict between workers and workers in the Communist society? (Because workers in control of production will work harmoniously?) Why should there not be conflicts between some working-men's interests and other working-men's interests? (Because abundance will make the fulfillment of human needs possible and fights among contending interests avoidable?) Why would there not be conflicts among different interpretations of freedom, peace, humanity, and fulfillment? (Because with the end of alienation and oppression, virtue will produce agreement?) Why should there not be different visions of how to organize and advance the Communist society? (Because a single vision would be overwhelmingly apparent to a redeemed humanity?)

Marx's failure to probe these questions—and suggested answers—is disturbing because it leaves a big gap in Communist theory. These questions point toward the reality of conflict even in the mature Communist society and, therefore, to the need for a mature democratic and constitutional theory to permit decision makers to make difficult judgments. There is evidence to support the view that Marx was striving, even if not always with success, to retain in his revolutionary communism some of the cardinal ideas of an older democratic and constitutional tradition. Clearly, he would radically democratize the economic system through worker control. He opted for universal suffrage. Genuine social and political equality would follow worker control of the economic system. He endorsed democratic representation, open government, and government responsiveness to human needs. What he failed to do, however, was to provide for continuing criticism of the operative Communist society. He neglected to provide for safeguards to ensure worker control, democratic rule, basic rights, and responsible supervision of government action to satisfy human needs. Marx, then, was not so much opposed to democratic and constitutional protections as convinced that they were not really necessary in the mature Communist society. And if Marx's assumptions about the classless, harmonious Communist society are correct, such protections really are not necessary.

Two additional points need to be made in connection with the decline of judgment in the utopian society. One of these relates to a disturbing consequence of utopian thinking: disillusionment. Disillusionment with the existing order can lead to fanaticism, violence, and death.[78] Again, Jonestown reminds us vividly of this consequence. Disillusionment also calls our attention to a second point: withdrawal from politics. Withdrawal may follow from disillusionment with the existing order. Or the utopian, disillusioned with utopia—usually after the demonic has demonstrated its fury in the utopian attempt—may turn away from all politics. And if politics is viewed as a powerful civilizing process, such disillusionment, fanaticism, violence, and withdrawal must be clearly antipolitical. Those who withdraw assume that ordinary democratic and constitutional politics is irrelevant, fruitless, worthless, impotent.[79] Such a view, ironically, is itself a judgment of the utopian's impotence. Such impotent withdrawal is the last refuge of the disappointed idealist.

This assessment of the weaknesses of utopian politics leads, initially, to a very gloomy set of conclusions. First, certain key utopian ends—about earthly harmony and salvation—may not be desirable. Second, even if utopian politics is desirable, it may not be achievable. Third, even if utopian politics is both desirable and achievable, the cost of its achievement may be too high and therefore unacceptable. Fourth, the serious utopian is confronted with bleak alternatives: disillusionment, impotence, or costly sacrifice.

But can more be said about striking a balance between the strengths and weaknesses of utopian politics?

CONCLUSION

The danger is not that we shall choose utopian politics but that we shall reject it completely. That would be a monumental mistake. Despite its weaknesses (which I have tried to emphasize), the utopian vision of a better world—the vision of an inspiring and life-sustaining future of liberating possibilities, of transforming power, of human and societal realization—is needed. We cannot be sustained by the vision of Machiavellian politics—the politics that focuses on the protection of the vital interests of the nation-state, by force or by craft, by fair means or by foul means. But we must not move from one flawed political pattern to another. From the weaknesses of Machiavellian politics to the weaknesses of utopian politics. From idolatry to hubris. From the effort to triumph in the inevitable struggle for power to the effort to overcome the struggle for power. From the harsh realities of lion and fox politics in the present to the beguiling fantasy of earthly paradise in the future.

But can we retain the strengths of utopian politics in a sensible alternative? Inspired by a larger vision, can we maximize freedom, peace, humanity, and fulfillment within political communities and in the larger world? Guided in our work by a more astute ethical and scientific theory, and by a keener theory of social change, can we move toward the more nearly perfect union and toward goals of peace and justice, freedom and happiness, prosperity and health, excellence and fulfillment? And without the costly sacrifice of democracy, constitutionalism, and wise judgment? Can we, in Tillich's phraseology, affirm the positive and transcend the negative aspects of utopian thought and behavior? And is Tillich right in concluding that we can do this only by rejecting the "expectation of perfection within history" and yet by demanding a "new order" in history—an order that is "provisional, not absolute," an order subject to ultimate criticism?[80]

What revised version of utopian politics would fulfill Tillich's hopes? Is it inevitable that when we try to raise our sights in any significant way we tempt disaster? Are we, like Icarus, doomed to plunge to earth when we seek to fly too high? Or is it the case that we can fly considerably higher than we now are without melting our utopian wings?

May it be the case that the democratic and constitutional welfare state is the safe semiutopia that may be the answer to our questions? Embodying older revolutionary impulses—of 1776, 1787, and 1789—and the watchwords of those revolutions (*life, liberty,* and *the pursuit of happiness*; *the more perfect Union*; *liberty, equality, fraternity*)—the modern democratic welfare state preserves the possibility of human and societal fulfillment. It holds open the possibility of transforming the given. Born with the ideals of the Enlightenment, it has been driven forward by a belief in progress. It has learned how to deal with a variety of interests—economic, social, and political—in a pluralistic setting. It was a constitutional state and, therefore, insistent upon limitations on power. Hence, it was able to guard against hubris. It could recognize and yet seek to harness the struggle for power among contending interests. It could recognize and cope with capitalist enterprise. It was democratic and thus committed to an enlarged suffrage and the widest possible involvement of citizens. It was anchored firmly in civil liberties. Pragmatic, it would be free to deal with problems, regardless of charges that its actions might be socialistic. Accepting the reality of conflict, it would seek superior patterns of accommodation. And given the work to be done to advance the ends of the more perfect Union, there would be challenge aplenty. In this way, then, the democratic and constitutional welfare state might overcome the weaknesses of utopian politics while retaining its strengths

But does a critical analysis of liberal democratic politics—on the model of the democratic welfare state—support the tentative proposition that it can indeed preserve the strengths and avert the weaknesses of utopian politics? And of Machiavellian politics? Let me address these crucial questions in the next chapter.

4 : Liberal Democratic Politics: The Conservative Politics of Pluralistic Balance

INTRODUCTION

In our search for a pattern of politics that may enable us to achieve a greater measure of civilized life, healthy growth, and creative fulfillment, we are drawn to modern constitutionalism and to its twentieth century expression, the liberal democratic state.[1] It seems to provide us with the right "idealistic-realistic" balance. Liberal democratic politics seems to be able to retain the strengths of Machiavellian and utopian politics without succumbing to their weaknesses. Liberal democratic politics seems to have incorporated the idealistic democratic impulses of 1776 and 1789 successfully; yet, as in the United States, these impulses were successfully tempered by the hardheaded realism of 1787. And, in twentieth century America, liberal democrats—in the interest of both an ethically desirable and an empirically accurate theory of politics—did not hesitate either to fulfill democratic and constitutional ideals or to reject others as naive, unscientific, and impractical.[2]

The attractiveness of liberal democratic politics was intensified by modern totalitarianism and reinforced by halting but eventually successful liberal democratic responses to economic difficulties. In comparison with the communism of Stalin or the fascism of Hitler, liberal democracy, despite its shortcomings, looked very good.[3] Its friendly critics—from Alexis de Tocqueville in the nineteenth century to Reinhold Niebuhr in the twentieth century—had noted and helped liberal democrats to face up to and deal with these shortcomings in the interest of a strengthened constitutional democracy. Critics, friendly and unfriendly, had been particularly prominent in the depths of the Great Depression in the 1930s; but while this depression had sorely tested liberal democracy, it had also led to pragmatic efforts to remedy the laissez-faire defects of liberal democracy. Moreover, the ability of the United States to move toward the welfare state suggested to many that a great liberal democracy could achieve a judicious balance between liberalism and democratic socialism, even if Americans would never dream of calling elements in the tradition of the Progressive movement, the New Freedom, the New Deal, the Fair Deal, the New Frontier, or the Great Society "socialism." Indeed, some observers in postwar America announced the "end of ideology"—announced that the United States had achieved the "good society."[4]

Of course, the announcements proved to be premature—as the movements in the 1960s for civil rights, against poverty, and against war demonstrated. Criticism was revived. And the criticism—we should not forget—came from the Right as well as from the Left. The criticism, nonetheless, was substantially *within* the democratic and constitutional tradition.

To set the stage for my own analysis of the idealistic-realistic vital center of liberal democratic politics, it may be helpful, briefly, to summarize the criticism of the 1960s and 1970s. The criticism, we should appreciate, revived the debate about the soundness of the idealistic-realistic liberal democratic balance. Liberal democrats, responding to this criticism, continued to emphasize the fact that the idealistic-realistic liberal democratic balance is a position that occupies the sound center of U.S. politics.

Aristocratic, individualistic, and procapitalist critics on the Right worried (and still worry) about the degeneration of liberal democratic politics into mobocracy, serfdom, and socialism. They worry about radical egalitarianism. They worry about the loss of equality of opportunity and its replacement by the doctrine of equality of results. They are hostile to "reverse discrimination" and other programs of preferential treatment. They worry, too, about the triumph of vulgarity, meanness, and mediocrity in the modern democratic state. They bemoan the loss of the sense of individual moral character and responsibility in the welfare state. They fear the growing bureaucratic power of the state in regulating our economic affairs and in undermining private property and enterprise as bastions of freedom. They deplore governmental controls and the encroachments of centralized state power. High taxes are anathema. Except for certain exceptions (for example, banning abortions, subsidizing tobacco crops, and protecting oil profits), they favor limited government. They are most content when government is in their hands and used for their purposes only. They are traditionally opposed to budget deficits and big spending for welfare purposes unless such spending is for their welfare.[5]

Radical democratic, communitarian, and democratic socialist critics on the constitutional Left attack on another front. They are concerned about too little—not too much—popular participation in the modern democratic state. They protest against a different kind of enslavement of the individual, rooted in an exploitative economic and social system, characterized by pervasive inequality, nourished by racism and sexism, and magnified by a lack of genuine concern for the "least free." While seeking to protect and expand civil liberties in the political, social, and cultural realms, they would not hestitate to use the powers of the democratic state to advance the cause of social and economic justice. They are unhappy about the adverse effects of a still largely laissez-faire economy, about the "vandal" aspects of the ideology of liberalism, and about the selfishness inherent in the liberal "theory of possessive individualism." They worry about ecological disasters. About human alienation. About elitism in our economic and political affairs. They seek an economy that can deliver satisfying jobs, decent housing, and better medical care. They seek a more generous community within which all individuals can develop their abilities in ways consistent with the common good.[6]

Of course, varying combinations and permutations of these two Right and Left positions are possible. I emphasize these two polar positions within liberal democracy to underscore an important point: Those who see liberal democracy as striking an idealistic-realistic balance see this balance as the vital center of liberal democratic politics.

The task of the analyst is to arrive at a just appraisal of liberal democratic politics, and especially of the idealistic-realistic balance within that liberal democratic pattern. Analysts must decide whether the adverse criticisms of liberal democratic politics are cosmetic or deep-seated. They must decide whether the strengths of this pattern of politics compensate for its weaknesses. They must decide what corrections are required. They must decide whether minor modifications or fundamental changes are in order. Above all, they must decide whether liberal democratic politics—as revised, corrected, changed—can (while true to its own idealistic-realistic commitments) incorporate the strengths and avoid the weaknesses of Machiavellian and utopian politics.

In addressing liberal democratic politics I propose to focus, then, on its enduring core of democratic and constitutional principles, and especially on those twentieth century (largely U.S.) writers who attempt to strike a sound idealistic-realistic balance. I will try to do justice to the idealistic commitment to freedom—religious, political, economic, social—of liberal democratic politics. I will note how those who practice this politics seek to preserve what ought to be conserved, particularly key constitutional principles and prescriptive institutions such as representative government and private property. I will also pay attention to the evolution of the "mixed economy" and the welfare state in liberal democratic politics.

Pursuant to these concerns, then, I will—in succeeding sections of this chapter—identify the distinguishing characteristics of liberal democratic politics (paying special attention to those twentieth century pluralists who seek to strike an idealistic-realistic balance). I will also examine both the strengths and the weaknesses of this pattern of politics (again with particular attention to twentieth century pluralists). Finally, I will attempt a reappraisal of liberal democratic politics. Such a reappraisal may more convincingly tell us if this pattern does indeed strike the right idealistic-realistic balance—not only between Machiavellian and utopian politics but also between Right and Left within the liberal democratic tradition. Such a reappraisal may also tell us if we have to continue our search for a better guiding model for the twenty-first century.

THE DISTINGUISHING CHARACTERISTICS OF LIBERAL DEMOCRATIC POLITICS

To set the stage for an examination of the distinguishing characteristics of liberal democratic politics, it may be helpful, initially, to compare the approaches to power in the Machiavellian, utopian, and liberal democratic models. Those engaged in Machiavellian politics seek to triumph in the struggle for power in order to protect the vital interests of the nation-state. The leaders of the nation-state act to protect the vital interests of the nation-state (by fair means or foul): this is the way things ought to be; this is the way things normally are; and this is the way things can wisely be. Those engaged in utopian politics seek to overcome the struggle for power in the interest of earthly salvation and universal harmony. They seek an earthly paradise for people and community: this, in their judgment, is the way things ought to be; this is not the way things are before the reign of utopia; but this is the way things can be if the utopian truth is pursued. By way of comparison: Those engaged in liberal democratic politics seek to regulate the struggle for power, by establishing known and fair rules of the political game, in the interest of balancing liberty and authority. Those engaged in liberal democratic politics seek such a balance in the interest of both legitimating necessary power and protecting individual freedom: this is the way things ought to be; this is the way things are in a democratic and constitutional political community (but not in all political communities); and this is the way things can be in all political communities—given the right principles, conditions, and leadership. But what, more fully, are the distinguishing ethical, empirical, and prudential characteristics of liberal democratic politics?

The More Nearly Perfect Political Community

The balanced vision of liberal democratic politics is an updated vision of Aristotle's *polity,* or constitutional government: dedicated to justice and the common good; representing an admixture of democracy and aristocracy; rooted in a strong, prosperous, well-educated middle class; reflecting a balance of economic, social, and political forces; and showing itself ever hopeful of achieving the politics of order and moderation. The vision is that of Aristotle as updated by John Locke and James Madison and John Stuart Mill and by the liberal democratic idealistic-realistic pluralists of the twentieth century. I call them *idealistic* because they are firmly committed to democratic and constitutional values; yet they are *realistic* in the sense that they accept the struggle for power among contending interests, reject naive liberal and democratic views about human perfectibility, and are skeptical about popular participation and an easily known and harmonious guiding common good. They are "pluralists" not only because they see politics in terms of contending interests but because they see the need for balancing a host of equities in politics. The polity is for Aristotle, as for his intellectual successors, the model of the best practicable state.

The Preamble to the U.S. Constitution captures the idealistic semiutopian ethical vision of liberal democratic politics in the modern democratic state. Not perfection. But a "more perfect Union," One that would "establish justice, insure domestic tranquility, provide for the common defense, promote the general welfare, and secure the blessings of liberty." The objectives for the American polity are plural; there is no "single vision" here. The democratic and constitutional vision is to be fulfilled, and a balance struck among potentially competing objectives, through known and fair rules of the games designed to validate the exercise of power by authority. Power is to be granted, denied, restricted. The rules are designed to ensure effective and regularized restraints on those who exercise power. The vision, in James Harrington's phrase (of which John Adams was so fond), is to be that of an "Empire of Laws" and not of arbitrary men and governments. The rules for the modern democratic and constitutional state are designed to ensure that government is limited, responsible, representative, and popular. The vision is of politics as a civilizing process—again, a Greek ideal that America's Founding Fathers were to find most congenial. A balance is to be struck, too, between individual "life, liberty, and the pursuit of happiness" (in Jefferson's glittering generality, which was not meant to downgrade the importance of property) and the general welfare. *Due process of law*—whose meaning had developed over centuries in British constitutional history—is to characterize the exercise of all power. The state is to be harnessed to the service of the people who, and the many and varied interests that, make up the political community. These people and interests reflected diverse economic, political, religious, social, geographical, and intellectual concerns.[7]

The Founding Fathers of liberal democratic politics in the United States (of whom James Madison was the keenest political theorist) were both realistic and idealistic political thinkers. It is with good reason that modern liberal democrats turn to them for inspiration. The founders were not naive republican theorists. Their vision of constitutional politics did not assume that all people (or, indeed, most people) would be saintly, informed, rational, altruistic, interested, and active. As Madison noted, people were, *in part,* revealed as passionate, fallible, shortsighted, unjust, ambitious, fickle, quarrelsome, opinionated, depraved, foolish, avaricious. Yet they were also, *in part,* virtuous, enlightened, energetic, concerned for others. These redeeming qualities, Madison insisted, made democratic and constitutional politics possible. Representative democracy rested on the proposition that "the people will have virtue and intelligence to select men of virtue and wisdom."[8] The realistic recognition of human shortcomings did not lead Madison to lower his vision of the liberating possibilities of constitutional politics. Rather it intensified his search for ways that would shore up virtuous, intelligent, freedom-loving, self-respecting, vigilant, and independent men through "auxiliary precautions," education as a means of popular enlightenment, and the freedoms of speech, press, assembly, and political organization. He did not bring his norms down so that they would square with uncomfortable realities. Instead—while granting the sometimes discouraging realities—he sought to transform, transcend, utilize, or alter them. People were free, rational, and ethical creatures who could, with the help of education and sound political activity, sustain a republican version of constitutional politics. Given their love of liberty, their reasonableness, their social character, and their civic effort, they could advance the end of intellectual, religious, political, and social tyranny, and the achievement of fuller realization. Republican constitutional politics was a feasible alternative.

Madison's theory of constitutional politics could also recognize, realistically, the fact that various interests, especially economic interests, struggle with each other to shape public policy in their own self-interest. He could do so, however, without accepting this proposition as a norm—as *necessarily* desirable. The struggle among contending interests in an extensive republic might make it less likely that a factional interest would prevail. This consequence was desirable. But he did not and could not endorse the view that somehow all will *necessarily* come out right if many interests struggle for power in the body politic. Madison recognized, but did not endorse, faction; and *factional interests* he defined as those that were "adverse to the rights of other citizens, or to the permanent interests of the community."[9] The task of government was to regulate faction in the public interest; it was not to succumb to factional domination of politics. A public policy in the public interest was not *necessarily* the resultant of group pressures, many of which were indeed factional. His constitutional theory of the "extensive republic" was designed as a "cure" for this disease.[10]

Modern liberal democrats—in the idealistic-realistic tradition—are very sympathetic to, but do not entirely endorse, the

Madisonian outlook. They seek to preserve—or advance—as many democratic and constitutional ideals as possible, but they insist upon facing up to the realities of actual political behavior.[11] They refuse to endorse modern democratic ideals that ignore these realities. They would modify naive democratic ideals so that they square with political reality. Thus, in some respects they would improve on the ideals of America's Founding Fathers—for example, in accepting suffrage for poor people, blacks, and women. Here they are clearly more democratic than the Founding Fathers. In other respects they seek to emulate the realism and pragmatism of the Founding Fathers—for example, in recognizing that people are often irrational, ignorant, uninterested, self-centered. Moreover, they do not hesitate to use these empirical observations to argue against the allegedly utopian ethical stance of those whom they call naive democrats—those who favor participatory democracy. The counterpart of the suspicions by liberal democrats of the limited capability of the average democratic citizen is their greater reliance upon wise democratic political leadership. Hence, they move away from the democratic goal of fuller citizenship participation and toward an endorsement of a theory of democratic leadership (which their adverse critics are to call a theory of democratic elitism).

If, in the interest of greater realism, the utopian vision of the participating democratic citizen is dimmed in the political theory of many modern liberal democrats, so, too, is their vision of the guiding common good. Without explicitly abandoning the older ethical vision of a common good or a public interest, or what Madison called "the permanent and aggregate interests of the community," they often tend to downplay this vision. Suspicious of fanatics who would "force us to be free," skeptical (in the positivistic tradition) of our ability to identify a standard of the public interest, open to political compromise, they are prone to accept as both norm and reality the proposition that public policy is, and should be, the resultant of group pressures.[12]

These points are important because they influence the modern liberal democratic interpretation of "the more perfect

Union." Liberal democrats are committed—they believe realistically—to the desirability of using wise democratic leadership to balance the inability of average citizens (lacking competence, interest, or time) to govern themselves sensibly. They also see a positive virtue in a system wherein public policy is (and should wisely be) the resultant of group pressures or the outcome of democratic compromises. In endorsing this outlook, liberal democrats seem to be trying to face up to Machiavellian realities and to avoid utopian illusions.

A third point, and commitment, must also be noted: the commitment to a stable, orderly, moderate, democratic welfare state as crucial to the vision of the more nearly perfect Union. This commitment also illustrates the pragmatic liberal democratic vision. Liberal democrats do not see the welfare state as an ethical ideal, as a foreign socialist import. Nor do they see the welfare state as built by doctrinaire architects according to a dogmatic blueprint. The welfare state was pragmatically hammered out in response to a host of pressing problems and a host of pressing interests. These included the clear need for government regulation of certain aspects of the economy; the cries for help of depressed farmers, unemployed and ill-treated workers, bankrupt businessmen, and cheated consumers; the manifest need for unemployment compensation, old-age and survivor's insurance, farm price supports, the right to organize and bargain collectively, jobs on public works projects, low-cost housing, income for the poor and the needy, medical care for the elderly, environmental protection; and so on. No vision of nationalization guided the evolution of the welfare state. A "mixed economy"—minimal public ownership or control, considerable regulation, and a large "free" domain—and a welfare state emerged pragmatically as a somewhat haphazard democratic and constitutional response to twentieth century realities overlooked too long by an earlier laissez-faire America. Pragmatic twentieth century liberal democrats gave meaning to the Preamble's vision of a "more perfect Union."

Let me now turn to examine more fully such key liberal democratic operative ideals as limited, responsible, representative, popular government. This examination will illuminate the empirical understanding and functioning of liberal democratic politics as well as throw additional light on its ethical vision. This examination will, furthermore, underscore the centrality of the concept of balance in liberal democratic politics. Finally, this examination may suggest how the liberal democratic view functions to strengthen the dominant forces of the status quo in liberal democratic politics.

Limited, Responsible, Representative, Popular Government

The key to the modern liberal democrat's empirical understanding of politics lies in the recognition that in society a multiplicity of interests exist and seek to protect and advance themselves. The struggles of these contending interests—some of which are, of course, more powerful than others—constitute the raw material of politics. These struggles are inevitable because they are rooted in liberty and diversity. Democratic and constitutional government functions to regulate the struggle among these interests on behalf of freedom and the common good, or, with modern pluralists, some approximation of the public interest. But government, to remain constitutional, must itself be controlled and kept honest. The struggle for power must be kept within bounds. It must be consistent with justice, domestic tranquility, the common defense, the general welfare, and liberty. The struggle for power must be civilized. Accommodation among contending interests must be sought. These objectives can best be achieved when government is limited, responsible, representative, and popular. These constitutional operative ideals help us better understand how the rules of the constitutional game function and how a judicious constitutional balance is struck between authority and liberty, higher law and man-made law, leaders and led, majorities and minorities, public interest and private interest, stability and change. It should also be noted that conflicts may break out between, say, popular government and limited government, or between responsible government and representative government, and that liberal democratic politics seeks to strike a judicious balance among these operative ideals in the continuing interest of striking a balance between liberty and authority.[13]

Limited Government

Historically, liberal democrats note, constitutional government emerged in order to guard against tyranny and the exercise of arbitrary power. Limits on governmental power were incorporated in constitutional agreements (whether in a written or unwritten basic charter of government or in unwritten consensus) and interpreted by governmental organs and political forces with the power to make them stick. In the modern world these limits were designed to exclude government from entering stipulated areas—for cxample, religion, thought, private property. In brief, certain matters were held to be outside the legitimate scope of governmental power. However, even in the exercise of legitimate and permissible powers, government was to operate in a nonarbitrary way to ensure the protection of life, liberty, and property. "Due process" was to prevail. Effective and regularized restraints on governmental power were to characterize constitutional politics. So it was, and is, in a system of constitutional politics that power is granted, prohibited, and restricted in the interest of delineating and legitimating the role of government and its kcy organs. Thus, the constitutional rules of the game establish what can and cannot be done by government, and what governmental organs are to do what in the exercise of power, and how those with power are to act. Moreover, because of the fear of omnipotent and arbitrary power, power (as in the American example) was itself divided and shared at the national level (separation of powers) and in the country as a whole (federalism). Here several different kinds of balance emerge: the balance of governmental organs (in the national government), the balance of geographical units (federalism), and the balance of social and economic and other forces. All contributed to the idea of limited government.[14]

Responsible Government

As the concept of limited government may involve pro-hibiting, granting, and restricting power, so the concept of responsible government may mean several things. And these several meanings illuminate another dimension of pluralistic balance. Responsible government may involve responsibility to a higher law (whether God or natural law or conscience). It may involve responsibility to the Constitution itself, and to the laws made under it. It may involve responsibility to the nation, or responsibility to the electorate, or responsibility to a majority within the electorate or within the legislature. It may involve responsibility to party. It may involve responsibility to the pro-fessional standards established by one's peers in or out of govern-ment. Here we see examples of ethical, legal, political, profes-sional, and economic responsibility. And here again—in response to the question: In the exercise of power, to whom (or what) is government to be responsible?—we note the relevance and operation (and ambiguity) of the constitutional principle of balance in working out an accommodation when clashes occur among the various senses of responsibility.

For example, what happens when responsibility to God, or natural law, or conscience clashes with responsibility to man-made law? When responsibility to nation clashes with respon-sibility to party? When responsibility to party clashes with responsibility to party leaders? When responsibility to capitalists clashes with responsibility to workers? When responsibility to producers clashes with responsibility to consumers? Or when responsibility to one group of industrialists, farmers, or workers clashes with responsibility to rival industrialists, farmers, or workers? And so on?

In constitutional politics the effort is made to ensure respon-sibility of government to the constitutional rules of the game through various effective and regularized techniques of account-ability: elections; public opinion; a free press; interest group pressures; the written or unwritten rules of the dominant economic, political, or social order; an independent judiciary;

legislative surveillance; impeachment; administrative superiors and peers; among others. These techniques ensure responsibility to key interests, citizens, the nation, party, law, and other governmental units and, indirectly, to God, natural law, and conscience. Patterns of accountability vary among constitutional systems (presidential or parliamentary); but most of these techniques are common to all liberal democratic constitutional systems. The key point is: Government recognizes that it is answerable for its performance. The fact that government (and also other political actors) may be answerable to more than one authority underscores the reality (and, its defenders would argue, the wisdom) of a pluralistic and balanced response. Monopoly—whether in religion, politics, economics—is therefore rejected as dangerous to freedom in any of these domains. Competition and choice are emphasized as positively good and as functioning to ensure the right balance between liberty and authority.[15]

Representative Government

In the modern democratic and constitutional world, governmental representatives are usually formally chosen by the electorate, with the organizing help of political parties. Leadership in government is determined, directly or indirectly, by majority or plurality decisions. But, again, we perceive the varying meanings of *representation* and, often, the representative's struggles to balance various factors in the conduct of his or her duties. For example, do representatives view themselves as trustees who, once elected, act on behalf of the higher interests of the whole political community—past, present, and future—pursuant to their own perception of the nation's good and to their own informed conscience? Or are the rules of the game best served, and responsibility best ensured, when representatives follow—as delegates—the will of the majority that elected them? (Or the will of the powerful political and economic interests that can make or break them?) Or, since parties make modern democratic and constitutional government free, possible, and responsible, do representatives as partisans follow the party at least on key issues? (And the party may itself be in conscious or unconscious accord with powerful economic and political interests; or the party may itself be attempting to form a coalition of diverse, and sometimes conflicting, interests and groups.) Or are representatives politicos who attempt, even more than the trustee, the delegate, or the partisan, the difficult job of balancing the varying responsibilities and pressures that face them: conscience, nation, constituency, interest group, party, and self-interest? Clearly, there is no easy answer in liberal democratic politics. Answers will vary from weak party to strong party system, from presidential to parliamentary system, from federal to unitary system, from one economic system to another. In the United States—as in other liberal democratic constitutional states—considerable balancing goes on. And, liberal democrats argue, such balancing achieves approximate justice for the many legitimate interests that are brought to bear on public policy.[16]

Popular Government

Such balance, however, must—pursuant to the Lockean (and democratic) principle that the people must judge—be in general accord with the popular will (however difficult it may be to identify such a will). This must be the case particularly when the people are interested in and informed about a given issue of public policy. And to ensure a prominent role for the popular will, the rules of liberal democratic politics require that the people participate actively within the framework of their competence. The people must be free, and have adequate opportunities, to express their needs, concerns, aspirations. The people must be free to judge policies, parties, and leaders; to debate and discuss; and to select among competing leaders, parties, and broad policies. To do so they must enjoy those civil liberties that permit them to evaluate the operation of government and the fulfillment of the objectives of a more nearly perfect Union and, especially, to assess the character and performance of parties and political leaders. Hence, we find in liberal democratic politics a commitment to functioning civil liberties, including robust debate and a widespread suffrage. Hence, too, a commitment to an informed and vigilant public opinion. And to a diligent and responsible press. And to the existence and competition of parties. And to a plurality of contending interests able to articulate and press their claims. In all these ways the people can protect their vital interests; in all these ways the needs and aspirations of the people of the political community can be served. Popular government is thus closely intertwined (and compatible) with representative, responsible, and limited government. A moderate and balanced constitutional interpretation of the rules of the constitutional game by a diverse citizenry (and by diverse economic, social, and political forces—none of which has a monopoly of power in the economy, in society, or in government) can effectively advance the "more perfect Union."

Liberal democrats (who have sought to revise the classical operative ideals sketched above in the interest of a better balance between idealistic goals and the realistic facts of political life) do not, of course, reject limited, responsible, representative, and popular government. But they do interpret these operative ideals in ways that support the status quo. Government is limited in its ability to invade individual rights and capitalist enterprise. Government is keenly responsible to, and tends to represent, powerful economic, political, and social interests. Representative government triumphs over popular government interpreted as direct, or participatory, democracy.

These interpretations—which reflect existing reality—are conservative. They are reinforced by skepticism about the ideal and practicality of more active popular participation; by doubts about the existence of a monolithic power elite ruling on all significant matters; by the recognition of "minorities rule" and the dispersion of power;[17] by convictions about the good sense and actuality of democratic leadership within a pluralistic setting; by the reality and good sense of public policy as a result of group pressure and democratic compromises; by suspicions of a clear truth in politics that is the common good.

These considerations reinforce the preference of liberal democrats for moderation and stability and encourage them to endorse the status quo of currently contending interests and to oppose significant reforms or radical changes in the dominant economic, political, and social system. In the interest of a more judicious balance between political idealism and political realism, liberal democrats adopt a more conservative interpretation of limited, responsible, representative, and popular government. Consequently, it is not surprising that their judgments in attempting to balance liberty and authority should illustrate considerable satisfaction with the existing liberal order, including a fundamental acceptance of welfare state capitalism. It is an easy step, for some liberal democrats, to the proposition that existing democratic and constitutional politics constitutes the best practicable life, if not *the* good life.[18]

The Crucial Role of Prudent Judgment

The very commitment to plurality, to balance, to tolerance, to self-interest, to accommodation, to the rules of the prescriptive liberal democratic constitution—this very commitment emphasizes the importance and crucial role of prudent judgment in liberal democratic politics. Judgments are required to protect one's legitimate self-interests. Choice is central in the politics of pluralistic balance.[19] Under the rules of the constitutional game and amid the pushes and pulls of conflicting interests, judgments are required in harnessing and umpiring the struggle for power. Judgments are required in balancing the equities: liberty and authority; justice and power; equality and freedom; individual and state; private interest and the public good; center and circumference; clashing economic, social, and political interests; party and nation; party and constituency; and so on. And in addition to difficult judgments on domestic issues, there are vexing problems of judgment called for in foreign affairs— troublesome judgments involving war and peace, economics, trade, monetary policies, and the like. These judgments can best be made by democratic citizens and leaders who have competence and sustained interest in these matters. According to the model of liberal democratic politics, judgments can, theoretically, be authentically prudential because the ends of the more nearly perfect Union are defensible, and the rational means employed are compatible with these ends.

The twentieth century liberal democratic gloss on this model reinforces the conservative, rather than the liberal or radical, commitments of this model. It is wiser for democratic leaders rather than the democratic rank and file to make key judgments. The role of the citizenry is to be restricted primarily to major elections that permit the citizenry to exercise a broad choice on top leaders, key parties, and simplified public policy issues. Moreover, the modern liberal democratic stress on stability, order, moderation, and equilibrium reinforces cautious judgments, political bargaining, compromises, coalition politics, and stalemates. Public policies are frequently the result of such judgments; and they tend to reflect the dominant forces in the community—political, economic, and social.[20]

So it is, then, that liberal democratic politics recognizes the importance—the ongoing importance—of prudent judgments in politics. The character of those judgments—as well as the quality of the ideals and the accuracy of the empirical understanding of liberal democratic politics—must now be carefully assessed. It is not easy, as my treatment above has perhaps already suggested, to separate completely the attempt simply to state the characteristics of liberal democratic politics from an implied assessment of the strengths and weaknesses of this pattern of politics. To a more direct and somewhat more complete assessment let me now turn.

THE STRENGTHS OF LIBERAL DEMOCRATIC POLITICS

Liberal democratic politics constitutes a great historical achievement in political history. It is a landmark in the evolution of human civilization. It constitutes a generally successful effort to work out rules of the political game that strike a needed balance between individual freedom and development *and* the vital interests that comprise the common good. Generous power on behalf of the political community is legitimized; yet individual rights are generally protected. Arbitrary power has usually been proscribed. Effective and regularized restraints on the exercise of power have been established and maintained. Generally, government has been made reasonably responsible to the people's representatives, and the representatives to the people. The state is not idolized, and the reign of earthly perfection is not expected or defended. From Aristotle to the modern constitutional world, the polity, and its contemporary liberal democratic expression, has been extolled as a political system able to ensure justice and order. Liberal democratic politics, it would seem, then, is able to avoid the worst features of both Machiavellian and utopian politics while realistically safeguarding vital community interests and sustaining the difficult quest for the more nearly perfect Union. Liberal democratic politics seems to have built into itself a realistic sense of the strengths and weaknesses of self-interest in society and politics as well as a hope for the progressive achievement of the constitutional mission on behalf of human freedom and community fulfillment. This, at least, is the correct assessment according to sympathetic theorists of liberal democratic politics in the modern world. And, many would argue, practice is substantially in accord with theory.

Modern idealistic-realistic revisions of classical liberal democratic politics serve to accentuate the traditional strengths of this pattern of politics. These revisions include the necessity of an expanded suffrage, protection for civil rights, the value of a mixed economy, and the sense of the welfare state. These revisions democratize and humanize classical laissez-faire liberal democracy.

Other revisions make liberal democratic politics more realistic. These involve, for example, a more realistic assessment of leaders and led; a rejection of the myth of a dogmatic common good in favor of the realistic proposition that public policy is, and wisely can be, the resultant of group pressures and the outcome of democratic compromises; and an acceptance of the possibility of achieving both stability and welfare in a system of regulated capitalism. Foolish expectations about popular participation are rejected. Democratic rulers are inevitable and can be held responsible through the competition of elites, parties, and elections. Messianic illusions about a dogmatic truth—a common good—are abandoned in favor of the sober effort to ensure a public policy agreeable to affected and dominant interests. A stable democratic welfare state can respond to the evils of capitalism and ensure a broader base of democratic support.

In this way stability and orderly progress are enhanced, divisive ideological conflicts are avoided, and authoritarianism and totalitarianism are rejected. A pluralistic balance of power contributes to social, economic, and political justice. The actual democratic and constitutional state becomes the model of the best practicable, if not the utopian, life. Vices—interestingly enough—become transformed into virtue. Popular apathy becomes democratic stability. Oligarchic rule becomes democratic leadership—and there is nothing to worry about with such leadership because no single, coherent, monolithic elite rules consistently on all the issues. The inability to identify clearly and pursue the common good becomes a sane tolerance for the many interests contending for power and advantage; and the resulting public policy—especially as it is expressed in a stable democratic welfare state—becomes the best approximation to justice on earth.[21]

THE WEAKNESSES OF LIBERAL DEMOCRATIC POLITICS

Despite its unquestionable strengths, liberal democratic politics is also characterized by certain weaknesses. From the perspective of prophetic politics, these weaknesses are clear: a faulty ethical vision, a deficient empirical understanding, and a timid prudential assessment. These weaknesses can be seen both in aspects of classical liberal democracy, understood in its historic relation to a middle-class economic, political, and social order, and in the modern idealistic-realistic version of liberal democratic politics.

First, the vision of liberal democratic politics is ethically faulty. Historically, the liberal democratic understanding of the "more perfect Union" has excluded Native Americans, blacks, women, and the poor. Recent efforts to correct for this faulty vision have been incomplete. Theoretically, liberal democrats are committed to an expanded suffrage, the protection of civil rights, and human welfare; but this theoretical commitment is offset by doubts about the wisdom of more popular involvement, by a lack of passionate concern for the least free, and by a generally uncritical understanding of the operation of a capitalist economy.

Of course, relatively speaking, working people (benefiting, as all Americans have, from a richly endowed land, agricultural and industrial frontiers to exploit, cheap food and energy, and a huge internal market) have fared reasonably well in liberal democratic America. It is the case, however, that the more perfect Union has never forthrightly faced the problem of worker alienation and democratic direction of the economy, or the problem of ecological malaise. Liberal democrats in the United States have been profligate in their exploitation of their God-given resources of land, water, timber, and minerals, and they have demonstrated a shocking disregard for the nation's ecological health. They may have limited the tyrannical power of government in most instances, but they have not seriously asked about abuses of human and natural resources. They have not adequately protected against the vandal aspects of the ideology of liberalism. Their sense of responsibility for the least free, for the environment, and for the future is weak. The least free, clean air and water, and posterity have lacked powerful representation in our liberal democratic politics. The people who have judged in the liberal democratic United States have most often been the rich and the powerful. Clearly, a more passionate concern for the quality of our more perfect Union, and for a just and caring community, has too often been lacking.

To note these matters is to underscore liberal democratic complacency in its own appraisal of its own ethos and processes. Liberal democrats have been too tolerant of existing evils. They have lacked a firm conviction of a common good that would ensure a more desirable future political order. So it is that liberal democratic politics today suffers from a too-easy acceptance of the going order, of the status quo, of the prescriptive constitution. Its practitioners too often act as if they had reached the end of the road of wise political evolution. They are prone to accept the rhetoric of liberal democratic ideals for the reality and thus to close their eyes to the often ugly reality.

Liberal democratic symbols—whether of individual, group, community, government—also need to be reexamined. Is the individual really free and capable of mature development? Are groups "factional" in Madison's sense (of being opposed to the common good), or are they legitimately protecting legitimate vital interests? Does a genuine sense of a caring and compassionate community exist? Does government really rest upon the consent of the governed? To raise these questions is not to indict liberal democratic politics as completely heartless but to suggest that it can too easily forget, neglect, become accustomed to, the difficult-to-deal-with evils of existing society.

Liberal democratic politics may be too willing, too easily, to settle for less. It may forget to dream dreams, may lack a true vision of individual realization within the framework of the common good, of a just and caring community, of a greater measure of democracy—real citizen involvement—in our social, economic, and political lives, of ecological sanity. Liberal democratic politics—smug and complacent about its accomplishments—may have lost a passionate and imaginative commitment to the achievement of a better future. Overly impressed by Machiavellian realism, it may have prematurely ruled out all the dreams of utopian politics as undesirable.[22]

Second, liberal democratic politics is deficient empirically. It has refused to see more deeply into the relationship between ethics and politics, economics and politics, ecology and politics. It has not probed significantly enough the consequences of public

policy as a resultant of group pressures. It has been blind to the
vandal aspects of the ideology of liberalism. It has often been falsely
realistic. By focusing too sharply on the status quo, it has ignored
the weak and the poor and the oppressed. It has often missed
recessive forces that have become, or can become, dominant. It has
overlooked new possibilities. It has rarely fully explored the relationship between a capitalist economic order and a democratic,
social, economic, and political order. It has been unwilling to explore economic alternatives to modern capitalism or modern
socialism. Its commitment to incremental change has deterred it
from more radical systemic criticism. It has missed the gulf between the principles of limited, responsible, representative, and
popular government and the practice of such government.

Clearly, to concentrate on the given—particularly the
powerful—is (today as always) to miss the often invisible forces of
politics, forces that do not come to attention except in periods of
crisis, riot, or revolution. To miss the recessive forces of today
that will become dominant tomorrow is to miss not simply future
possibilities but future actualities. This deficient empirical
understanding is manifested in a wrongheaded view of change.
Politics is too often seen in terms of balance, or equilibrium, and
hence in terms of the maintenance of the status quo. If politics is
seen in terms of progressive change, it is rarely seen in terms of
radical and rapid change—the kind of radical and rapid change
that may sometimes be required to handle not only some crucial
contemporary problem but also key problems of the twenty-first
century.

The details that flesh out these generalizations are seen most
dramatically in the empirical neglect of black people, of other
nonwhite people, of women, and of poor people in an often racist,
sexist, and blindly affluent dominant society. These details are
also seen in the failure to conquer unemployment; and in what
seems to be a congenital failure of liberal democratic politics to
face up to the problem of satisfaction and creativity in work—our
most basic life activity.[23]

And third, liberal democratic politics is too timid prudentially. It is too often wrongly conservative instead of rightly

conservative: for example, it may preserve poverty, racism, and sexism instead of civil liberties, economic well-being, or the environment. It is too often hesitant: particularly in its unwillingness to try new and bold economic, social, and political experiments—especially in its preference for stability over change, the known over the unknown. It is too slow in responding to admitted evils, for example, high levels of unemployment, ecological disasters, and rank racial and sexual discrimination. Liberal democratic politicians may lack the passion as well as the vision to act wisely. They may be wrongly convinced that most of the ways ordained by the liberal democratic prescriptive constitution are sound for the present and the future. They may even be too hesitant in fulfilling the best in the tradition of liberal democratic politics.

Consequently, liberal democratic politics is today less open to creative breakthroughs in politics: breakthroughs to broadened conception of limited, responsible, representative, and popular government; breakthroughs to more genuinely participatory communities; and (surprisingly for aristocratic and conservative critics) breakthroughs to a heightened concern for republican virtue and quality of life. Unfortunately, the injunction of liberal democratic politics—"to get along one must go along" often transforms genuine prudence into weak-kneed timidity and makes courageous and bold political wisdom impossible. And so a desirable tension between what ought to be and what is—a tension that nourishes courageous judgment in politics—disappears.[24]

Twentieth century revisions in liberal democratic theory—those presumably designed to advance a more realistic understanding of liberal democratic politics—have facilitated the disappearance of this tension. These revisions reflect adverse judgments on the intelligence and capability of common people, on the possibility of identifying a common good, on alternatives to the economic, political, and social status quo. These realist revisions call for democratic elitism, a recognition of the rough justice in a public policy hammered out by contending interests, and an appreciation of the good life in the welfare state.

Unfortunately, the judgment of the "best and the brightest" turns out to be defective in the Vietnam War. The temptation to guard the security of the state by fair means or foul—in moments of crisis—also reveals the loss of devotion to higher ethical standards. Vietnam and Watergate illustrate the persistence of Machiavellian judgments in the liberal democratic state. The emphasis on stability, order, and moderation—so noticeable in modern liberal democrats—clearly contributes to a loss of tension between what ought to be and what is in liberal democratic politics. So, too, does the press of everyday political business, the conviction about the difficulties and dangers of change, the doubts about the feasibility of suggested reforms, and the skepticism about radical political moralists.

Generally, liberal democrats—largely because of their greater tolerance of the existing order and its considerable virtues—are less predisposed to make those bolder judgments that are the very stuff of creative breakthroughs in politics.[25] There may, of course, be virtue in balance (understood as respect for many contending interests; as juxtaposing power and power; as equilibrium of conflicting pressures; as enhancing economic, political, and social stability); but preoccupation with any virtue may transform it into a vice.

So it is that emphasis upon democratic elitism, skepticism of an unmistakable common good, and preference for a stable, moderate welfare state in a system of regulated capitalism affect the ethical vision, the empirical understanding, and the prudential judgment of modern liberal democrats. These factors operate to strengthen the dominant forces of liberal democratic politics. They make it more likely that liberal democrats will fail to approximate more fully the more nearly perfect Union. They suggest why limited, responsible, representative, popular government will function to preserve the status quo in sometimes questionable ways. They make it more likely that government will be limited, responsible, representative, and popular only insofar as dominant political, economic, and social groups are concerned. That the populace, in general, and the least free, in particular, will not have their genuine needs considered. That workers will not have greater control over their economic lives. That the scientific, economic, and technological challenges of the late twentieth century—in education, industry, agriculture, and trade—will not be met. That liberal democratic nations will remain crassly indifferent to ecological depredations. That representatives will be partly blind and partly deaf to weak minority groups and to women. That power will not be employed safely to achieve greater economic, social, and political justice. That quality of life—as reflected in a significant decrease in crime and in a significant increase in highly literate, socially caring, and culturally endowed people—will not be appreciably enhanced.

CONCLUSION

In my presentation of liberal democratic politics, I have deliberately stressed the importance of democratic and constitutional principles. Constitutional principles preceded the liberal democratic state. They were incorporated within liberal democratic politics. And they will, and must, endure in any future democratic political order. But if the self-interest of the bourgeoisie led them to advance the cause of constitutionalism and popular rule, the self-interest of workers, consumers, blacks, women, environmentalists, peace advocates, may lead them, in turn, to use constitutional and democratic principles on their own behalf—and on behalf of a common good that transcends all classes, whether a capitalist class or a working class, whites or blacks, men or women. Historically, excluded classes, groups, and interests have broadened our understanding of both constitutionalism and democracy—and of the common good— by demanding that they be included. Ironically, these self-interested claims have enhanced our understanding of the common good, of a broader range of legitimate human interests and needs, of the linkage between democratic power and constitutional protection, of the larger community in which we live. Any guiding pattern of politics for the twenty-first century must remain committed to the progressive flowering of soundly prescriptive constitutional and democratic principles.

Liberal democratic politics must be seen as a stage in the flowering of constitutional and democratic principles. Despite its weaknesses, those guided by this pattern have learned to live amid, and to deal with, the harsh realities of Machiavellian politics but without sacrificing too much of a higher political ethics. Important vital interests have been protected, even if not all such interests adequately. Religious, economic, and political interests—suspicious of state interference—did not idolize the state. Leaders of the state were limited, restrained, and made accountable. The "beastly" world of Machiavellian politics was, generally, made less beastly and somewhat more human.

The practitioners of liberal democratic politics have also been very successful in avoiding the weaknesses of utopian politics, even if they have been less successful in incorporating its strengths. Guided by the cautionary Niebuhrian judgment that in politics we can seek only proximate solutions to insoluble problems, they have resisted falsely messianic passions for earthly paradise. Yet, to some modest degree, they have been able to move toward some semiutopian approximations of justice, domestic peace, security, general welfare, liberty, equality, and fraternity. Certainly, the common person, the ordinary citizen, has improved his or her lot in the modern democratic and constitutional state. And there are a number of liberal democrats—for example, J. Roland Pennock and Robert A. Dahl—who strive to improve on liberal democratic theory and practice. But what of the weaknesses of liberal democratic politics?

These weaknesses suggest that—and where—we can do better in politics. The weaknesses of liberal democratic politics are significant, but they must not be exaggerated. In our zeal to improve on liberal democratic politics, we must be careful not to weaken or destroy its sound principles and practices.[26] In comparison with authoritarian regimes of the Right or Left—whether they are semifascist or semi- or full-fledged Communist regimes—liberal democratic regimes merit support.

On the other hand, a misguided complacency, a thoughtless tolerance, a restricted future vision, can threaten the continued existence of liberal democratic regimes themselves. So can a distorted and often false understanding of present and future. So can wrongly conservative judgments on policy responses to clear-cut evils. As I have argued, too many modern liberal democrats illustrate a limited ethical vision, deficient empirical understanding, and timid prudential judgment. They are willing to settle for less. Their vision of the "more perfect Union" is dim. Their bolder exploration of the fuller meaning of limited, responsible, representative, and popular government is either nonexistent, incomplete, or tardy. Their judgments are unimaginative. They seem to have lost faith in common people and a common good and breakthroughs beyond a welfare state and mixed economy characterized by large-scale unemployment, large pockets of poverty, and persistent economic and social inequities. They may grumble about the abuse of the welfare state and excessive government regulation, but they still accept the idea of a welfare state and a mixed economy as a good and necessary modification of the older liberal laissez-faire order. They pay lip service to popular government, but they really mean representative government; they are very suspicious of a greater measure of participatory democracy.

Here we see their overly conservative understanding of limited, responsible, representative government. They are reluctant to confront and upset powerful economic interests. They seem tuned in to the dominant: to the strong, the wealthy, the visible. Preoccupied with dominant interests and appetites, with tidying up the normal liberal democratic paradigm, they are ill-equipped to face up to the larger ecological, economic, international problems that threaten the ability of liberal democratic politics to guide us in the twenty-first century.

Liberal democratic politics, then, even as revised by those who would fulfill some ideals and adjust theory and practice to empirical reality in other key respects, seems incapable of the judgments that are called for today and tomorrow. In the economic sphere liberal democratic politicians have glossed over the systemic weaknesses of capitalism and the effect of its operation on a healthy economy, a healthy environment, and a healthy social system; and they have failed to press for a greater measure of industrial democracy. In the social sphere liberal democratic politicians have failed to move toward a healthy and more meaningful community that would do justice to bona fide human needs. In the political sphere they are allergic to creative breakthroughs in political participation and public policy. And, finally, in the intellectual sphere they have failed to articulate a more prophetic politics.

Our difficult and creative task is to build on the strengths, as we seek to overcome the weaknesses, of liberal democratic politics. We can wisely recapture the bolder, courageous vision of outstanding theorists and practitioners of early epochs in democratic and constitutional politics, even as we recognize their historical shortcomings. Inspired by their creativity, in their own time, we can be encouraged to articulate, again, a superior vision of democratic and constitutional politics which, to differentiate it from liberal democratic politics, we might call *prophetic politics*. But what, in more detail, is the style of politics that I have called *prophetic politics*? To that question I now turn in Chapter 5.

III : Prophetic Politics: The Radical Politics of Life, Growth, and Fulfillment

5 : The Prophetic Paradigm

INTRODUCTION

Two key questions concern us in Chapter 5. First, what vision of civilized survival, healthy growth, and creative fulfillment will ensure the future of the democratic revolution? By *civilized survival* I mean more than sheer physical existence; I mean a human life that enables political actors to carry on their political—and social and cultural—business in a humane way. By *healthy growth* I mean development free of war, oppression, and exploitation that permits one political community to enlarge its capacities, increase its wealth and power, or enhance its fulfillment—but at the expense of other political communities, groups, individuals, or nature itself. Positively, *healthy growth* means development toward sounder ways of dealing with the struggle for power, of enhancing prosperity, of achieving a harmonious ecological balance. By *creative fulfillment* I mean the progressive achievement of excellence in all domains of human endeavor—in the arts and sciences as well as in politics, economics, and social life. Second, does prophetic politics provide us with that vision? These are the question that trouble us.

It is clear—if my argument up to this point is persuasive—that we must move up to a new level of politics. It is equally clear that Machiavellian politics, utopian politics, and liberal democratic politics are far from adequate and may, indeed, be disastrous. We have seen that moving from Machiavellian politics to utopian politics only makes matters worse. This we might seek to avoid by placing our faith in liberal democratic politics; but, upon closer examination, we have discovered that liberal democratic politics, although very good, is simply not good enough. We seek, ideally, to avoid the weaknesses of all three of these patterns while yet incorporating their undoubted strengths. But is it possible to do this in that pattern we have identified as prophetic politics?

To begin to answer these questions we will attempt in this chapter, and in the next three chapters, to spell out a little more fully the distinguishing characteristics of prophetic politics and to identify its strengths and weaknesses. In this chapter we will explore the prophetic paradigm—its origins, strands, development, and cardinal features. In Chapter 6 we will investigate the nature and uses of prophetic criticism, a criticism that blends ethical concerns and modern social science. In Chapters 7 and 8 we will probe the meaning—and indispensability—of prophetic constitutional breakthroughs, particularly on four crucial fronts (peace, human rights, economic well-being, and ecological balance). In Chapter 9 we will examine continuous prophetic scrutiny and futuristic projection in an effort to test the value of futuristic scenarios and to underscore the need for continuous scrutiny, even of the strengths and weaknesses of prophetic politics itself. In these chapters we will be particularly concerned with how this pattern blends ideals, realities, and judgments.

To set the stage for a fuller exposition of prophetic politics, let me again juxtapose the four patterns we are seeking to analyze in this book. As I have noted earlier: whereas the Machiavellian seeks to triumph in the inevitable struggle for power (by force and craft), and the utopian seeks, often after one last, great battle, to abolish the struggle for power (in a fulfilled, harmonious community), and the liberal democrat seeks continuously and judiciously to adjust power to power (within the framework of a liberal and largely capitalist status quo), the prophetic politician seeks to transform the struggle for power in radical but sane ways (in the interest of civilized life, healthy growth, and creative fulfillment). It has been difficult for the prophetic politician to move beyond the competing patterns I have identified because of the attraction of the "realism" of Machiavellian politics, because of the fears of a naive "idealistic" utopian politics, and because of the virtues of the "idealistic-realistic" balance of liberal democratic politics.

It becomes important, therefore, to demonstrate that prophetic politics is in tune with a genuinely realistic protection of the vital interests of the political community. It is also important to distinguish convincingly between utopian and prophetic politics—particularly between unsound utopian and sound prophetic ideals—in order to demonstrate that the weaknesses of utopian politics are not to be found in prophetic politics. And, finally, it is important to emphasize that prophetic politics—as a superior democratic and constitutional politics—incorporates the virtues of liberal democratic politics, especially its efforts to achieve a sensible balance between political ideals and political realities.

The failure to distinguish between the utopian and the prophetic can lead to the rejection of prophetic politics along with utopian politics and to an unthinking acceptance of liberal democratic politics. The blurring of important differences between the utopian and the prophetic may lead the uncritical observer to fail to see that the legitimate criticisms leveled at utopian politics do not hold for prophetic politics. The consequences of this failure and blurring are inhibiting and conservative. We may become convinced that since utopian politics is dangerous, and Machiavellian politics is disastrous, the only acceptable alternative is liberal democratic politics—the conservative pluralistic politics of the capitalist welfare state. Indeed, the adverse critic of prophetic politics may maintain that prophetic politics, in order to avoid the weaknesses of utopian politics, must be substantially identifiable with liberal democratic politics. Hence, in outlining the distinguishing characteristics of prophetic politics, it is crucial to differentiate not only between prophetic and utopian politics but also between prophetic and liberal democratic politics.

THE MAJOR STRANDS OF, AND INFLUENCES ON, PROPHETIC POLITICS

But how are we to understand the strands of prophetic politics? And will this understanding also help us to distinguish prophetic politics from both utopian and liberal democratic politics? We should also appreciate that the identification of the strands out of which this pattern is woven will also serve to highlight its sources and other factors influencing its development.

Prophetic politics is fashioned by a number of interrelated strands: (1) the soundly religious, (2) the constitutional, (3) the democratic, and (4) the scientific. These strands in turn, have been influenced by certain (5) philosophical and (6) historical movements that reinforce these strands in important ways. Let me examine each of these strands, in turn, and then the reinforcing movements of thought and action.

The Soundly Religious Strand

The soundly religious strand—crucial in the development of Western constitutionalism and of liberation movements in the Judaic-Christian tradition—has its origins in biblical monotheism as refined by biblical prophetic faith.[1] This faith looks to human and societal fulfillment in accord with a divine, a transcendent, paradigm. The soundly religious is passionately concerned with the achievement of the kingdom of righteousness and—in the Judaic-Christian tradition—is intimately related to the messianic idea, what Jacob Talmon has called the "finest original form" of messianism.

> In its final original form Messianism was a vital aspect of the Judeo-Christian tradition, a witness to the depth and intensity of its conscience. It was an extreme expression of that obsessive preoccupation of the Western World with the question of the legitimacy of power, of that irresistible need to submit its thoughts and actions

to the criteria of some ideal, of that urge to justify ourselves before some higher tribunal, and to try to realize the ideal of righteousness on earth.[2]

The biblical concept of covenant illuminates the meaning of the soundly religious and helps us to see the link between the religious idea of covenant and the secular idea of a superior political constitution. Central to the idea of covenant is the voluntary but enduring compact (between God and the people of Israel) to fulfill an agreement by which higher rules for living, as prescribed by God, are freely accepted by the people of Israel in the contractual expectation that honoring God's commandments will bring them the good life—a life of peace, freedom, justice, abundance, fulfillment. The covenant establishes a loving relationship between God and the people of Israel; this relationship is a prototype of the relationship between God and all humankind. The covenant calls into existence a holy community whose people are obligated to live in a holy way. The relationship between God and human beings becomes the model for all human relationships—individual, social, economic, political. By the terms of the covenant, human beings are obligated to act within certain limits. They are free to honor or violate covenantal requirements; but if they violate the requirements, they will, of course, be punished. But because the covenant is a loving relationship, God is forgiving and holds out hope for redemption if human beings sincerely repent and renew their covenantal obligations.[3]

The biblical prophets play a crucial role in developing soundly religious ideas within the covenantal framework. They both conserve and transform key covenantal ideas. They function to keep alive the great covenantal values for Israel and for all humankind. They return, again and again, to the ethical core of the covenantal message: to the affirmation of life and quality of life, to divine love as a model for human relationships, to the commandment to do justice, to the imperative to enhance freedom (particularly for the "least free"), and to the surpassing importance of securing peace. They criticize violators of the convenant and warn of God's wrath and punishment. They both warn of the dreadful prospect of disaster and hold out hope for redemption. They call for action to avert the threatened catastrophe. They demand a higher level of worship at a higher level of human behavior. They keep before humankind the vision of peace and the end of fear, of justice and the end of oppression, of love and the end of hate. They keep alive the *b'rith* (covenant) of *chesed* (love), of *tzedekah* (justice or righteousness), of *shalom* (peace and harmony). Covenant love goes beyond the strictly legal requirements of a contract by insisting upon generous concern, forgiveness, mercy. It helps to transform narrow conceptions of justice into compassionate righteousness. Similarly, covenant love influences the fuller harmony among human beings—and in the universe—that is peace. The prophetic interpretation of covenant thus powerfully stimulates the humane imagination and keeps the covenant idea alive and vital over time.

If the biblical prophets are incomprehensible without the covenant, so we cannot imagine the Messiah and the messianic vision without the prophets and the covenant. And, of course, there is a link between prophet and Messiah insofar as the prophets keep the messianic idea alive by keeping the covenantal vision alive. The Messiah is the powerful leader who will assist the Children of Light to triumph over the Children of Darkness. He will lead the children of Israel to victory over their enemies. He is the righteous figure whose coming and action will result in the glorious fulfillment of the covenant. With the advent of Christianity, one interpretation of the messianic idea achieves a wider audience and increased potency, first in the Western world and then throughout the globe.

A critical examination of the messianic idea, however brief, helps us to distinguish—as we must—between the soundly and unsoundly religious. Clearly, messianism has been a most powerful force in religion and politics—for good or for evil. On one hand, the Messiah's association with the covenant (as understood by the biblical prophets) illustrates the truth, power, and fruitfulness of covenantal ideals. On the other hand, the

Messiah's association with Armageddon—and with that millennial interpretation of the "end of days," which actually looks to the repeal of covenantal law among the victorious saints—illustrates the dangers of the messianic imagination. The dream of the absence of law, interdiction, restraints, limits, and conflicts in a society of saints can easily become a dreadful nightmare. Given these considerations, we can appreciate the importance of the struggle to harness the power of the messianic idea in the right way. Indeed, we could argue that the central question before Western civilization (and, now, since the advent of Marxism in the nineteenth century, before world civilization) is whether we shall be successful in that struggle. Within the covenantal (the genuinely prophetic) harness—which in secular politics means the constitutional harness—messianic power has a fantastic ability to accomplish sane transformation. Outside that harness, messianism—either a perverted religious or secular messianism—can destroy the world and its peace, justice, freedom, and resources in falsely "righteous" battle against the enemies of "righteousness."[4] This examination of the uses of the religious idea of messianism may help to clarify the distinction between the soundly religious and the unsoundly religious, as it may also serve to distinguish between prophetic and utopian politics.

A soundly religious interpretation of the covenantal idea is the prophetic interpretation; it is not the false messianism portrayed above. The prophetic interpretation of covenant insists upon wise limits. It avoids the danger of hubris. It does not presuppose, even though it aspires to, the fulfillment of the harmonious community. The coming of the Messiah does not mean the repudiation of the covenant, but its fulfillment; not the end of Torah, but its effective power. Peace, virtue, freedom, and prosperity are only meaningful within the framework of the covenant. Their coming will not abolish the covenant. So understood, the covenant idea as it becomes the animating power of the secular constitution holds open a genuinely fruitful alternative for humankind. Most significantly, by harnessing the power of what Talmon has called the "finest original form" of

"Messianism," by putting that power to work within the framework of covenant/constitution, as prophetically interpreted, that power can be made safe and fruitful for humankind. The soundly religious would thus simultaneously emphasize release and restraint: unprecedented realization for every person's inalienable rights within a framework of both aspirations and limitations—both of which are ordained by a divine order and wisely accepted by free and rational (if fallible) human beings.[5]

The relevance of this soundly religious, prophetic interpretation of covenant to contemporary politics should now be clear. It is a "radical/conservative" interpretation. It is an interpretation that commits us to choose and conserve (preserve) life, to make more secure our capacity to grow, and to encourage the fulfillment of our human potentialities for ends compatible with covenantal standards. Such a biophilic ethics must be the root of any defensible political philosophy. Given the threats to such ethics, we may be obligated—always within the wise limits of the covenantal framework—to adopt some "radical" measures to secure the values of the covenant. For example, under appropriate safeguards we may have to dismantle the war machine—the modern equivalent of beating swords into plowshares and spears into pruning hooks. We may have to opt for a more humanistic economics—to ensure prosperity, greater job satisfaction, economic democracy, a prudent steady-state economy—the modern equivalent of the land of milk and honey and a caring community. We may have to universalize the protection of basic rights—to make freedom for all meaningful, to ensure the modern equivalent of protecting widows, orphans, strangers, and the poor. We may have to learn to make courageous, farsighted decisions on behalf of ecological health via biospheric balance; and on behalf of the achievement of wise regulation of God-given resources, a sensible balance between population and resources, and an end to disastrous pollution—the modern equivalent of respect for God's good earthly creation. These illustrations may thus serve to clarify the meaning of the soundly religious.

The Constitutional Strand

The constitutional strand is not, of course, unrelated to the soundly religious—as its treatment above should have made abundantly clear. The constitutional strand rests upon, and emphatically underscores the need for, a fundamental covenant to establish ends and mean in politics: respect for the integrity of the individual and for the common good that must illuminate our communal association. The constitution thus serves to provide just, known, orderly, regular rules of the political game: rules to legitimate power, rules to establish bounds for power, rules to establish effective restraints upon the exercise of power, rules to protect basic rights, and rules to encourage the maximization of individual realization within the framework of the common good. Carl J. Friedrich and a number of scholars have convincingly demonstrated the important linkage between what Friedrich calls the "religious dimension" and constitutionalism. Friedrich maintains: "Constitutionalism, understood as the belief in the basic features of a constitution, such as human dignity and the rights implied in it, and the lust for power and the need for restraining it, is a central feature of Western civilization and its Judeo-Christian belief system. It might disintegrate and pass away, if that belief system were to die."[6]

The constitutional strand in prophetic politics helps to translate into political practice the covenantal emphasis on both release and restraint. Here a fuller comparison of covenant and constitution (based on the Sinai Covenant and the U.S. Constitution) and an examination of the prophetic interpretation of constitution serve to underscore this emphasis and help us to distinguish prophetic politics from both utopian and liberal democratic politics.[7]

Superior Origin and Standard of Judgment: The Higher-Lower Contrast

The Sinai Covenant comes to us (if we are traditional believers) through divine revelation; or, if we are skeptical, through inspired prophetic leadership. The U.S. Constitution was drafted by our Founding Fathers, an unusually gifted group of men, and ratified by (relatively) popular conventions in the several states. Its immediate legitimacy comes from the ultimate source of legitimate secular power in a republic: the constituent power of the people themselves. However, insofar as the Constitution is inspired by a "Higher Law," its truly ultimate source is also transcendent.[8] The Declaration of Independence, which provides the argument for the new "station" of the Americans and is the first of the national covenants that culminated in the Constitution of 1787, makes clear that Americans are entitled to their "station" by "the Laws of Nature and of Nature's God," that it is their "Creator" who has endowed them with "unalienable Rights—Life, Liberty and the pursuit of Happiness," and that they appeal to the "Supreme Judge of the World" as witness and protector. The superior standard of judgment in the Sinai Covenant is, of course, the divine paradigm, or, if you will, the prophetic paradigm—the divine paradigm as expressed by the most ethically sensitive humans: those who spoke God's word. The Sinai Decalogue is the vital heart of the covenant: the relationship of God to humans, of humans to God, and of humans to humans. The prophetic paradigm keeps our eyes continuously focused on the heart of the covenantal relationship: God's love; God's commands to do justice, love mercy, walk humbly; God's prohibitions of idolatries; God's promise of peace and freedom and prosperity for fulfilling his law. In the United States the Constitution is the "supreme Law of the Land." It is dedicated to the fulfillment of the great ideals of the Preamble: a more perfect Union, justice, domestic tranquility, common defense, general welfare, liberty.

The points made above underscore the fundamental contrast between a higher and lower law, with the lower subordinated to the higher.[9] In the Sinai Covenant the contrast is between the divine and the human; divine law must prevail over human law if there is a conflict between the two. With regard to the U.S. Constitution, the contrast is between a superior and an inferior law. Federal law or action in conflict with the Constitution must fall. The Constitution is the higher standard used by Congress, the president, the courts, and the states.

Agreement: Free Popular Choice

The Sinai Covenant is an agreement between God and the people of Israel. It is freely entered into; it is not based on coercion; it is based on consent. The people of Israel voluntarily choose to accept, and abide by, the Covenant. Similarly, the Constitution is a voluntary agreement among the people—of course, a fairly restricted electorate in the late eighteenth century—of the several states. They freely enter into the constitutional agreement; this agreement, too, is not coerced; it, too, is based on consent. The people of the several states voluntarily choose to accept, and abide by, the Constitution.

Community

In each case—Covenant and Constitution—a community, a people, a nation, is established. The community becomes a lasting relationship. The Covenant endureth forever. Similarly, the Constitution creates "an indestructible union of indestructible states." The Covenant community is a holy community. It is united by common values. People in it are suffused by a sense of belonging together. They are conscious of their birth in freedom. They possess a vivid historical memory; they are conscious of their obligations and destiny to be a "holy people." Similarly, the community—the nation—that becomes the United States is a community called to higher responsibilities. Certain (if not all) common values, a sense of belonging together (at least for the dominant ruling elite), a vivid historical memory, a consciousness of a destiny as an experiment in republican freedom (at least for white males)—as a light unto the nations—these, too, characterize the American people at their best.

Obligation

Acceptance of the Covenant obliges the people of Israel to fulfill the commandments. This is central to the covenantal relationship.

Effort, action, and activity on behalf of covenantal values are demanded. Life must be chosen. Justice must be pursued. Freedom must be sought. Peace must be obtained. The biblical prophets remind the people of Israel and their rulers of these obligations. Similarly, the people of several states—through the federal government they have established—are also committed to the fulfillment of the objectives of the Preamble. Legitimate power must be exercised within the framework of due process. Illegitimate power—abuse of power—must be avoided. Congressmen, presidents, and Supreme Court justices take a solemn oath to protect the Constitution of the United States.

Rightful Power, Wise Limits, and Due Process

The Sinai Covenant thus demands the exercise of rightful power to fulfill the commandments of the Covenant within the framework of wise limitations set forth in the covenantal relationship. The same is true of the Constitution. Rightful power—the commerce power, the taxing power, the spending power, and so on—is to be exercised, but within the framework of the Constitution's limitations, rules, and requirements of due process. The Preamble's objectives do not constitute an independent source of power; but they illuminate the ends on behalf of which rightful power can be exercised.

The Sinai Covenant explicitly places limits on what people can and cannot do. Its famous interdictions are designed to guard against the wrongful exercise of power. They are designed to ensure the highest level of conduct for humans always capable, according to the rabbinic tradition, of succumbing to the *yetzer hara*—the evil inclination. The interdictions are purposely designed to advance and protect both individual integrity and the common good. They thus guard against sin, against pride—against what the Greeks called hubris. The Constitution also imposes limits. It limits the power of the central government, the power of states in the federal union, and, in some instances, the power of individuals. (State constitutions, of course, have greater powers, theoretically, in protecting the rights of their citizens against violations.) Federal law, passed under the Constitution, and in fulfillment of its objectives, may also limit groups, corporations, and individuals.

Both the covenantal tradition, as it develops in Talmudic literature, and the constitutional tradition are deeply committed to due process of law. Thus, even within the framework of legitimate powers, certain procedures must be followed to ensure that legitimate power stays legitimate. Of both Sinai Covenant and Constitution (as they develop over time), it can be said that "liberty is secreted in the interstices of procedure."[10]

The Mingling of Democratic and Aristocratic Elements

One must be careful; we must remember that the Sinai Covenant is not a democratic document in the modern sense. The Covenant does not provide a mandate for popular rule, and its understanding of basic rights is not our modern liberal democratic understanding. And, of course, the U.S. Constitution once sanctioned slavery. Yet both Sinai Covenant and U.S. Constitution are deeply committed, under God and a higher law, respectively, to the principles of human integrity and free choice—but without prejudice to genuinely aristocratic leadership. Prophets and priests, kings, judges, rabbis, provide leadership under the Covenant. Madison and most of the other Founding Fathers argued on behalf of wise leadership. Thomas Jefferson and John Adams (who were not at the Philadelphia Convention) looked to a natural aristocracy to provide wise leadership for the republic.[11] Basic rights—to worship God, to life, to liberty, to justice, to property—are to be protected by the Covenant. The Constitution of 1787 quickly added a Bill of Rights (in which religious freedom is the first mentioned in Article 1) to a document that already contained a number of key rights (for example, the writ of habeas corpus). If the Sinai Covenant is more compatible with theocracy than democracy, and the 1787 Constitution is more compatible with polity than modern democracy, we can still argue that the logic of both Covenant and Constitution demands a democratic evolution: satisfying legitimate human needs, extending human rights, encouraging popular education, extending popular participation. Both Covenant and Constitution call for creative dialogue and human fulfillment. A concept of what is best must suffuse all the people in the community.

Universality

The Sinai Covenant, although it begins with the people of Israel, clearly points toward the embrace of all humanity on the globe. The Covenant is a Covenant for all peoples. The Constitution is, of course, a document for a specific people, a nation on the North American continent; but the founders saw it as a light unto the whole world. Although both the people of Israel and the people of America looked upon themselves as chosen people, they also recognized themselves as chosen to illuminate Covenant and Constitution, respectively, for the entire globe.[12]

Worship and Love

The people of Israel, and then all humankind, are to worship God. The Torah is a tree of life. Similarly, Americans have, under God, revered the Constitution.[13] The Constitution is a cherished document. It, too, is a tree of life to which Americans have felt they must hold fast, particularly in times of adversity. Love of God demands love of neighbor. This is a convenantal imperative. Love of country—patriotism—cannot, of course, be equated with the love of God. But when the Constitution is seen, as it has been, as an expression of higher law, the idolatry of narrow patriotism, the inadequacies of the "civil religion," can be transcended. Love of one's fellows who share the covenantal/constitutional relationship then comes close to love of God and neighbor. This kind of love that demands the extra responsibility, the extra step, on behalf of fellow human beings and the common good can be illustrated (sometimes if not always, and partially if not fully) in U.S. history.

*The Recognition of Conflict and the
Imperative of Peaceful Accommodation*

The Sinai Covenant does not assume a conflictless society—certainly not before the "end of days." The covenantal tradition sees conflict as a fact of life, but an unhappy fact. The persistence of murder, robbery, injustice, reinforces the widsom of covenantal interdictions. Humans respond by seeking, as well as mortal and fallible creatures can, to overcome the worst conflicts and to achieve peaceful resolutions of inevitable, but tolerable, disputes. Wise patterns of accommodation are, therefore, necessary. But if a sinful inclination produces conflict, a good inclination (*yetzer tov*) also makes peaceful accommodation possible. The acceptance of the divine/human contrast would have led the prophets to endorse Madison's dictum that if men were angels, no government would be necessary, and his observation that we cannot presuppose, in society or politics, harmony or total unanimity. Madison would conclude that since we must, in politics, rule out unanimity and anarchy, and since minority rule violates the republican principle, we must accept majority rule as a sensible technique of practical accommodation.[14] Constitutional government constitutes the ongoing search for wise and effective patterns of accommodation among inevitably conflicting interests in human society. However, it should be clear that neither the biblical prophets nor the Founding Fathers accepted the desirable inevitability of all conflicts—especially war. The Sinai Covenant outlawed murder. The prophets sought to end war. So, too, the Founding Fathers saw the Constitution as an effort to overcome the worst conflicts—especially civil war—and to bring other conflicts under the control of patterns of peaceful accommodation.

Creative Tension

The points above about conflict and accommodation underscore the tension that exists in both the covenantal and constitutional relationship. Tension will always exist in the relationship between a perfect God and an imperfect human being, between a superior standard and a sinful, fallible people obliged to fulfill that standard. We should note, however, that this tension is by no means an unmitigated evil. Indeed, such tension can function magnificently to guard against complacency.[15] We sin. We violate the Covenant. But, under the standard of the Sinai Covenant, we cannot be complacent—or, to use the more arresting theological concept, guiltless—about our violations. We are, indeed, compelled to repent, to right the wrong, to work out a better pattern of accommodation among conflicting interests within the framework of the Covenant. A comparable tension exists between a higher constitutional law and the law of our daily lives—our often fallible, shortsighted, selfish lives. The higher constitutional standard constantly reminds us of wrongs committed in the name of nation, class, race, and sex, and reminds us, too, of a common good that transcends immediate pleasure and profit.

Change: An Open, Self-Correcting System

Backsliding is an omnipresent reality in human history. We do violate covenantal commandments. But the covenantal tradition holds out hope for redemption after repentence. If we are open to God (and therefore to our better selves), we can amend our ways; we can correct our mistakes. Similarly, the Constitution provides a framework for corrective action. We, too, in the constitutional arena must first turn away from mistaken acts before we can achieve redemption. Change is inevitable; but it is safest in an open, self-correcting system modeled on our openness to God and redemption.

Appeal to People Sober

The people consent to the Covenant. But we should note that this is an appeal to the people sober, not to the people drunk. Moses, on his first trip down the mountain at Sinai with the Torah, finds the people whoring after false gods. In anger he breaks the tablets. He then ascends the mountain and only returns later with another Decalogue—and to a people sober.

The Constitution, by way of comparison, was first written by a gravely deliberate body of remarkably wise men and then put before specially elected representatives of the people in the several states. These representatives soberly debated the new Constitution before approving it. The Constitution thus constitutes the sober judgment of what was, for the time, a relatively large proportion of the people.

This comparison of Covenant and Constitution strongly emphasizes the link between the soundly religious and constitutional strands of prophetic politics. This comparison is also designed to emphasize how prophetic politics seeks to incorporate the strengths of both utopian and liberal democratic politics while avoiding their weaknesses. This comparison has contrasted utopian and prophetic politics. But a few more words are in order to contrast prophetic and liberal democratic politics and, particularly, to emphasize how prophetic politics—while endorsing the soundly religious and the constitutional—may avoid the weaknesses of liberal democratic politics. This may best be accomplished by noting that both Covenant and Constitution can be interpreted by complacent priests as well as by fearless prophets. Let me also—in the interest of realistic perspective—redress my glowing picture of the U.S. Constitution and note the reality of priestly interpretations of both Sinai Covenant and Constitution.

At the risk of obscuring the very serious shortcomings of 1787 and America's subsequent constitutional history, I deliberately emphasized similarities between Covenant and Constitution. But, clearly, it would be a major mistake, in both theology and politics, to ignore some vital differences. And these differences must be stressed if we are to avoid the idolatry of the "civil religion" and the occasional tendency of liberal democracy to lapse into Machiavellian politics.[16] (The "Civil Religion" is the concept that Rousseau first talked about in *The Social Contract* and that has had such an uncritical vogue among social scientists and students of religion interested in bringing religion back into the center of American life.)[17] Not even the most liberal democratic nation is God. The Constitution is not the Covenant. Washington is not Moses. Lincoln is not Isaiah. The worship of the Constitution can be an idolatry, especially if the Constitution treats blacks as slaves, disenfranchises women, ignores the poor, misinterprets plutocracy for aristocracy and oligarchy for democracy, destroys Native Americans or Vietnamese in the name of "pacification," and tolerates the violation of rights in the name of national security. *Chesed*—Covenant love—is not patriotism. The United States is not the world. If we forget these differences, we forget the unique character of the Sinai Covenant. These key differences require us to be on guard not only against nationalistic idolatry, even if practiced by a liberal democratic state, but also against priestly liberal democratic interpretations of the U.S. Constitution.

Both Sinai Covenant and U.S. Constitution can be interpreted to endorse the status quo of rich, powerful, white, male, satisfied people. Or they can be interpreted to demand change to achieve their own inner dynamic of life, growth, and fulfillment. Covenant and Constitution can be sanctified by smug, complacent priests celebrating the existing order; or they can be invoked by prophets demanding freedom for the least free, justice for the oppressed, peace for the war afflicted, food for the hungry, clothing for the naked. Unfortunately, the too-often dominant priests of Covenant and Constitution have lowered their ethical sights, are blind to the enormities of existing reality, and timid in their assessments of what is feasible. They fail to see the catastrophic shortcomings of the war system, the nation-state system, the economic system, the social and political system. Unlike the prophets, they no longer put before us a powerful image of possibilities that can be wisely achieved, a truth about human potentialities that can be sanely fulfilled, a course of action that is fruitful and feasible.

The Democratic Strand

The democratic strand in prophetic politics is also closely linked to the soundly religious and the constitutional. All people are children of God. All individuals, in a modern constitutional system, are to receive the equal protection of the laws. Democracy is to be understood in terms of both popular rule and the protection of basic rights. And although some would limit the people—and popular rule and basic rights—to the propertied middle class, to the educated ("the wise and the honest"), and to white men, the logic of democracy—in a society committed to the soundly religious and the constitutional—forces an extension of the suffrage to those of less substantial property, to those who are not white, to those who are not male. A comparable logic calls for an extension of basic rights. These extensions serve to protect the integrity, autonomy, power, and opportunity for realization of all individuals in a genuine community

The democratic strand in prophetic politics is not to be understood in terms of Greek democracy, or Communist democracy, or Third World democracy. Democratic rule, in the prophetic tradition, does not mean the class rule of the (usually poor, often ignorant) many in their own interest; nor does it mean the dictatorship (or, later, the alleged harmonious rule) of the proletariat; nor does it mean the free and independent rule of the people of the nation pursuant to a Rousseauistic conception of the "general will."

Moreover, the democratic strand in prophetic politics carries us beyond the modern liberal democratic facade of popular rule and basic rights (usually in selected affluent First World countries) to a passionate concern for human integrity, voice, and fulfillment for all peoples in all countries. A special concern of prophetic politicians is the least free—and their political power, their rights, and their needs. Concern for enhancing the freedom of the least free becomes a touchstone of democratic politics in the tradition of prophetic politics. I will have more to say about the democratic strand of prophetic politics when I set forth the distinguishing characteristics of this pattern. Emphasis on the least free here may help to distinguish prophetic from liberal democratic politics.[18]

The Scientific Strand

The scientific strand in prophetic politics calls attention to this pattern's respect for the realities of politics and human life, and also for the importance of experimenting in politics (or living prudently in the political community) on the basis of sound knowledge. These realities we must stress—involve physical, social, and intellectual being and becoming.

Political values and principles are abstract; they need a concrete reference if they are to be more meaningful. We need to be able to operationalize glittering prophetic values and constitutional principles. Only in this fashion can we communicate more clearly, can we criticize more effectively, can we argue more persuasively.

We must also appreciate how the scientific strand in prophetic politics reinforces the soundly religious, constitutional, and democratic strands. Thus, scientific openness to inquiry reinforces the soundly religious commitment to truth. Scientific appreciation of limits reinforces the constitutional commitment to law and human fallibility. Scientific appreciation of human life and potentiality reinforces the democratic commitment to individual realization within the framework of common good.

The scientific strand embraces both the social and the physical sciences. Social science, rightfully employed, is a powerful tool for human understanding, social criticism, and human prognosis. Social science, too, rests significantly upon the principle of keeping the doors to inquiry open and upon respect for evidence, for consequences, and for rational argument, in measurement, generalization, and assessment. At its best it is not afraid of affirming life, of seeking creative breakthroughs in politics, and of pragmatically assessing what political actors do.[19] In Chapter 6, in our examination of prophetic criticism, we will more fully elaborate on the importance of the scientific strand in prophetic politics.

In calling attention to these religious, constitutional, democratic, and scientific strands in prophetic politics, I inevitably oversimplify. Yet singling out these strands will, I believe, help the reader to understand better the sources of, and influences shaping, prophetic politics. The biblical prophets are clearly a major source. The basic outline of the model of prophetic politics (values, criticism, constitutional action, future orientation) is adumbrated by the biblical prophets. Because of their emphasis upon divine commandments and values, criticism of violations of those *mitzvoth*, the idea of covenant or constitution, and future scenarios, they give form and meaning to the soundly religious, influence constitutional development in the West, point toward the universality of democratic ideas, and help us look to the future with hope.

Greek Philosophy and Natural Law

Yet it should also be clear that the pattern of prophetic politics—including each of those strands we have just examined—is also influenced by other philosophical and historical movements that make for a more fulfilling constitutional and democratic politics. To call attention to these movements is also to emphasize that prophetic politics is not an exclusively orthodox religious pattern rooted only in political theology. Politics remains a secular subject; but, as I have tried to make clear, it is a subject clearly not immune from religious inspiration and influence, especially certain prophetic insights in a given religious tradition in our prescriptive constitutional history.

Without doubt, however, it is the case that the fuller development of the model of prophetic politics owes a great deal to Greek philosophy and the tradition of natural law, each of which developed independently of the Judaic-Christian tradition and yet linked up with that religious tradition in Western thought. The concept of *areté* (excellence), of the fulfillment of individual potentiality, of the rational pursuit of truth, of dialogical criticism of conventional wisdom, of high regard for the constitutional rule of law, of justice as harmony—these the model of prophetic politics owes to Greek philosophy. Moreover, the belief in a higher law and in right reason (in the tradition of natural law) links up with the search for the "divine center" in Greek thought and with the concept of divinity in Jewish and Christian thought. Thomas Aquinas illustrates these linkages. These linkages—which can be seen in Aquinas and traced from him to Thomas Hooker and John Locke and Jefferson and

Madison—make it easier for those in the natural law tradition to insist upon constitutional limitations on rulers in the interest of religious freedom and political liberty.[20]

The Influence of the Enlightenment

Historically, the model of prophetic politics owes a great debt to those movements of philosophical, social, and political thought we call the *Enlightenment,* especially as the Enlightenment encapsulates, and brings to fulfillment, aspects of a superior constitution. The thought of the Enlightenment, particularly as it flourishes in the nineteenth century, helps significantly to translate constitutional theory into constitutional practice and to ease the way for the fuller democratization of the political order.[21]

Although I have, by no means, done full justice to the strands of, and influences upon, prophetic politics, this sketch may, nonetheless, partly satisfy those who are curious about the intellectual antecedents of this model of politics. Further clarification will come as I elucidate a little more fully the four distinguishing characteristics of prophetic politics. In doing so I will simultaneously be giving fuller meaning to the strands of, and influences upon, prophetic politics. As I develop these distinguishing characteristics, I will also attempt to differentiate prophetic politics from utopian and liberal democratic politics.

THE PROPHETIC PARADIGM: THE STANDARD OF A SUPERIOR UNIVERSAL ORDER

The first major commitment—the first distinguishing characteristic—of prophetic politics is a commitment to the standard of a superior universal order. This universal order must extend the great prophetic values—of peace, freedom, justice, love, truth, prosperity—to all.

The Old Testament prophets first develop forthrightly the concept of a superior universal order that constitutes a superior standard of judgment. They also first articulate the key values of prophetic politics. Thus, of peace: "And they shall beat their swords into plowshares, And their spears into pruning hooks; Nation shall not lift up sword against nation, Neither shall they learn war any more."[22] And justice: "do justice, and . . . love mercy. . . . "[23] And freedom: "let the oppressed go free. . . ."[24]

As my earlier discussion of the strands of, and influences on, prophetic politics has made clear, Christianity carries these prophetic values into Western thought. The development of constitutionalism makes these ideas more effective within political communities. The Enlightenment recaptures earlier glimpses of universalism even as it secularizes prophetic ideas. Democratic and constitutional theory helps to make key aspects of the prophetic order operational. Democratic socialism contributes to the advance on the prophetic front by emphasizing the need to emancipate working people. In the modern world, world order advocates, liberation theologists, civil rights workers, feminists and ecologists illustrate the persistence of the prophetic paradigm. They illustrate the call for a global covenant of peace, human rights, prosperity, and ecological balance. For the Old Testament prophets, of course, the superior constitution is rooted in the Sinai Covenant. Over time the religious constitution becomes secularized and democratized. When God's law becomes not only the higher law of religious sects but links up with the higher law of natural law, the force of the covenant idea carries beyond the maintenance of right worship (narrowly understood) and sustains the development of constitutionalism and the democratic state.

The universalistic element in the prophetic tradition is unmistakable; and so, too, is the prophetic concern for the least free. The commandment is to "loose the fetters of wickedness," to "undo the bands of the yoke," to "break every yoke," to "deal thy bread to the hungry," to "house the poor, to cover the naked."[25]

I am aware that the fuller meaning of these values still calls for clarification. Before I am finished with the distinguishing characteristics of prophetic politics, I will advance that understanding even more.

I do appreciate that, at first glance, this first commitment—as indeed, each of the other three prophetic commitments that I will outline in succeeding chapters—is perhaps not easily distinguishable from that of utopian politics at its best. After all, Plato was committed to justice, the Grand Inquisitor to happiness, and Marx to freedom, peace, abundance, and fulfillment. And Skinner was committed to the "Good Life" that is "truly happy, secure, productive, creative and forward looking." Hence, it is important to comment more fully on these values and to distinguish the prophetic paradigm from the utopian outlook.

Those in the prophetic tradition insist that prophetic values, which are to apply to all, can only be advanced under a superior democratic constitution. Such a constitution must keep the doors of inquiry open. Must ensure popular rule. Must guard vigilantly against the abuse of power. Must develop sane patterns of accommodation for inevitably conflicting interests. And must honor the individual's right to say no to those who claim the individual's obedience when such obedience is not merited. Moreover, prophetic values are appreciative of human fallibility and hence provide room for the qualities of compassion, mercy, and repentance. Above all, prophetic politics rejects the very possibility of the completely harmonious community, of the conflictless society, of the end of alienation, of human perfection. In human affairs the dangers of the abuse of power will persist. In the present and future we will need a constitution to ensure effective and regularized restraints on those who exercise power to protect our individual and collective right to safeguard popular rule and to help us resolve our conflicts sensibly. This is *not* the order of a Plato, a Marx, a Grand Inquisitor, or a Skinner!

The prophetic standard may also have to be distinguished from that of liberal democratic politics at its best. Again, at first glance, the distinction is not too clear. At least some of the following traits characterize both liberal democratic and prophetic politics. Prophetic politics calls for a universal, not a national or parochial, standard. It insists upon civilized life, healthy growth, and creative fulfillment for all peoples. It is rooted in such concepts as the goodness of human life, the holiness of community, and creative fulfillment. It takes seriously the commandment to act to maintain prophetic values. It sees the modern constitution as a serious modern covenant that provides a framework for creative conflict and accommodation. It accepts, unequivocally, the idea of selective and conditional political obligation. This idea denies a particular political community a monopoly on the individual's obligation. This idea permits individuals to choose which government, group, or individual they will be obliged to obey on the basis of the performance of such claimant in satisfying such individual's informed conscience or such individual's informed (and always conditional) judgment about the claimant's contribution to fulfillment of individual realization within the framework of the common good. Prophetic politics, moreover, emphasizes the urgency of the recalculation of a society's calculated risks.

This prophetic position differs from that of liberal democratic politics insofar as—in degree, if not in kind—it emphasizes a commitment to the least free worldwide; insofar as it does not hesitate to assess adversely the balance of the existing order's accommodations in politics (or economics or society); and insofar as it constantly prods existing rulers to overcome the gulf between the prophetic paradigm and contemporary performance. In this fashion, then, prophetic politics militates against the limited ethical vision, the deficient empirical understanding, and the timid prudential policies of liberal democratic politics. The distinction between prophetic and liberal democratic politics will become even clearer as I move on to outline the other commitments of prophetic politics.

CONCLUSION

The prophetic paradigm establishes a standard for prophetic politics. It is a demanding universal standard. It is thoroughly democratic in the sense that it holds for all peoples. It is a constitutional standard that draws support from religious, philosophical, and scientific traditions. It has a live and active history. To the extent that it can be sustained, it provides a sound basis for prophetic criticism—the second distinguishing characteristic of prophetic politics, which we will address in the next chapter.

6 : Prophetic Criticism

INTRODUCTION

In this chapter we shall explore a little more fully a second major distinguishing characteristic of prophetic politics: fearless criticism of the existing order. The prophetic paradigm illuminates the ethical imperative in politics. It outlines a standard for judgment. Only in the light of the prophetic paradigm can criticism go forward. But criticism also needs an empirical referent. There must be an empirical witness to the behavior of political actors in accord (or not in accord) with the prophetic paradigm. Fearless criticism helps to fulfill the function of the empirical witness. Values, behavior, and judgment are all open to criticism. The foundations, the operations, and the policies of the existing order are all open for surveillance. Such critical surveillance is the second commitment of prophetic politics.

Again, the Biblical prophets illustrate some of the cardinal features of fearless criticism. They criticize the existing order in the light of the covenantal model. They do not hesitate to criticize pharaoh or king. They warn of doom but hold out hope of redemption. They are commanded to speak out and particularly against those who would "eat the flesh of my people," who would "make the fatherless their prey."[1] The prophets see themselves as watchmen—warning humankind but holding out the promise of a better world. They unmistakably attack idolatry, pride (what the Greeks called hubris), and complacency.[2] They adumbrate, if they do not elaborate, a philosophy of history that can provide "meaning to the past," "urgent importance to the present," and "ultimate significance to the future."[3] They thus provide inspiration for those in the tradition of prophetic politics who can never rest content with Machiavellian idolatry, utopian hubris, or liberal democratic complacency.

But for such criticism to be effective, there must be reliable evidence of such idolatry, hubris, and complacency. And there must be understanding of such behavior. Clearly, those committed to prophetic politics are obligated to criticize the dominant order—as it has been, as it is, and as it will be—but empty indictments are not enough. Criticism of the past, present, and future must rest upon persuasive empirical evidence and upon sound theoretical explanation.

Let me outline four of the major concerns of prophetic criticism and illustrate some of the key empirical factors that are relevant to these concerns. This outline will point toward the kind of empirical evidence that is relevant and toward the explanation that prophetic criticism seeks.

FOUR MAJOR CONCERNS OF PROPHETIC CRITICISM

Peace

Six factors guide empirical criticism in connection with the prophetic value of peace. They underscore the gulf between ideal and reality and press the prophetic critic to speak more cogently to the "why" and "what" questions—both "Why the gulf?" and "What can be done to narrow or bridge the gap?" The six factors that sensitize prophetic empirical research are: (1) the mortal threat of nuclear war, (2) the disastrous consequences of conventional wars, (3) the onerous burden of the arms race, (4) the dangers of the sovereign nation-state system, (5) the uncertainties of the balance of power, and (6) the weakness of the United Nations as a global organization.

Nuclear war in the closing decades of the twentieth century threatens to destroy the only globe we know. The biological destruction of the species Homo sapiens is the dreadful scenario that prompts our efforts to break through to a more peaceful world. This is a worst-case scenario. But even if humanity is not literally wiped out in the event of an all-out thermonuclear war, the devastation wrought by such a war, or even a limited nuclear war, is almost too horrible to contemplate. Our empirical knowledge of Hiroshima and Nagasaki and of the potential of new and improved atomic bombs make the control, and eventual elimination, of nuclear arms a prophetic necessity.

The record of conventional wars in the twentieth century—in massive deaths, injuries, and incredible human suffering and in human, monetary, social, and physical costs—is difficult for our limited human minds to grasp. Yet this record must be grasped if the urgency of the quest for a better way to handle international conflicts is to be maintained.

One questionable current way involves the onerous burden of the arms race. Economically, politically, and socially, the arms race is costly. What is most disturbing is that the arms race—in rich and richer countries in the First and Second Worlds and in the poor and poorer countries of the Third World—drains resources from the fulfillment of basic human needs: for constructive jobs; for food, clothing, housing, education,and medical care; and for social and cultural development. The arms race distorts human priorities. Military spending in the arms race hurts the battle against inflation, militates against healthy economic growth, and wastes valuable money, manpower, and resources.

The threat of nuclear war, the disastrous consequences of conventional wars, and the burden of the arms race are all intimately tied up with the existence of the sovereign nation-state system. This system requires no peaceful appeal to a supranational authority or global law in the event of a serious conflict between nations. The struggle for power among nations may be carried out in peaceful ways or by force and violence; but there is no prohibition on the ultimate resort to war to protect a nation's vital interests. And of course national rivalries have played a major role in triggering catastrophic warfare. And such warfare is not a monopoly of the powerful and wealthy nation-states.

Nations seek national security not only in self-defense but also in alliances and in the balance of power. However, the balance of power operates very uncertainly. We cannot confidently guarantee the stability of any balance of power. And the actual operation of the balance of power—even when it maintains an uneasy peace (at least averting a World War III between the United States and the Soviet Union)—exacts enormous costs. Given shifting political, economic, scientific conditions, the balance of power is inherently unstable. It may have helped so far to avert World War III, but it has not prevented warfare in Korea, Vietnam, or Afghanistan. It has not prevented the cold war all over the globe. And its costs are distressing: the price of armaments to maintain the balance; jockeying for power in the Middle East, Asia, Africa, and Latin America; military interventions by the Soviet Union in Czechoslovakia, Hungary, and Afghanistan; interventions by the United States in Latin America as well as in Korea and Vietnam.

Moreover, despite modest successes, the United Nations has not been able to function to advance the objective of genuine collective security. It has not been able to dispel the mortal threat of nuclear war. It has not been notably successful in averting a number of conventional wars or other aggressive acts. It has not been able to move the world successfully toward disarmament. It has not been able to cope with the dangers of the nation-state system as it leads to war or violates human rights. It has not been able to deal with serious East-West conflicts. All of these factors highlight the status of peace in the world and point toward the need for a satisfactory empirical theory (difficult as it may be) that might illuminate the necessary and sufficient conditions of peace and highlight the means by which we can move toward the kind of peace we want.[4]

Human Rights

Regarding human rights, the prophetic critic focuses on violations of human rights and the battle of the least free to achieve fuller emancipation. Again, this focus should lead to answers to: Why do violations of human rights occur? And how can they be prevented? Five factors merit attention: (1) the dreadful reality of genocide, (2) the struggle to achieve national freedom and independence, (3) the ugly persistence of racism, (4) left-wing and right-wing human rights violations, and (5) sexism—offenses against women. Let us briefly indicate how these factors help us to understand the status of human rights.

The dreadful reality of Hitler's murderous extermination of 6 million European Jews is difficult to grasp. It is an ugly reality—this planned, calculated, systematic extermination. Hitler's campaign against Jews started with prejudice, was stimulated by propaganda, led to political, social, and economic persecution, and ended in mass murder. Even though the Holocaust is unique, the murderous actions of the Nazis extended to massive violations of the human rights of millions of other civilian Europeans. And although nothing quite comparable with the Nazi Holocaust has occurred since World War II, there have been attacks on national, ethnic, racial, and religious groups in a number of countries. And a fanatical ideological genocide—such as the murderous actions of Stalin against the kulaks, of the Chinese Communists against their opponents, or of Pol Pot's regime in Cambodia (Kampuchea) against its own citizens—is not unknown.

The struggle of peoples to achieve national independence and freedom is a bittersweet story, involving—as it sometimes has—war as an instrument to achieve national self-determination. Since World War II almost all of the colonies of the Western European powers have achieved independence. Yet important questions must be asked about the ability of these new nations to make good on their right to determine their political status freely and to pursue their economic, social, and cultural development independently. The unhappy reality is that many of the new nations—and indeed a number of older developing nations—although legally free and independent, have not proved to be politically stable, economically viable, or socially cohesive and thus able to use the right of national self-determination effectively.

And their vulnerability underscores the vulnerability of human rights in many of these countries. Moreover, questions can be raised about the real freedom of the peoples of countries such as Poland and Czechoslovakia and other Communist countries in Eastern Europe, as well as about those little nations—Lithuania, Latvia, and Estonia—that were absorbed into the Soviet Union.

Similarly, serious questions must be asked about the ugly persistence of racism. Slavery and discrimination, based on race, is an old chapter in the history of humankind. Slavery was only legally ended throughout all the United States in 1865; second-class citizenship lingered on until the mid-twentieth century; and discrimination against nonwhites still persists. Slavery still persists in some parts of Africa and the Arabian peninsula. And apartheid, as a legal doctrine, prevails in South Africa in blatant disregard of world opinion. People of color throughout the world have suffered and continue to suffer social—if not always legal, political, and economic—discrimination.

Although we have come a long way in articulating human rights standards (in many national communities and in the international community), and although we have turned our backs resolutely against genocide, colonialism, and racism, persistent and flagrant violations of human rights are still widespread throughout the world. They occur in both left-wing and right-wing authoritarian regimes: in Communist nations; in Asian, African, and South American countries. One expert has written: "There are probably more countries where fundamental rights and civil liberties are systematically violated than there are countries where they are effectively protected."[5] The record of political massacres, disappearances, torture, imprisonment without trial is ominous and distressing and demands redress.

So, too, the violations of one-half of the human race —women—demand redress. This is the reality despite the pronouncements of national constitutions. Even in such countries as the United States, despite significant gains, women still face a daily reality of discrimination, limited opportunities, economic hardship, and degrading culture. The 1977 Declaration of American Women maintained, and quite accurately, that women "lack effective political and economic power." "We have only minor and insignificant roles in making, interpreting, and enforcing our laws, in running our political parties, unions, schools, and institutions, in directing the media, in governing our country, in deciding issues of war and peace."[6] These human rights issues constitute a second major area of prophetic concern.

Economic Well-Being

Human rights cannot, of course, be separated from economic well-being. Indeed, one cardinal ingredient of human rights is the *"right to the fulfillment of such vital needs as food care, shelter, health care, and education."*[7] In our outline we will focus on five factors: (1) the persistence of poverty; (2) the scourge of unemployment, hunger, ill-health, illiteracy, and poor housing: (3) the unsettling reality of inequality; (4) the difficulties of lifting the level of economic well-being; and (5) the agonizing calculus of costs and benefits.

There are approximately 600 million to 1 billion poor people in the world. This means that about one person in five lives in shocking and degrading poverty. They have minimal per capita income and inadequate diets and live in substandard conditions of health and housing. They are overwhelmingly illiterate. They lack the basic necessities of life. Permanent insecurity is an ongoing fact for them. They are unemployed or underemployed. They have high birth rates and infant death rates. They suffer from preventable disease. They have shorter life spans than people in affluent countries. The bulk of the world's poor live in Southeast Asia and in rural areas. However, there is a considerable percentage—about 10 percent—that may live in poverty in affluent countries; and mass urban poverty now afflicts many cities in the world.

People lack money because they are unemployed or underemployed, or because they are not receiving a fair share for the produce of their labor. Unemployment, in turn, mirrors industrial stagnation, sectoral depression, economic recession, low agricultural productivity and rates of growth, and inadequate use of human and material resources. In 1980 there were 20 million persons out of work in developed countries and a huge 455 million jobless or underemployed in developing countries. Hunger remains an agonizing problem for the world's poor. This is true despite the fact that food stocks are reasonably high. The food problem today is largely one of inadequate purchasing power and inadequate and inequitable distribution. According to one estimate, 450 to 750 million people are seriously malnourished. And, of course, hunger is related to disease. In the developing world poverty and hunger, the lack of clean water and effective sanitation, the absence of immunization programs, and the shortage of trained health personnel contribute to high infant and child mortality, to a host of debilitating diseases, and to shorter life expectancy. Water-related diseases—cholera and typhoid, for example—kill 10 million people yearly in developing nations. Some 5 million children die every year from diseases that could be prevented by immunization. In developing nations there are 109 deaths among infants under one year per 1,000 births; the comparable figure for the developed world is 19. Illiteracy in the poorer countries of the world—as high as 95 percent in Niger or Somalia—hampers efforts to achieve greater economic and social well-being. Illiteracy makes it difficult for people to get and hold jobs; it hampers productivity; it works against family health and population control; and it hinders intelligent participation in politics. Poor housing also militates against economic well-being. And poor housing—inadequate space, sanitation, and protection—is the lot of millions worldwide, and particularly of those in poor developing nations.

No treatment of the struggle for economic well-being can ignore the persistence of inequality. Serious inequalities exist within both rich and poor nations, and between rich and poor nations. The gap is ominous and shows no appreciable sign of disappearing. It is quite common for the richest fifth of a developing country to command 60 percent or more of the national income, whereas the poorest fifth has only 3 to 5 percent of such income.

The poor nations of the world face enormous difficulties in lifting the level of economic well-being. They often lack political stability and a competent civil service. They frequently suffer from the absence of crucial economic, educational, and social institutions as well as health and transportation facilities. They may suffer from the fluctuation of commodity prices and an adverse balance of trade. Their populations may be growing in excess of their resources. These considerations underscore obstacles facing policymakers concerned with improving economic well-being.

The calculus of costs and benefits is perhaps most agonizing in the poor developing nations; but it is not absent in relatively affluent countries, such as the United States, which must also face problems of unemployment, sectoral depression, foreign competition, pockets of poverty, and an inadequate welfare system.[8]

Ecological Balance

The key factors that the prophetic critic must address concerning ecological balance are: (1) the problem of scarce resources; (2) a population out of balance with resources; (3) the catastrophes of pollution; (4) the reality or myth of a scientific/technological "fix"; and (5) the challenges of ecological politics. Ecological concerns, as we shall see, cannot be entirely separated from the issues of peace, human rights, and economic well-being.

The prophetic critic notes, with grave concern, the depletion of valuable nonrenewable resources. Oil, for example, will not last forever. Its increasing scarcity will increase its cost and hence affect the fate of industry, agriculture, highways, our budget. Other renewable resources—for example, land, water, forests—have been ruthlessly exploited, wasted, and exhausted. The "tragedy of the commons" threatens to become a global tragedy. We have not yet really confronted the problems of "human survival on a finite and destroyable planet with limited resources."[9]

Sensible survival is aggravated by population growth wildly in excess of resources. Although there are signs that population growth, at least in the richer developing countries, is slowing, the gravest population problem exists in the poorer developing nations. There is where it is difficult to feed people and sustain them. World population is approximately 4.5 billion today. What will happen—particularly in the developing world—when this figure becomes 6 or 7 billion?

This problem is also complicated by global pollution, which threatens our resources in another way. Modern war and modern industrialization have contributed to the catastrophes of pollution. The problem affects capitalist and Communist societies, developed and developing lands. If we are concerned with the quality of human life—and therefore with clean air and water, healthy soil and forests—we have an obligation to be concerned about pollution.

There are those, of course, who believe that our ecological problems can be solved by modern science. Modern science and technology—they maintain—can produce substitutes for oil, repair or replace our ravaged resources, bring population growth under control, lick the pollution problem. But is this belief a belief in a reality or in a "fix"? Science has helped us in these matters; but can science come up with a miraculous fix? The prophetic critic tends to be skeptical.

What the prophetic critic cannot be skeptical of, however, are the challenges posed by key ecological considerations. Ecological scarcity, the imbalance of population and resources, and pollution pose challenges to liberalism and socialism, capitalism and communism. Again, prophetic criticism must go beyond the candid statement of ecological realities and explanations and probe alternative responses to anticipated consequences. Will all countries (whether liberal democratic, Communist, right-wing authoritarian, or Third World) be forced to be more regulatory, coercive, and harsh—or inequitable—than they are now in order to ration scarce resources, impose population controls, and curtail pollution? Will the modern dream of freedom in abundance prove to be illusory?[10]

A PRELIMINARY CONCEPTUAL
FRAMEWORK FOR CRITICISM

As we reflect on these four concerns of prophetic criticism, we must not lose our perspective. Prophetic criticism—guided by prophetic values, resting as it must on a solid understanding of crucial empirical realities, informed by relevant empirical explanations, and pointing toward alternatives responsive to anticipated consequences—must often be adversely critical of existing arrangements; but it need not be inevitably adverse. Beneficial as well as detrimental aspects of the dominant order may be perceived. Such criticisms, too, rest upon truthful empirical evidence and understanding. Nonetheless, those committed to fearless criticism will be most sensitive to existing evil because of the gap that prevails in every existing order between the prophetic standard and the contemporary reality, and because of their commitment to close that gap. The breadth or narrowness of the gap cannot, however, be ascertained without convincing empirical evidence, and the feasibility of bridging the gap cannot be judged without the help of empirical theory.

The character of prophetic criticism has already roughly been suggested by the dialogue between prophetic politics and Machiavellian, utopian, and liberal democratic politics. Thus proponents of prophetic politics are sensitive to, but cannot accept, Machiavellian brutality and deception; merely utopian promise or frightening utopian performance; and liberal democratic myopia, deficiency, and timidity. They must protest against the lowering of sights and standards and the cruel and uncivilized behavior that characterize Machiavellian politics. They must speak out against the maddening pride, the divorce from a more discriminating sense of the possible, and the unwillingness to calculate human costs that mark and mar utopian politics. And they must bemoan the blindness and conservative bias that blemish liberal democratic politics. They must criticize basic norms and ethical premises, actual behavior and projected consequences, judgments of feasibility and practicality. In all this they are guided by a prophetic ethics and good logic. But their criticism will be more compelling if it draws upon a rich body of empirical evidence and empirical theory.

Criticism does not operate under any statute of limitations. All political actors are subject to criticism. Prophetic critics train their sights on rulers and ruled—at kings, princes, priests, presidents, premiers; at all the groups and institutions that, and all the individuals who, make up a society; at those pumped up with pride, privilege, and possessions; at the sometimes short-sighted and presumptuous populace; at false prophets; at all those who deviate from the prophetic constitution. Prophetic critics can never accept falsity, illusion, sham, or any activity that militates against a fulfilling life. They must see the emperor's nakedness. They must speak the often unpleasant and bitter truth. It will not do to cry peace when there is no peace. Thus it is that the prophetic vision of a better way for mankind makes them searing and relentless critics of war, injustice, poverty, ecological malaise, and the other evils that plague humankind and threaten the prophetic aspirations of our common humanity. Mortal citizens and mortal institutions are not immune from such criticism—nor are nation-states and their rulers. And a particular concern of prophetic critics is the plight of the least free: the captive, the poor, the weak, and the needy.

Such criticism, moreover, must be truly discriminatory and thus genuinely responsible. There is a difference between personal inconvenience and public disaster. Between private tragedy and global catastrophe. Between deviation from a sound principle and action in accord with a depraved principle. The critical punishment should fit the critically determined crime.

A preliminary conceptual framework for criticism has already been suggested by our previous analysis of Machiavellian, utopian, and liberal democratic politics. Let us here recapitulate this framework.

Apropos Machiavellian politics, the prophetic critic attacks the worship of the nation-state: the commitment to its success regardless of the ends of the nation-state and the means to obtain those ends. Here "reason of state"—and the behavior of rulers of nation-states—is a primary object of criticism. The behavior of nation-states (and particularly its commitment to war as a ultimate weapon in the struggle for power) is examined in the light of the question (whose negative answer is taken for granted by the advocates of Machiavellian politics), Is there a better way? A particular target of adverse criticism is the brutality, cruelty, and suffering that characterize the operation of the nation-state, especially in time of war. The evidence that can be abundantly adduced here then becomes crucial in the argument on the question, Must we continue to accept or endure such brutality, cruelty, and suffering? The deceptions practiced by the nation-state are also open to criticism. So, too, is the general lowering of standards in nation-state politics. But before evidence is forthcoming and abundant on these points, one cannot talk intelligently of the argument of the Machiavellians that political realism requires these harsh but necessary concessions to force and craft. Of course, the balancing of equities calls for more than empirical evidence of the extent and duration and costs of force and craft. But that evidence is vital in the complicated critical assessment required in any calculation of costs and benefits.

However, criticism of Machiavellian politics must also take account of its strengths: its focus on protecting the genuinely vital interests of the political community, its appreciation of the importance of the struggle for power, its wisdom in avoiding the confusion of what ought to be and what is in statemanship. Prophetic criticism must concentrate on how these strengths can be retained in a system of prophetic politics. Prophetic criticism suggests attention to the protection of the vital interests of people in a global community. It also suggests a broader understanding of the struggle for power and, particularly, the inclusion of the least free in this struggle. It also recommends that visions of a better future can prudently influence the transformation of the unhappy present.

Aspects of utopian politics are also fair game for prophetic criticism. Utopians may defy wise bounds to human action. In their pride, conceit, arrogance, they may attempt to play God. In attempting to achieve the perfect society on this earth, they may succumb to fanaticism, authoritarianism, totalitarianism.

In the zealous quest for their harmonious society, they may sacrifice free debate in favor of dictatorial edicts, an open society for a closed one. Prophetic critics are obligated to expose false and misleading promises. If, on one hand, they are adversely critical of Machiavellian "realism," so they are also critical of utopian fantasy. If the advocates of Machiavellian politics may make too much of human depravity, so some of the proponents of utopian politics may make too much of human goodness. And seeking harmony, the utopians may be tempted to impose it. Rejecting conflict, they may miss its creative function. Intolerant of the existing order, they may be undiscriminating in their rejection of everything in it, including the decency, sense, and civility of many established ways. Failing to attain their utopian ends easily in a world of fallible, finite, and mortal people, they are tempted to reject politics entirely as too dirty for good people and, hence, to retreat passively into a purely selfish world of their own. If they keep a distance from politics, and talk only in platitudes, their vagueness can become a convenient cover for sterility and inaction. But, again, before this critical analysis of utopian politics can carry conviction, more complete and illuminating evidence and explanation must be forthcoming to support the argument that this adverse criticism is correct.

Prophetic criticism must also endeavor to understand the strengths of utopian politics more fully—its ability to inspire us to dream of a better world for human fulfillment, its fruitfulness in opening up "possibilities which would have remained lost if not seen by utopian anticipation," its power in being able "to transform the given."[11]

Prophetic criticism must attempt to discover how these strengths can be disengaged from the weaknesses of utopian politics and incorporated into a system of prophetic politics. Historically, prophetic criticism points to the conclusion that this can be done only within the framework of a covenant relationship, which is the essence of the superior constitutional relationship. Again, evidence and explanation must be forthcoming to sustain the truth of this proposition.

Prophetic critics must also turn their attack on the complacency, blindness, and hesitancy of liberal democratic politics.

There often is in such politics an uncritical commitment to the existing balance of power and, consequently, an unreflecting tolerance of the persistent evils of that balance: war, injustice, poverty, and ecological malaise—evils by no means restricted to the Second and Third Worlds. Prophetic critics must look to the life of the least free—poor people, nonwhite people, especially, but also women—and set forth their condition, and the reasons for their condition, in liberal democratic politics. They must probe recessive as well as dominant forces. They must examine potential as well as actual dangers. And they must inquire into the hesitancy of the practitioners of liberal democratic politics in acting to overcome clearly identified ills. They must be prepared to probe the struggle for power, and the sources of power, in radical ways. They may have to make searching investigations into the economic and social systems, as well as into the political system. Here, too, a host of empirical questions about the functioning of liberal democratic political institutions, of capitalist economics, of social systems in the predominately white, rich, and male social world, cannot be answered convincingly without more reliable empirical investigation.

The considerable strengths of liberal democratic politics must also be critically assessed: the sensible commitment to the more nearly perfect Union; to limited, responsible, representative, popular government; and to the exercise of prudent judgment in balancing competing values and interests in a pluralistic, tolerant community. These strengths are considerable. And dogmatic, unsubstantiated socialist attacks on capitalism can be no substitute for fair-minded and penetrating ethical and scientific analysis. The relation of capitalism to liberal democracy and constitutionalism must be realistically probed. And alternative political, economic, and social principles and systems must be courageously appraised.

So it is, then, that in order to move beyond prophetic self-righteousness, to be able to move beyond merely moral exhortation and glittering prophetic pronouncements, and to be able to distinguish true and false prophets, it is important for ethical criticism to link up with modern social science.

The modern theory of prophetic criticism that emerges from the linkage of ethics and social science has five main tasks. These tasks give a modern meaning to the ancient concept of prophetic witness, and they also serve to ensure healthy self-criticism of prophetic politics itself. These tasks include: (1) clarifying prophetic standards that orient empirical investigation; (2) obtaining supporting evidence of fulfillment of, or deviation from, the prophetic paradigm—with the help of social science indicators that can be used to make prophetic values operational; (3) developing norms to assess the practical meaning of empirical evidence bearing on the necessary and sufficient conditions for civilized life, healthy growth, and creative fulfillment; (4) formulating scientific hypotheses and scientific theory—to permit generalizations, explanations, and (if possible) predictions—about the necessary and sufficient conditions of peace, freedom, justice, prosperity, ecological balance, and excellence and about the vital (but neglected) subject of social change; and (5) pointing toward wise public policy alternatives—to narrow the gap between prophetic values and existing reality. In this fashion, wise, radical, and constructive criticism can go forward, and always with a special concern for the least free who remain a touchstone of a genuinely prophetic politics.

CONCLUSION

Thus it is that the prophetic paradigm sets the stage for empirical investigation by identifying what is significant and by focusing attention on the status of prophetic values. Fearless criticism must look to the operational meaning of such values. This will require attention to social science indicators, which may permit more precise measurement and testing. However, the evidence alone is not enough. We must have a better way of knowing what the evidence means. With the aid of appropriate indexes and norms, prophetic critics are in a better position to evaluate the evidence and to warn of political health or illness. Moreover, prophetic critics will make a more convincing case when their case is built on solid empirical generalizations and theories that illuminate, in a more reliable way, the process of social change. Finally, criticism will be more effective when it points toward action soundly based on careful exploration of alternatives.[12]

Prophetic criticism, although guided by ethical values, draws heavily on modern social science to illuminate the actual gap between prophetic values (and often professed values) and actual values as revealed in actual behavior. Prophetic criticism cannot, however, rest content with the scientific demonstration of this gap; such criticism must also explore scientific hypotheses about the necessary and sufficient conditions of political health. And beyond that, prophetic criticism must illuminate the debate about wise public policy alternatives. It must point toward prophetic constitutional breakthroughs—creative breakthroughs—to narrow the gap between prophetic values and existing reality. In the next two chapters we will begin our fuller exploration of those breakthroughs.

7 : Prophetic Constitutional Breakthroughs: I

INTRODUCTION

Prophetic criticism sets the stage for the third commitment of prophetic politics—the commitment to superior constitutional action. It does so by calling attention to problems that demand our attention and to the need for political alternatives addressed to these problems. These problems, we have suggested, involve the quest for peace, human rights, economic well-being, and ecological balance. The fuller articulation of these problems and the testing of constitutional alternatives invite a prudentially creative response, a prophetic judgment that may constitute a creative breakthrough in politics. The breakthrough may be, and usually is, ethical and empirical, as well as prudential. The breakthrough builds on, but carries us beyond, ordinary liberal democratic politics and toward a more prophetic constitution.

The prophetic breakthrough generally follows a particular model. It is invariably a response to a troubling problem that seems to defy resolution, a problem that the political priests of the existing order are not able to cope with. For example: How can we overcome war? Or how can we make the protection of human rights more secure? Or how can we overcome poverty? Or how can we achieve a sensible ecological balance? Many other smaller problems—some of which might be parts of these larger problems—could also be identified: How can we significantly reduce the incidence of crime? How can we significantly reduce unemployment? How can we significantly reduce the danger of pollution? How can we significantly reduce disease, poor housing, illiteracy? How can we improve the cultural quality of life?

The prophetic alternative will usually constitute (as I have suggested) a breakthrough on three fronts: ethical, empirical, and prudential. It will usually involve superior ideas as to what we ought to do; a superior understanding of political phenomena (what has been, is, and will be); and a superior judgment of what is feasible—of what is wise public policy.

In prophetic politics creative constitutional breakthroughs to a superior constitutional order are mandatory. But, unlike some utopian remedies, prophetic action *must* be constitutional. There can be no sacrifice of basic rights, especially of freedom of religion, of thought, of speech, press, assembly, of due process of law. There can be no dreadful but "necessary" sacrifices in the "higher" interest of utopian harmony and earthly salvation. However, such breakthroughs carry us beyond the liberal democratic politics of the existing order in countries such as the United States. We must appreciate that we had constitutions before we had religious liberty. We had constitutional monarchy before we had the federal republic. It took prophetic figures—such as Roger Williams or James Madison—to move their societies toward a superior constitutional order for their own day, a new constitutional order that would include religious liberty and that would be able to reconcile liberty and local self-government with order and federal power.

The alternatives that are to be explored, in liberal democratic countries, do not call for the scuttling of the best features of liberal democratic politics. They must be maintained. But we may have to move, with the help of creative breakthroughs, beyond liberal democratic politics. We are certainly obligated to overcome the weaknesses of such politics. These creative breakthroughs must succeed in dealing more effectively and more sanely with those problems that frustrate or baffle liberal democratic politics.

On the American scene—in the twentieth century—creative breakthroughs in politics may be illustrated by the progressive income tax, social security legislation, the Wagner (Labor Management Relations) Act, *Brown* v. *Board of Education,* and the Civil Rights Act of 1964. The progressive income tax provided for a more equitable sharing of wealth. Unemployment compensation helped to sustain workers thrown out of work. Old age and survivor's insurance aided older workers in retirement and widows and orphans. The Wagner Act helped to remove a cause of industrial strife: the strike to achieve union recognition. *Brown* v. *Board of Education* served to overturn the pernicious doctrine of "separate but equal." The Civil Rights Act functioned to make the access of black voters to the ballot a more effective reality. These are but a few illustrations.

Often challenged at the time as impossible, disastrous, radical, these measures—in historical perspective—have been hailed as significant breakthroughs. They indicate the prophetic spirit at work in a system of liberal democratic politics. These breakthroughs are not apocalyptic in the sense that they usher in the millennium. They do not come after Armageddon—and after the Children of Light have slain the Children of Darkness. But they do move us forward (often too slowly and not completely enough, I grant) toward a more prophetic political, economic, and social order.

To illustrate the concept of prophetic constitutional breakthroughs more fully—and to set the stage for an examination of some needed contemporary breakthroughs—let me employ Roger Williams and James Madison to illuminate the character and possibility of genuine creative breakthroughs in politics, and John C. Calhoun to illustrate a spurious breakthrough.[1] This analysis will also give me the opportunity to define and illustrate such key terms as *creative* and *breakthrough* more fully. In the following chapter I will—building on the base established in this chapter—move on to examine key problems, alternatives, and suggested breakthroughs in the four crucial areas of peace, human rights, economic well-being, and ecological balance. Confidence in our ability to deal with those key problems will be enhanced by examination of Williams, Madison, and Calhoun and the breakthroughs, genuine or spurious, that their thought and action represent.

ON CREATIVE BREAKTHROUGHS
IN AMERICAN POLITICS

Creative breakthroughs are prompted by difficult practical problems—involving concepts of the good life, of political behavior, and of wise policy. Here I will focus on two genuine creative breakthroughs (Roger Williams's theory of religious liberty and James Madison's theory of the "extensive republic") and one spurious one (John C. Calhoun's theory of the concurrent majority).

By *creative* I mean significantly constructive, orderly, fruitful, productive, novel, distinctive, unique. By *breakthrough* I mean a resolution or discovery or invention or experiment that results in the overcoming of a major problem, difficulty, obstacle, or roadblock and that results in a momentous change in outlook and behavior. Creative breakthroughs are prophetic when they are in accord with, and advance, prophetic values. A *prophetic creative breakthrough* would mean a significantly fruitful resolution of a major problem in connection with one or more of the major interrelated tasks of politics: the tasks of ethical recommendation, empirical understanding, and prudential judgment. These are the tasks that involve the prescription and justification of prophetic values in our public life; the comprehension of superior patterns of cooperation, accommodation, and handling the struggle for power in politics; and the making of wise public policies. These tasks are interrelated; and, of course, the ethical and empirical concerns are brought to focus in dealing with the prudential task.

Prophetic and creative constitutional breakthroughs thus require us to focus on problems in politics and how they can be resolved successfully. As one not unaware of Reinhold Niebuhr's strictures, I do appreciate that most often in politics there are only proximate solutions to insoluble problems. Yet this realistic warning should not deter us from seeking to attend to our political business in a better way, even as we eschew final, perfect, utopian solutions.

Clearly, there are crucial problems in politics that need our attention, problems that we can handle better than we do at present, problems susceptible to significantly proximate solutions. These problems involve conceptions of the good political life; they involve the necessary and sufficient conditions of political health; they involve wise practical decisions on peace and war, liberty and tyranny, prosperity and poverty; they involve the balancing of claims of freedom and order, of community, group, and individual, and of liberty, equality, fraternity, and justice. The theoretical integration of *ought, is,* and *can be* in the context of a practical political situation poses yet another significant problem. The greatest breakthroughs—those of the first magnitude—would involve successfully dealing with problems that embrace all four tasks. Here, although I will call attention to the ethical and empirical tasks (which I have examined in Chapters 5 and 6), I will be primarily concerned with the prudential task.

Problems involving these tasks come to our attention because of a difficulty we have experienced in politics. In politics these difficulties are most often rooted in conflicts: conflicts over values, behavior patterns, and policies; conflicts over the possession of resources, the protection of vital interests, the satisfaction of needs, the distribution of benefits; conflicts between liberty and authority; conflicts between competing political actors, interests, political communities; conflicts involving the character and power of the political community. The creative breakthrough results in a better way of handling the conflict; it enables citizens to live together better in the political community. The fruitful resolution of a real problem in politics inevitably involves *ethical* considerations—considerations of how men ought to live together and, most frequently, conflicts about the good political life. Fruitful resolution also inevitably involves *empirical* considerations—empirical theory, hypothesis, generalization, measurement, and, most often, the illumination of the character, conditions, causes, and consequences of conflict and accommodation. A fruitful empirical theory is future oriented; it is concerned with what will be, as well as with what has been and what is. These ethical and empirical considerations are then brought to focus on the prudential problem. For clearly fruitful resolution also involves *prudential* considerations—considerations of practical wisdom, of feasibility, and, most often, of action, not fully scientific, about conflict and conflict resolution.

The most fruitful resolutions will invariably have a major impact on scope, substance, and methodology in the discipline of political science and on the nature and character of politics. Problem resolution can lead to momentously new and fruitful changes in outlook, behavior, and judgment. It can lead to significantly altered political values, to a new world of understanding of political phenomena, to the testing and confirmation in action of novel practical possibilities. These outcomes can result in the contraction or expansion of the theoretical and operational meaning of *politics,* of *public,* of *public policy,* of *political community.* Problem resolution can also illuminate dark substantive areas of concern, uncover additional problems that call for attention, and place in an entirely new perspective commonplace values, facts, and judgments. Problem resolution also invariably suggests diverse and powerful methodologies—approaches to (and tools for) articulating ethical recommendations, enhancing empirical understanding, and making prudential judgments.

The greater the impact, the more significant the breakthrough. And the impact itself is measured by success in overcoming the major problem, handling the significant difficulty, roadblock, or conflict. The breakthrough may initially be at the level of theory, but, sooner or later, if it is to be a genuine political breakthrough, it must be tested in practice. This test in practice, if it is a constitutional test, serves to guard against a cardinal weakness of utopian politics: a refusal to come to grips with political reality in a sane way. In saying this I do not mean to downgrade the dazzling brilliance of a Plato, a Rousseau, or a Marx. I do mean to underscore that the test in practice constitutes the major test of fruitfulness. The genius of a Plato, a Rousseau, or a Marx—or of a Hobbes—can be acknowledged even as we raise questions about their success or that of their followers in dealing sensibly with major practical problems. To express this reservation is not to foreclose the possibility of utilizing some of their insights or contributions in dealing with contemporary political problems; and it is certainly not to foreclose bold and daring explorations in political philosophy and politics. It is to urge the importance of a sane linkage between theory and practice in relation to the sound and fertile resolution of our major political problems.

Practical success in problem resolution need not be either blindly worshipped or cavalierly and contemptuously dismissed as unworthy of higher minds. Moreover, we can consider the impact of the breakthrough on political actors and political scientists in terms of both immediate and long-range influence. Practical success can involve the fruitful influence of the larger political philosophy—its metaphysics, its ethics, its political science, its key concepts, its central empirical propositions, its approach and methods—as well as the operational political theory. In either case, the breakthrough is tested by political actors and political scientists who find the breakthrough relevant to their problems.

With these introductory comments in mind, let me next turn to an examination of two genuinely creative breakthroughs in Western constitutional politics. In each instance (and I will repeat this pattern in my analysis of Calhoun's spurious breakthrough) I shall initially identify the problem that called for a breakthrough; articulate the theory (or alternative) that addressed itself to the problem; highlight the breakthrough's related ethical, empirical, and prudential contributions; and then appraise the breakthrough in the light of our continuing need for creative breakthroughs in politics. I hope that my analysis of these concrete historical cases will not only clarify the meaning of prophetic consititutional breakthroughs but also help us to distinguish between true and false political prophets and to be willing to explore the possibility of contemporary breakthroughs with greater confidence.

Roger Williams and the Theory of Religious Liberty

The problem that prompted Roger Williams's creative breakthrough involved a dominant paradigm of sixteenth century thought.[2] It involved, specifically, two cardinal propositions of that paradigm: (1) that there is only one true faith and (2) that it is the duty of the Prince (ruler or state) to uphold the true faith. Both Catholics and Protestants adhered to these propositions. Theirs (of course) was the true faith; and it was the duty of the Catholic (or Protestant) Prince to uphold the true Catholic (or Protestant) faith, as the case might be.

However, given the existence of substantial numbers of people in disagreement about which, in fact, was the one true faith (that is, the Catholic or Protestant version, or which Protestant version), and given, too, the will of the Prince (ruler or state) to carry out his duty according to the conventional wisdom and dominant political paradigm, the outcome could only be conflict, persecution, bloodshed, and civil war. And events in the sixteenth century testify eloquently to the ugly reality of this outcome. Despite the bloodshed, advocates on both sides refused to budge. After all, the one true faith must be upheld against disbelievers and heretics and schismatics. People must live by the one true faith. They certainly cannot live by the false faith. Moreover, unless the Prince (ruler of state) upholds the one true faith, disbelief, heresy, and untruth will spread; and this is intolerable to God and to truth and to peace.

In addition—so the advocates of the dominant Christian paradigm argued—the political community cannot endure unless it is founded on, and guided by, the one true faith. Harmony, good faith, justice, prosperity—these would be undermined and destroyed unless the one true faith prevailed. These at least were the arguments of the conventional wisdom. And they seemed most persuasive to Christians in Western Europe who were absolutely convinced that belief in and practice of the one true faith were of transcendent importance. A person's life on earth, after all, was brief; but life after death opened up the glorious vision of immortality to those of the true faith and the horrible vision of eternal punishment for disbelievers and sinners. Consequently, the cost of bloodshed was a small price to pay to maintain the one true faith.

However, the fact of disagreement on basic religious matters persisted, despite persecution and bloodshed and savage civil war that set person against person, family against family, town against town, country against country, and that, moreover, divided men and women, families, towns, and countries. And Princes could be found who were convinced of the duty to uphold the true faith by sword and prison.

There were, of course, voices other than the dominant voices of persecution. For example, a minority spoke up for a policy of expediency. They would persecute or practice a policy of enforced religious uniformity only when they could do so without jeopardizing civility, order, strength, and prosperity in the state. Otherwise, they deemed it wise to practice a policy of toleration of religious dissenters. Those who held to this outlook recognized that a blind and dogmatic policy of persecution, regardless of consequences, would undermine peace, order, law, justice, strength, and prosperity in the state; and this, they argued, was an evil greater than the toleration of religious dissenters.

An even smaller minority, especially at the beginning, advocated a policy of religious liberty. The tiny handful of advocates of religious liberty (with help from the *politiques*, the shrewd advocates of a policy of expedient toleration) usher in the new religious and political paradigm. They are primarily responsible for the creative breakthrough here.

The advocates of religious liberty propose to have the best of two seemingly contradictory worlds. They maintain that it is possible to pursue the one true faith without insisting upon coerced religious conformity. They maintain that religious diversity is not incompatible with the enjoyment of a good, moral, peaceful, constitutional, prosperous political community. They challenge the conventional wisdom, the dominant religious and political paradigm. They do not necessarily deny (at least at the beginning) that there is only one true faith. They do assert that people cannot be absolutely sure of what the one true faith is. Only God perfectly understands the true faith; and only God—on Judgment Day—can confidently say whether an individual has lived according to the true faith. Consequently, these advocates of religious liberty reject the view that it is the duty of the

Prince—or ruler or state—to uphold the one true faith by persecution, with sword and prison.

Roger Williams—drawing upon the thinking of the advocates of religious liberty—excellently illustrates a powerfully articulated argument in the seventeenth century on behalf of religious liberty and against the dominant paradigm of persecution. Is it not anomalous, he deftly pointed out, for Christians—in the name of Christ, the Prince of Peace—to persecute, to wield the sword, to spill blood, to divide brother against brother? What would Christ's answer be on the question: Who really are the true believers? Are they Catholic or Protestant? And which Protestants? If some of each group are being persecuted, then some must be persecuted even if they are the true believers. But only God on Judgment Day—not human beings in this world—can make the decision on who the truly faithful are. Hence, how can a policy of persecution, which may result in some true believers' being persecuted, be defended? Indeed, Williams argued, given doubts as to God's true children, persecution cannot be defended. It is malicious and vicious. It is counterproductive. Moreover, Christ himself indicated that disbelievers must be allowed to live in this world and that their punishment would come in the next. In any event, it was clearly contrary to God's message to coerce conscience. Individuals could only come to God freely, not because of fear of earthly persecution, punishment, and coercion. Rape of the soul—Williams's vivid image for religious persecution—was incompatible with God's message that people be drawn freely to Divinity.

Furthermore, the political community did not require enforced religious conformity for its continuance. The Prince, Civil Magistrate, or state had limited responsibilities: to preserve peace and order in the political community. Religious uniformity was neither a necessary nor a sufficient condition for such peace and order. Indeed, when the Civil Magistrate persecuted for cause of conscience, he undermined peace and order. The sword and the prison could not, and should not, be used to enforce the alleged one true religious faith. In brief, matters of religious faith were to be left to the individual person and to God. The practice of religious faith was not a matter of concern to the Civil Magistrate; religion was to be placed beyond the power of the state.

Here, of course, are ideas that contribute to the paradigm of constitutional government: of a government limited in its powers and of a government effectively and regularly restrained even in the exercise of those powers granted. Certain matters (here, religious matters) are to be beyond the power of the state. Later, of course, these matters will become rights, and they will be broadened to include freedom of speech, press, and assembly, as well as religious freedom; and the right of revolution will be enshrined as a way to protect these rights against tyranny.

The achievement of Roger Williams, and other advocates of religious liberty, is highly significant. By challenging the dominant paradigm of Western Christendom—a paradigm that had seemed so logical and so persuasive—the advocates of religious liberty were able to articulate a new paradigm that would protect the rights of conscience, and the search of human beings for the true faith, while simultaneously eliminating from the political arena a vital source of discord and division—harmful, indeed potentially fatal, to the peace, law, order, justice, civility, prosperity, and strength of the political community. They articulated a theory of religious liberty and constitutional protection for the rights of religious conscience; and they helped to shape that theory of resistance, revolution, and constitutional government necessary to ensure the successful practice of religious liberty. Their activities led to a momentous change in outlook, behavior, and judgment in both religion and politics. The results of their activities were fruitful: in ending, in time, religious persecution; in securing the effective exercise of religious freedom; and in constitutionalizing the exercise of power. They contributed mightily to the resolution of a deeply troubling problem that had badly split Western Christendom since the Protestant Reformation and that had led to catastrophic religious warfare in Europe.

The breakthrough was a breakthrough along several fronts. Putting the matter differently: The prudential breakthrough (not of course to be more fully realized until the late eighteenth century, with enshrinement of the principle of separation of church and state in the U.S. Constitution) rests upon ethical and empirical breakthroughs. Ethically, a more satisfactory philosophy of politics was articulated: of people of different religious faiths living freely, happily, harmoniously, civilly, peacefully, prosperously together in the same political community. This political philosophy held, crucially, that certain beliefs ought to safeguard religious liberty—and then other liberties—and ensure the right of revolution against tyrannical rulers. Empirically, a new hypothesis was articulated and, in time, tested: that in Christendom people of different religious faiths, enjoying religious liberty, could in fact live together without the evil effects that some feared (lack of civility, morality, respect for law and order, peace, prosperity); and that in fact religious persecution was the great enemy of societal harmony and a major cause of war. Prudentially, the judgment was made that it would be wise to ensure religious liberty: by calling attention to the ill effects, hypocrisy, and illogic of persecution; by acting to limit the power of the state in religious matters; and by endorsing theories of resistance and revolution to secure a return to constitutional government in the event that the state violated certain basic rights.

In reflecting on this particular creative breakthrough, we note that, initially, the ethical recommendation on behalf of religious liberty seems outrageous; that the empirical proposition that religious liberty and political peace are compatible seems false; that the prudent judgment that religious liberty is wise seems absurd. However, when the decision on behalf of religious liberty is tested, it works. This suggests the need in political science to be willing to test new possibilities for living together better in the political community. These new possibilities are suggested by new ethical views; they are reinforced by a willingness to try new patterns of conflict resolution; and these new possibilities are, initially, suggested for testing by people searching for wise solutions to live political problems. These people are not discovering a scientific mystery long shrouded in our past and present—in nature. They are, in a significant sense, inventing the future. They are divining political becoming. They are discerning future possibilities. They are, at the highest level, prophetic. They are significantly influenced by untried ethical possibilities, by a glimpse of new empirical possibilities, by an intimation of a novel (but sound) wisdom.

This perspective should hearten those who look to creative breakthroughs. It should hearten those with a soundly radical ethical vision, those who challenge the harmful empirical realities of the status quo or the status quo ante, and those who have prudential intimations of wiser political action for untried human and humane possibilities.

This creative breakthrough also illuminates the conflicts of faiths—political if not religious—in our own century. And here I do not want to be misunderstood. I do not equate authoritarian communism (as practiced, for example, in the Soviet Union) with liberal democracy (as practiced, for example, in the United States). But I do see a conflict of faiths, and I do see some both in the Soviet Union and in the United States committed to the proposition that there is only one true political faith and that it is the duty of the rulers of the state to see that faith prevail, even if victory calls for force and violence and war.

Thus, if we interpret communism and liberal democracy as faiths, we immediately see some parallels that make the religious battles of the sixteenth to the eighteenth centuries very current. Is communism (or liberal democracy) the one true faith? And is it the duty of the Communist (or liberal democratic) state to uphold that true faith? And how? Does this mean, therefore, that conflict, including war, is inevitable between Communist and liberal democratic states?

And are we moderns in trouble, and unable to make Roger Williams's argument about freedom and peace in this world, because we no longer believe in a God who forbids "soul rape" (or political rape) and who will judge us—whether we are Communist (or liberal democratic) believers—only at Judgment Day? If we lack faith in a transcendent deity, must we (and can we) come up with a convincing secular substitute, or at least consider what standard we shall employ to challenge the dogmatism and fanaticism of ideological and nationalistic idolatries?

Must we seriously confront the reality that we are modern-day *politiques*—advocates of "peaceful coexistence" on purely expedient grounds? Do we then have to live with the possibility that one side or the other will risk war if the costs are minimal and victory seems likely? Or—following Williams—do we have to reject forceful conversion on the ground that neither side can be absolutely certain of the true faith? And can this conviction—which works against religious and political dogmatism and fanaticism— be reinforced by a scientific conviction opposed to imposition of alleged truths?

And can we move from a religious to a scientific and human refusal to coerce conscience and to persecute nonbelievers, heretics, schismatics? Can we not only place religious, scientific, political, economic, and social beliefs beyond the power of the state, or of would-be rulers of the state, to enforce against a person's conscience but also establish peaceful and constitutional means of handling inevitable conflicts about matters legitimately in the public arena? Or are we unable to learn the lessons of the bloody religious wars of the sixteenth century? Will Williams's arguments on behalf of freedom of conscience and peaceful accommodation prove unavailing until our reaction against a twentieth century nuclear war—a war produced by twentieth century fanaticism—produces a new constitutional receptivity (assuming there are people and communities surviving a nuclear holocaust)?

These questions adumbrate the character of a major creative breakthrough in the future, a breakthrough to genuine peaceful accommodation among the lethally armed superstates of the modern world. We need to reject both "better dead than red" and "better red than dead." We need to constitutionalize the international stuggle for power. We need to make the world safe for the eventual triumph, by peaceful and constitutional means, of prophetic values.

Madison's Theory of the Extensive Republic

In Madison's case, the problem was this: How reconcile

liberty and large size? Or how reconcile liberty and authority in a large state?[3] But why was this a problem? It was a problem for Madison (as it was for all republicans in the United States) because he was (as they were) committed to republican government (that is to say, to government by the many and protection of basic rights for all) in a new American nation that required requisite power and authority for survival. Was it possible, however, to reconcile liberty and authority in a large state? This was a real problem because the conventional wisdom—according to the dominant paradigm, the prevalent concept, the evidence of history, the testimony of political theorists—indicated the impossibility of reconciling liberty and authority in a large state. According to the conventional wisdom, republican government (based on self-government and liberty) was possible only in a small political community—a city-state such as Athens or Venice or Geneva. But, alas, the new United States of America was a large state! Moreover, according to the conventional wisdom—the political science of the day—a large state could only be governed under the authority of a monarch or a despot and within the framework of a nonrepublican empire, one incompatible with self-government and liberty, at least the degree of self-government and liberty that the Americans had presumably fought their revolution to secure. Anything less than such republican self-government and republican liberty was a state of affairs that good American republicans could never accept.

How, then, deal with this problem? How get out of this dilemma? Could American republicans have the best of two, seemingly contradictory, worlds? Could they have self-government and liberty in a republic and also enjoy legitimate power, authority, order, and security in the large country that the United States was?

Others had refused to face up to the problem because they believed it to be insoluble. Patrick Henry and other anti-federalists argued that republican government is possible only in a small political community. They did not lift their sights beyond the loose political confederation of the Articles of Confederation. They rejected the possibility of a greatly strengthened central government. Alexander Hamilton and John Adams and other advocates of "high-toned" government maintained that only an empire, or a strong central government on the British model, could hold together a political community as large as the new American nation. Confederations, they insisted, were notoriously weak and unstable and detrimental to the interests of justice. If Henry and his friends argued that great strength in a central government jeopardized republican self-government and republican liberty, Hamilton and Adams and their friends held that faction prevailed in small political communities and jeopardized both the public good and the Union.

Neither Henry nor Hamilton challenged the accepted political science of their day or perceived that the traditional statement of the problem of how to reconcile liberty and authority (in the large expanse of the new United States) had to be reexamined. Only Madison challenged the conventional wisdom and was bold enough to look at the problem in a new light and to ask if a new political concept—the concept of a new federal republic—suggested a way out.

Madison's theory of the extensive republic—the theory of the new federal republic—constituted a creative breakthrough because he proposed that Americans could work out a new political synthesis. They could have liberty and self-government, at the local level, and yet enjoy justice in the 13 states and a powerful central government able to protect the common interests of the whole Union, by adopting the model of the new Constitution of 1787. This new federal model continued control by the states over their local affairs and yet gave the new central government authority in matters of concern to all members of the Union. For good measure, the new federal republic operated to control the effects of faction, primarily but not exclusively at the state or local level. The Constitution of 1787 created a central authority—the new federal government—that rested more legitimately on popular consent and the Union's component states, and yet possessed greater strength than any confederation in history. The features of the Republic are today well known; but in 1787 they constituted a breakthrough in governmental theory and practice: the unique division and sharing of powers; constitutional limitations on federal and state governments; a federal government with significant powers operating directly on the people; a strong chief executive in the president; and so on.

Ethically, Madison's theory, particularly as fully developed, included broadened conceptions of liberty, self-government, pluralist democracy, and the good political life: specifically, conceptions of religious liberty, freedom of speech, press, assembly, and other constitutional protections against violations of liberty; an explicit acceptance of interests, parties, and public opinion in the process of government; and a more enlightened conception of popular rule, governmental power, and national union.

Madison's theory of the extensive republic also involved an empirical hypothesis designed to explain how Americans could enjoy the best (and escape the worst) of two worlds: how they could enjoy liberty without fear of anarchy and the adverse affects of faction; how they could enjoy authority without fear of tyranny and the adverse affects of an overpowerful central government. The large size of the political community plus the diversity and multiplicity of interests in the political community—these factors would defeat or inhibit the operation of factions and thus ensure greater success for the public good. Representation would also operate to filter the evil effects of faction. Constitutional limitations on power and separation of powers were additional "auxiliary precautions" that would help to ensure the successful reconciliation of liberty and authority in the new Republic. Moreover, a loyal republican and constitutional opposition party would guard against tyranny at the center. The constitutional operation of majority rule; a sound public opinion, based upon a free press; a healthy two-party system; the federal judiciary; a wise statesmanship that could distinguish between a usurpation, an abuse, and an unwise use of constitutional power—these would protect against the evils of monarchy, plutocracy, and tyranny in the central government and against antirepublicanism and anarchy in the component states of the Union. Given the assumption of this theory, generous and necessary republican power could be safely exercised by the central government.

Prudentially, Madison's theory constituted sound political judgment on a number of crucial matters, not only in the crucial year 1787 but in the 1790s and later in the 1820s and 1830s. In 1787 Madison saw the need to strengthen the powers of the central government. He wisely insisted on the possibility of a new federal system that would do a better job of reconciling liberty and authority. He refused to listen to those who denied the possibility of republican government in an extensive country. He was willing in 1787 to settle for a central government not as strong as he had wanted it to be because he perceived that the Constitution of 1787 was at least a step in right direction. Guided by his political theory, he acted to articulate key features of the new federal republic in Philadelphia in 1787; to defend the new Constitution eloquently and effectively in *The Federalist* and in the Virginia Ratifying Convention; to establish the new Constitution on a firm foundation with a Bill of Rights and with other supporting legislation at its beginning; to exercise leadership on behalf of a constitutional opposition party in the 1790s; and to defend the Union against nullification and secession at the end of his long life. Madison's theory constituted a generally successful guide to prudent action throughout his lifetime effort to demonstrate that Americans could reconcile liberty and authority in a large state.

Madison's theory of the extensive republic illustrates the intimate connection of the ethical, empirical, and prudential components of politics. A thorough appreciation of this connection is crucial to a full understanding of prophetic constitutional breakthroughs. Madison's theory is grounded in an ethical commitment to republican liberty and self-government and to the common good. His theory faces the empirical realities of faction and large size and posits both the multiplicity and diversity of interests and the extensive terrain as factors that will serve to guard against factional mischief. It holds that republicans can wisely reconcile liberty and authority in a large state by adopting a federal and republican constitution with certain unique features and by interpreting this constitution in the proper republican spirit. Boldly, Madison moved beyond the thinking of contemporary political priests in the nascent liberal tradition, yet without succumbing to either utopian illusions or Machiavellian temptations.

Madison's creative breakthrough is to be found in the new political paradigm he enunciated for political science and American politics: that which we associate with the concept of the federal republic. No one can deny that he built upon the constitutional and republican tradition of the past. But we must also appreciate his (and America's) boldness, inventiveness, openness to political experiment. Madison did not hesitate to develop a new theory to achieve a more nearly perfect Union amidst the conditions of America. He was conscious both of his indebtedness to the past and of his (and America's) creative experiment with the model of a new federal republic. Moreover, he had (as did many of his republican colleagues) a keen sense of America's "becoming," of America's future, of the creative process in politics, of the need to test new values, behavior, and judgments in the crucible of politics. Madison appreciated the need, in his lifetime and by his political action, to solidify the breakthrough by attending to additional problems that faced the new Republic as it continued to seek to reconcile liberty and large size.

Today we still continue to struggle with the reconciliation of liberty and authority, liberty and large size. And Madison would be the first to concede that we have to ask hard questions about the adoption of his model to the changing conditions of modern America and of the twentieth and twenty-first centuries. Can Madison's model for a late eighteenth century America be successfully adapted to the decreased size of America brought on by science and technology? To the powerful demands of contemporary interest groups? To the demands of the welfare state? Is Madison's theory too negative in character to do justice to maltreated minorities, to the poor, to the politically weak, to women? Does Madison's theory (despite his own strong nationalism in 1787) vest too much power in the states? Can Madison's theory really function to guard against factions in the modern world? Can we adjust the Madisonian model, or is a new creative breakthrough called for? A breakthrough that will enable us to speak to this reformulation of our problems: Can the modern democratic state reconcile advanced ideas of social, economic, and political justice with the pluralistic, constitutional, and capitalist operative ideals of modern America? We can also ask about the relevance of federalism to the larger world. To ask these questions is to carry on in the spirit of prophetic constitutional breakthroughs.

What, indeed, is the future of the paradigm of the federal republic? Can it be utilized not only at the national level but also at the regional or global level and at very local levels through new patterns of popular participation? These questions suggest intimations of what the future might hold but, as yet, no clear-cut breakthroughs. Regional federal government seems more plausible than a global federal government. New patterns of participatory democracy are currently open to people at local levels, but they have not been fully explored. Yet, in all these arenas, we would be naive to assume that the problems of modern federalism are easily solved or that current objections are easily overwhelmed. Nonetheless, Madison's theory and practice encourage us to investigate the continuing fruitfulness of his model and to search for comparable breakthroughs relevant to our concerns. As Madison drew upon the theory of religious liberty (by making a virtue out of the multiplicity of religious sects or of economic, political, and social interests), so may we draw upon Madison's theory of the extensive republic. And we do so best when we look upon creative breakthroughs in terms of the testing of future possibilities.

But we may not want to test all alleged breakthroughs or possibilities. Some breakthroughs may not be in the prophetic tradition. To distinguish between genuine and spurious breakthroughs, let me turn from Roger Williams and James Madison to John C. Calhoun.

A Spurious Breakthrough: Calhoun's Theory of the Concurrent Majority

We can, I believe, profit from an examination of both genuine breakthroughs and false breakthroughs. We can learn from successful as well as from unsuccessful breakthroughs. With this in mind let me now turn to a false candidate for creative breakthroughs in political science and in politics: John C. Calhoun's theory of the concurrent majority.[4]

Superficially, the problem that Calhoun posed is a major one: How protect the vital interests of the minority in a majority rule system? Phrased differently—and more accurately—Calhoun's question, his real question, is less appealing: How protect the vital economic, political, and social interests of the slaveholding, agricultural South in a Union more and more dominated by a Northern and Western majority favorable to free labor in factory and on farm; to industrial, commercial capitalism; and to the republican principle of majority rule? Calhoun wanted the best of two worlds: perpetuation of the institution of slavery, of the South's social institutions, of the South's political power; and, simultaneously, enjoyment of the blessings of liberty, constitutionalism, and federal union.

Calhoun, too, proposed to achieve his objective by means of a new political paradigm, a new majoritarian model, a new concept of constitutional government: the theory of the concurrent majority. According to this theory, the South would obtain a concurrent voice in the passage of public policy or a veto on its execution. This would clearly solve Calhoun's problem of how to protect the vital interests of the minority. The majority would not be able to pass or execute any policy without the concurrence of the South or, indeed, of any state in the South. Free white men, constitutionally, would be able to preserve their rights—and their political, economic, and social power—in the Union.

Calhoun rejected the majoritarian model of the going American system—the conventional wisdom—precisely because it permitted the majority to take action at the expense of the vital interests of the South (as determined by majority rule in the South). There are, of course, a number of factors that limit the operation of bare majority rule in the United States: for example, the special majorities (two-thirds or three-fourths) needed for certain actions, the president's veto, judicial review, the process of elections, party mores, the power of committee chairpersons, the filibuster, and so on. But Calhoun was not satisfied with these limitations on majority rule. He sought to strike directly at the operation of the principle of the numerical majority: decision based on sheer numbers. Calhoun sought what he called *decision by a true constitutional majority*—that is, a majority based not on numbers but on the vital interests that held a society together. If these vital interests were not protected (and against the numerical majority, if necessary), the society could not be held together. Hence, only a concurrent majority could be endorsed if truly constitutional government—government that would protect the vital interests of all vital groups in the political community—were to prevail.

Ethically, Calhoun's theory is defective because it is dedicated not to the protection of all minority interests, or all minority rights, or individual rights such as freedom of speech, press, assembly, and so on, but to the protection of slavery. Calhoun's vision of the good life did not anticipate a good future; it sought to reassure the continuance of an evil past. It was not simply conservative; it was deeply reactionary. His grounds for the defense of the slave system were deeply reactionary even at the time he made his argument. Moreover, he proposed a reactionary alliance between the slaveholding South and the capitalist North against the interests of the working person, free and slave. I use the word *reactionary* advisedly. Madison and Jefferson—and the enlightened Founding Fathers of 1776 and 1787—were opposed to slavery and looked forward to its demise. Calhoun turned his back on these men and resurrected less enlightened arguments in defense of slavery. Similarly, capitalism in Calhoun's time was premised on free labor and a free market and was opposed to governmental attempts to regulate and control the economy. Calhoun's efforts, if successful, would have sought to go back to an earlier period of restrictions on labor, to impose, via government, an economic system hostile to free labor, a free market, and private enterprise—in the interest primarily of a slaveholding elite.

Empirically, Calhoun misconceived the dominant forces of his time and the political, economic, and social forces that were to shape America's future. He misconceived the nature of democratic patterns of conflict and accommodation. He did not understand the empirical impossibility of a permanent veto over such issues as slavery, or even over higher tariffs, or over changes in the Southern way of life. He did not appreciate fully enough the practical difficulties of achieving unanimity on vital issues. He misunderstood the possibilities of compromise, which would protect Southern interests and prevent violation of genuinely defensible vital interests. He misunderstood the dynamic nature of American capitalism and its lack of interest in perpetuating slavery and the plantation system. He misunderstood capitalism's hostility to governmental efforts to hold back the clock of economic development. He misread the power of nationalism, the democratic temper, the social conscience in America.

My comments in the preceding two paragraphs also highlight Calhoun's lack of prudent judgment. They also underscore the ethical and empirical contributions to wise judgment. Calhoun's basic failure of judgment was that he sought, futilely, to protect anachronistic interests such as slavery by means of a veto incompatible with democratic rule. He simply did not understand the character of the new federal republic created in 1787. Ethically, politically, economically, socially, he was trying to push the clock back. He never perceived that the principle of the concurrent majority that he sought to use to protect slavery against majority decisions in the Union could also be used by whites and blacks to oppose slavery itself. For if human freedom is a vital interest, then majorities in Southern states should not be able to perpetuate slavery. Indeed, even one black slave should be able to veto the action of that majority that keeps him or her a slave.

Calhoun's values were at odds both with the libertarian and egalitarian trends of democratic America and with the individualistic and capitalist trends of the industrial East and the agrarian West. His reading of America's operative ideals, its economic interests, and its political patterns was simply wrongheaded empirically. Hence, his prudential recommendations were bound to fail; the theory of the concurrent majority was simply not a possibility for America.

Calhoun failed. And he failed despite the efforts of those twentieth century thinkers who have tried to see his success in those devices that, practically speaking, limit, inhibit, and defeat majority action in the United States. Calhoun himself was not happy with these devices, and he was not convinced that they operated to give him the kind of constitutional government he wanted.

Calhoun's failure—interestingly enough—was foreseen by Madison, who first clearly criticized and exposed the theoretical and practical weaknesses of Calhoun's theory. Madison was convinced that the theoretical weakness of Calhoun's argument foreshadowed its practical failure. Madison maintained that Calhoun's theory led to either anarchy or tyranny. Both, for Madison, were incompatible with republican and constitutional government. If the South could veto Union policy contrary to the South's vital interests, why could not a state in the South veto policy contrary to its own interests? And if a Southern state could veto the actions of the Union or of the South, why could not a county within that Southern state? And then a city within that county? And a ward within that city? And a group within that ward? And, ultimately, an individual within that group, within the ward, within the city, within the county, within the state, within the South, within the Union? The path led to anarchy when one departed from the majority principle. Diversity of interests made unanimity impossible; and Calhoun was really seeking unanimity. To depart from the majority principle, as Calhoun suggested, was to move toward anarchy, and this would mean the death of republicanism, which was based on the majority principle.

Moreover, given the impossibility of anarchy—and the inability to act when a majority sought to act—those seeing the need for action, when Calhoun's theory foreclosed effective action, would opt for tyranny rather than accept anarchy. Hence, the twin evils of anarchy and tyranny—traditional enemies of republican government—were theoretically rooted in Calhoun's theory and vitiated his argument. Madison foresaw, prophetically, what would happen if the Union refused to accept Calhoun's theory of the concurrent majority, and the South insisted on following Calhoun down the road of nullification and secession, ultimate weapons that Calhoun's followers in fact endorsed to protect the vital interests of the slaveholding South against majority rule in the Union. Madison saw the breakup of the Union in nullification, and civil war in secession. These indeed were the practical consequences of Calhoun's efforts to ensure the operation of the theory of the concurrent majority: the anarchy of nullification and secession, and the dangers of tyrannical actions (in both the Confederacy and the Union) required to maintain unity in the light of nullification and secession.

Calhoun's theory was not a creative breakthrough. It was defective in theory. It did not work in practice. It was partly responsible for the catastrophe we oddly celebrate as the American Civil War. Despite the arguments of those who see in other devices (the party system, the power of the chairpersons of key committees based on seniority, the filibuster) the accomplishment of the objectives of Calhoun's theory of the concurrent majority, the fact remains that no section, state , or vital interest has a secure permanent veto on policy and execution in the U.S. polity. In brief, we have not followed Calhoun's interpretation of constitutional government.

To argue against the weaknesses of Calhoun's theory of the concurrent majority is not to say that prohibitions against certain majority action should not be institutionalized. But we must distinguish, in the tradition of prophetic politics, between protecting slavery and protecting religious freedom. And we must distinguish between institutionalizing a veto on all matters of vital interest and prohibiting political action on a limited range of freedoms.

The problem of how to protect minority or individual rights in a majority system is still a problem that challenges our ingenuity. We have not yet worked out a foolproof system to ensure such protection. The exploration of past creative breakthroughs, genuine or spurious, stimulates our critical imagination and invites us to continue to explore for such protection in the future. As we continue to explore possibilities here,

we must be clear on the worth of the vital interest to be protected
and on the effectiveness of the mechanism we choose to achieve
the desired protection. The real problem that should engage us
should be this one: How secure the more adequate protection of
the weak against the strong in the interest of justice? Here there
is need for continuing breakthroughs—to safeguard the poor,
disadvantaged minority groups, women, and particularly these
people in the developing nations.

CONCLUSION

The three case studies in this chapter call attention to the
argument that creative breakthroughs in politics involve better,
more fruitful ways of handling troubling questions, of dealing
more successfully with disturbing problems, in politics. The
problems must be major ones; and major problems are most
often practical problems that involve, for example, peace and
war, liberty and authority, prosperity and poverty, accommodation and conflict. Often the creative breakthrough occurs when
the old question or problem—say the reconciliation of liberty and
authority in a large state, or the reconciliation of truth and
freedom— is approached in a new way, is seen in the light of a
new possibility, is appreciated in terms of a different understanding of political becoming. The new approach may call for the rejection of old premises. The rejected premise may be ethical—the
ethical view that it is the duty of the state to enforce the true
religious faith. The rejected premise may be empirical—the empirical view that liberty is incompatible with large size. The rejected premise may be prudential—the prudential view that
democracies cannot overcome the fatal disease of faction. The new
approach usually calls for experimentation with new governmental operative ideals: for example, experimentation with the concept of a federal republic or with the concept of religious liberty.
These are the new paradigms that constitute ''answers'' to troubling questions, ''resolutions'' of disturbing problems. Most often
they enable political actors to grapple more successfully, more

fruitfully, with political conflicts. They carry us beyond the conventional wisdom of ordinary constitutional politics toward a superior constitutional order and without the dangers of utopian or Machiavellian politics.

The radical examination of major questions and problems must, therefore, be a top priority for those concerned with prophetic constitutional breakthroughs. The political scientist must be sensitized to explore and identify the deficient ethical, empirical, and prudential responses that have made past answers and resolutions ethically unacceptable, empirically false, and prudentially foolish. The political scientist must also be aware of new ethical, empirical, and prudential possibilities: a new way of looking at things and a willingness to experiment with new concepts, premises, paradigms. Creative—and prophetic—possibilities build on what is sound in past and present, but they are future oriented. The problem is resolved in the future, not in the past or present. Success will be measured by fruitfulness; and in politics this most often means practical success. The practical, prudential success, however, rests significantly on bold and advanced ethical recommendations and on a scientific willingness to test experimentally new political values, new patterns of handling conflict and achieving accommodation, and new wise public policies.

In taking the position on prophetic and creative constitutional breakthroughs in politics that I have advanced in this chapter, I do not mean to deprecate either the seminal contributions of the great political philosophers in the classical tradition or the useful contributions of the outstanding behavioral political scientists of the contemporary world. I do mean to underscore the importance of the real problems of politics for political scientists, problems that are primarily practical in character. I do also mean to focus attention on the ethical, empirical, and prudential dimensions of these problems. I do mean to emphasize the importance of imaginative possibility in politics, the importance of discerning political becoming, the importance of exploring the prophetic intimations of politics. I do mean to underscore the testing of creative possibilities in politics, testing in the spirit of creative political evolution. Viewing creative prophetic constitutional breakthroughs in this way, we can be encouraged to overcome the timidity, blindness, and complacency of liberal democratic politics, without succumbing to the dangers of Machiavellian politics or the illusions of utopian politics. Guided by a prophetic politics attuned to all the vital concerns of political science and of politics—ethical, empirical, and prudential—we can address ourselves more ably to the quest for civilized survival, healthy growth, and creative fulfillment.

In the next chapter, I will bring this perspective on prophetic constitutional breakthroughs to bear on a number of contemporary issues that disturb the prophetic imagination.

8 : Prophetic Constitutional Breakthroughs: II

INTRODUCTION

As we saw in the last chapter, historical perspective enables us to see past breakthroughs and to distinguish between genuine and spurious breakthroughs. The task of identifying present and future breakthroughs is more difficult. Although we can identify the big problems that concern us, we cannot confidently say which of several alternatives will constitute the prophetic constitutional breakthrough. In this chapter, therefore, we will state those problems as they relate to four major areas of concern (peace, human rights, economic well-being, and ecological balance), pose and examine key alternatives with regard to problems in these four areas, and then indicate what prophetic constitutional breakthroughs, if any, may now seem prudent and feasible.[1]

1. *Peace.* Can we safeguard the very life of humankind on earth? How can we obtain a more secure peace among sovereign nation-states within a framework of freedom and at a sensible cost?
2. *Human rights.* Can we advance greater human freedom throughout the globe? How can we more effectively translate global rhetoric into effective and regularized mechanisms for maximizing human rights?

164

3. *Economic well-being.* Can we overcome poverty and the disastrous consequences of poverty? How can we establish and effectively maintain, worldwide, minimum standards of income, health, housing, education, and other basic human needs?
4. *Ecological balance.* Can we ensure the ecological health of the planet earth? How can we sensibly husband our resources, protect our air and water and land, and bring population and resources into better balance?

It is, of course, easier to pose these problems than to answer them. But, clearly, these questions suggest the need to correct or move beyond current political ideologies, policies, and institutions that are malfunctioning. Key premises of the war system, nation-state policies, dominant economic behavior, and prevalent ecological practices need to be critically assessed. In each of the four areas of concern, we need to be searching for prophetic constitutional breakthroughs that enable us to move beyond the idolatry and narrowness of the often power-mad and deceitful nation-state without succumbing to falsely utopian notions about creating an angelic new person in a miraculously new earthly society where all conflict, tyranny, want, and imbalance have been entirely eliminated; and that enable us, too, to take bolder and wiser steps than conservative liberal democrats or violence-prone Communist revolutionaries. Given the commitment to prophetic values, we are obligated to seek those constitutional breakthroughs that would reduce significantly the dangers of nuclear war, abolish gross tyrannical acts, satisfy human needs more equitably, and enable us to clean up our ecological home. But before reaching some judgments on steps to be taken, it will be helpful to review alternative policies that address problems in our four selected areas of concern and the arguments that might be made, pro and con, on these alternatives.

THE QUEST FOR PEACE

In the quest for peace five alternatives can be briefly examined.[2] They do not by any means exhaust the possibilities. Some may seem more sensible than others. All, however, even the most outlandish, bear critical examination. And critical examination is crucial because it points toward the prudent and feasible breakthrough.

The Balance of Power

Is a modified balance of power (based on positions of strength or the balance of terror) the most sensible way to maintain peace in the modern world and, simultaneously, to protect a nation's vital interests? Let us reflect on this question, for a moment, as Americans. Some argue that such a policy is the only one that can deter a massive conventional Soviet attack against Western Europe, or even Soviet nuclear aggression. They insist that the cost of such a policy, although high, is worthwhile because it protects the security and freedom of the United States and its allies. They minimize the risk of either conventional or nuclear war by underscoring the improbability that the Soviet Union would launch an aggressive attack in view of the terrible damage it would suffer (in retaliation) if it did so. They maintain that such a policy—which requires that the United States strengthen both its nuclear and conventional forces—will in time permit arms control and real disarmament. They note that there has, in fact, been no World War III; and contend that the balance of terror (however we dislike the thought) has prevented Soviet domination of all Europe and has curtailed overtly aggressive actions by the Soviet Union against other key centers of power. They hold that, given the realities of international politics, we must accept the inevitability of the present sovereign nation-state system, the struggle for power, and some variation of the balance of power.

Those opposed to the positions of strength policy call attention to the catastrophic consequences of nuclear war and urge that we devise a better policy. They emphasize both the dangers and the costs of present policy. They maintain that détente (a real relaxation of tensions) is impossible in any balance-of-power policy that calls for a continual military buildup and thus another suicidal arms race. Some of these critics call for a modification of the present bankrupt nation-state system or, at a minimum, for the removal of nuclear arms from the arsenals of all nations.

The United Nations

Apropos the United Nations, I focus not on the Security Council, which many thought would be the agency able to preserve the peace against aggressors, but upon the third-party activities of the United Nations, a UN role, keen students argue, more in keeping with the United Nations' record and its real potentiality. Here the key question is: *To what extent can we wisely rely upon a policy based upon the strengthened third-party activities of the United Nations?*

Those who defend this option contend that it is based upon a realistic recognition of what the United Nations can in fact do. They argue that a strengthened secretary-general can serve as a resourceful global leader on behalf of peace. With a properly equipped staff the secretary-general can persuade parties in conflict to use negotiation, conciliation, arbitration, or judicial settlement to work out their disputes. This approach can work, they maintain, especially if the Security Council itself backs this third-party role vigorously.

Those opposed to this option argue that third-party activity does not get at the root causes of war. It deals with symptoms, not causes. It does not seriously address East-West conflicts of interest, the rivalries of other nation-states, North-South tensions, the issue of internal suppression of peoples. Such an option cannot deal successfully with the problem of disarmament, especially the crucial issue of nuclear disarmament. Moreover, they insist, such a policy places too much reliance upon one person (the secretary-general), upon a veto-ridden Security Council, and upon a sometimes irresponsibile General Assembly. Finally, such a policy, however well intentioned, is too weak insofar as it depends upon the consent of the disputants and rejects sometimes necessary economic, diplomatic, or military sanctions.

The Functional Approach

How effective is the functional approach to a peaceful world? Those who support this approach argue that pragmatic success in working on common problems in a host of fields (in health, education, agriculture, communications, transportation, and so on) is the only way to build trust among peoples in the global community. They insist that such functional successes can in time overcome nationalistic suspicion and rivalry and facilitate the emergence of a global order also capable of attending to the function of security. This process may be slow, but it will pay off in the long run as mutual benefits build mutual trust. In this process, moreover, it is possible to have people working together to address the root causes of war in very practical ways.

Those who are skeptical of the functional approach doubt whether nationalism—and the determination of the sovereign nation-state to rely upon its own power to protect its vital interests—can be overcome when nations work together on common problems in health, agriculture, broadcasting, postal service, and the like. They emphasize that smaller functional successes in these areas will flounder on the rock of superpower rivalry, nation-state suspicions, North-South tensions involving the big, really vital, issues. Even if nations cooperate on certain functional tasks, they will not be able to do so when it comes to the crucial function of security. Moreover, they insist that we do not have sufficient time to await the building of functional networks, given the explosive global situation in which we currently live.

A New Global Security System and Radical Disarmament

Is a dependable peace possible only if founded on a global security system that has made radical disarmament a central policy? Those who argue on behalf of this alternative emphasize the bankruptcy of the present sovereign nation-state system and especially the danger of reliance upon nuclear arms to achieve national security. They call for bold steps to reduce and eventually eliminate nuclear weapons. They would then move on to reduction of other weapons of mass destruction and the establishment of a global security system with effective authority to maintain the peace. Their global authority would operate, of course, in a democratic and constitutional fashion.

Those who are skeptical of this alternative doubt both the desirability and the feasibility of this approach, which, they content, is naive and utopian. They point out that we cannot speedily enough raise national consciousness, mobilize regional interests, and transform global institutions in order to build a more durable world order system. They are not persuaded by the theory of transition of this approach: they do not find that it informs us clearly and realistically as to how we can move from where we are now to where we would like to be. They do not believe that we can build and trust a new global order system, especially one with crucial powers in the domain of security. Given the strength of the national suspicions of "the other side," radical disarmament is impossible; to trust the other side is flagrantly dangerous. Finally, they strongly emphasize that freedom might be jeopardized in a world in which the United States is disarmed.

Nonviolence

Is nonviolence the policy we must adopt in order to build a more peaceful world? Those who advocate this position hold that we must turn away from violence before it consumes us. Nonviolence is desirable because it protects the integrity of human life. It is feasible because it can work to achieve peace and resist aggressors through protest, noncooperation, and peaceful intervention. This policy recognizes the reality of conflict but would use nonviolent means to deal with it, especially such means as conversion; political, economic, and social accommodation; and nonviolent coercion. These methods would lower the level of violence and still permit people to resist aggressors and advance the cause of freedom. By moving away from war, violence, and arms, a policy of nonviolence would free human monies and energies to address the unmet human needs of the world's peoples.

Those opposed to this policy argue that it is neither desirable nor feasible. They insist that neither the Americans nor the Soviets—nor the French, Chinese, British, Indians, Iranians,

South Africans, and Israelis—are willing to rely upon nonviolent civilian defense as a dependable way to deter or defeat aggression. They hold that the costs of this policy (for example, in the loss of freedom under an aggressive occupying power) are too great to warrant trying this policy. Any probable benefits—for example, the end of nuclear war—are not worth the risk to national security inherent in this option. People are simply not yet ethically strong enough to carry out this policy successfully. To adopt such a policy would be an invitation to the triumph of the militarily powerful.

Conclusion

Do any of these alternative policies suggest a prophetic constitutional breakthrough? Is our best alternative, the balance of power, understood as the balance of terror? Or the modest third-party activities of a strengthened United Nations? Does the functional approach make sense and can it work speedily enough. Or must we move dramatically to secure a new global organization that can take bold steps to ensure disarmament and then guard the peace against aggressors? Or must we take an even more radical step and opt for nonviolent defense as the way to stop the savage cycle of war and destruction and introduce more humane ways of dealing with human conflict?

The acceptance of the ethical vision of a more peaceful world order is central to a prophetic breakthrough here. We have no difficulty in articulating this vision; we do have difficulty in getting major political actors to act upon this vision. By a more peaceful world order, it should be clear, we do not mean the end of all conflict, competition, and tension. Rather, we mean the elimination of catastrophic world wars, of major regional wars, of devastating civil wars, of the need for wars of national liberation. We mean the minimization or general reduction of the level of armed conflict. We also mean a world in which significant arms control and genuine disarmament are possible. We mean, then, a world in which major disputes (between and within nations) are settled without resort to violence and bloodshed, in which dangerous international tensions are considerably reduced, and in which world energies and monies can be put to use constructively in addressing unmet human needs for food, housing, medical care, education, community, and rich human social and cultural development.

To accomplish such a more peaceful world order we have to move away from the balance of terror and toward a new pattern of accommodation that will permit a variety of mechanisms to operate in the interest of peace—including the third-party activities of organizations such as the United Nations, a host of functional organizations, and bold radical disarmament. The habit and practice of a wide range of techniques of nonviolence (including dialogue, voting, economic pressure, and non-cooperation) remain as options in selected cases and as examples of preferred ways of dealing with conflicts. The long-range goal is the development, over time and with the help of intermediate successes, of a global community that is constitutional, democratic, federal, and equipped with minimal but effective powers to preserve the globe. An indispensable first step toward this goal of preserving the globe is nuclear disarmament. And here we may propertly heed the counsel of a realist with solid credentials as a statesman and student of foreign affairs: George F. Kennan.

Kennan holds that nuclear weapons are dangerous, improper, useless, defensively ineffective, redundant, risky, provocative. He advocates a policy of "no first use" of nuclear weapons and "the complete elimination of these and all other weapons of mass destruction from national arsenals"; and states that "the sooner we move toward that solution, and the greater courage we show in doing so, the safer we will be." Kennan would move by stages to the elimination of nuclear weapons. He would, initially, have the president of the United States, "after proper consultation with the Congress," "propose to the Soviet government an immediate across-the-board reduction by 50 percent of the nuclear arsenals now being maintained by the two superpowers—a reduction affecting in equal measure all forms of the weapon, strategic, medium-range and tactical, as well as all means of their delivery—all this to be implemented at once and without further wrangling among the experts, and to be subject to such national means of verification as now lie at the disposal of the two powers." Then "if this first operation were successful, I would then like to see a second one put in hand to rid us of at least two thirds of what would be left." And so on, to "complete elimination!"[3]

Of course, no one can say with confidence that the Soviet Union would respond—and thus make Kennan's "modest proposal" possible. What is clear is that this proposal, if effected, would safeguard the planet earth. Kennan speaks out of a realistic concern to protect the vital interests of the United States. He does not advocate unilateral disarmament. Indeed, he favors strengthening our conventional armaments in Europe. But he does see nuclear disarmament as crucial for the United States and for our posterity. Such disarmament would diminish a real danger and buy the time for other processes of accommodation to operate. It is a prophetic breakthrough worth trying.

THE QUEST FOR HUMAN RIGHTS

Concerning human rights, here again we will only be able to sample a few alternative approaches.[4] And even here our selection will focus on what might be done on behalf of the "least free." We will thus examine what might be done by the United States (as a leading nation in the world), by the United Nations, by nongovernmental organizations, by the least free themselves, and by a new world organization. Again, too, we should appreciate that these several approaches are not necessarily exclusive; they may reinforce each other.

The United States and Human Rights Policy

Should the United States rely primarily on "quiet diplomacy" toward offending friends? Or should the United States criticize friend and foe alike and not hesitate to invoke sanctions to punish human rights offenders? Those who favor quiet diplomacy emphasize that our national security interests, and not abstract morality, must guide our foreign policy. Hence the United States must be tactful and not scold publicly those who support our foreign policy even as we seek privately to get them to respect human rights. They argue that we may harm our own vital interests if we cut off military or economic aid to right-wing regimes that help us in foreign affairs. They point out that right-wing authoritarian regimes (for example, Spain or Portugal) may be replaced by more democratic governments, whereas left-wing Communist totalitarian regimes hold out no such prospect.

Those who favor a stronger and more evenhanded position on human rights argue that the United States cannot adhere to a double standard. The United States must exert its influence to protect human rights against both semitotalitarian states on the Left and authoritarian governments of the Right. Quiet diplomacy has its uses, but the United States must be prepared to utilize political, economic, and legal sanctions as well. If, ultimately, the United States is to move toward real respect for human rights under international law, there can only be one standard of law for all violators.

The United Nations

Should the United Nations resign itself to the articulation, and rhetorical acceptance, of human rights standards in the international community? Or should it concentrate on devising wise and effective legal, political, and economic remedies for clearly confirmed, consistent, gross violations of human rights? Those in one school of thought argue that the United Nations has an important job to do in articulating standards for the global community. These standards, they insist, shape the consensus that will make international freedom a reality. At this time, they maintain, the United Nations is unable to go beyond this very important task without meddling in the internal affairs of nations. At a future date, perhaps, the United Nations may acquire a real power to investigate complaints of violations of human rights and to fashion effective remedies for such violations.

Those in another school of thought favor the wise and effective remedies now. They would not only strengthen the power of the United Nations to investigate complaints; they would also establish machinery for the protection of human rights after persistent and gross violations have been established. They would, if necessary, amend the UN charter to make it possible for the UN (in clearly delimited areas) to overcome the current prohibition against interference in a nation's internal affairs. In the meantime, they would develop the United Nations' growing power to investigate and to use its considerable influence to stop violations of human rights.

Nongovernmental Organizations

Can the nongovernmental organization (NGO) stop as well as publicize violations of human rights? Those who are highly impressed by the work of the NGOs—such as Amnesty International—argue that their careful work in documenting and protecting violations has had a most salutary effect in protecting human rights. They make violating governments take notice. The NGOs cannot perform miracles, but they make actual or potential offenders think carefully about their practices. They may, in fact, prevent violations that would otherwise have occurred. And they do secure the release of at least some victims.

Others—who applaud the limited good that the NGOs do—may, nonetheless, emphasize the weaknesses of the NGOs. They note, for example, that although the NGOs can organize influential, and even mass, memberships in the United States and Western Europe, they cannot do so in the Soviet Union or China or Argentina or Indonesia or either North or South Korea. They do good work, but their effectiveness is limited. Moreover, they hold that, ironically, it is the case that even the limited effectiveness of the NGOs would diminish if they turned their attention from publicizing specific violations of human rights to a broader concern for the underlying causes of political, social, and economic injustice.

The Least Free

Can the least free themselves achieve self-consciousness, mobilize effectively, gain allies, and exert power to transform their condition by using the strategy of slower, incremental, constitutional, peaceful reform? Or must they turn to speedy, wholesale, extralegal, violent revolution? Those who argue on behalf of reform believe that it is important to obtain, and then build on, institutions of freedom in all countries. They concede that the battle on behalf of human rights will be easier in those countries with a constitutional tradition and more difficult in authoritarian nations. But they assert that peaceful reform can be achieved at less cost, and with more benefits, than by following a strategy of violent revolution.

Those who favor a more militant policy point out that those who now keep the least free powerless will not easily permit peaceful and constitutional change. They underscore the fact that repression will continue until power is mobilized to overturn repression. Because those who now oppress the least free do so by explicit violence, or threat of violence, it may be necessary to use violence to defeat the oppressor. The degree of militancy will depend upon the character of the oppressor, and different strategies may be called for by different categories of the least free—for example, by blacks or women or political dissidents—as they confront different types of repressive regimes.

A New World Order

Can we devise a new world order that will permit us to overcome, or deal with, violations of human rights at national, regional, and global levels? Those who support a new world order maintain that the protection of human rights calls for moving beyond the historical principle of national sovereignty. Nations can no longer have complete authority to violate the rights of their own citizens. When nations fail—when they engage in gross, persistent, and systematic violations of the rights of their own citizens—there must be a recourse to higher constitutional authority (either at the regional or global level) to protect human rights. There must be an effective constitutional mechanism to receive complaints of violations, to engage in investigations of such violations, and to secure protection for those whose human rights have been violated. They argue that we can slowly extend this rule of law throughout the global community.

Those who are critical of this approach note the persistence of the fact of jealous national sovereignty and argue that a new world order is a utopian dream. The world is not even ready for more modest efforts by the United Nations to protect human rights. It is certainly not ready for a more ambitious global order. Given the strength of the nation-state system, it is unlikely that a new global order will be able to invoke legal, political, or police powers successfully to protect human rights if voluntary consent or publicity fails. No feasible strategy of transition to such a new global order is in sight.

Conclusion

Life, growth, and development clearly call for the protection of human rights. Ethically, a civilizing politics must give top priority to the least free and the worst evils: nuclear war, official genocide, starvation, brutalizing racism, legal apartheid, savage colonial repression, torture, political persecution, inhumane sexism. Consistent, systematic, persistent, gross violations of human rights must be opposed and ended. A civilizing politics should prefer lawful, constitutional, nonviolent means to protect human rights.

Empirically, we recognize that the global community has now articulated splendid standards for human rights. But nations in too many countries fail to honor these standards. And the United Nations has not been effective in implementing protection of those human rights. In the 1970s the United States did adopt policies to enhance the safeguarding of internationally recognized human rights, but it remains to be seen whether this more vigorous, but prudential, policy will prevail. NGOs such as Amnesty International and other private groups have done a fine job of publicizing violations, but the scope of their power is limited. The least free themselves face serious handicaps in their efforts to protect themselves. In too many instances national security and political considerations take precedence over human rights in the behavior of nation-states and of international organizations. There is, however, developing a theory of legitimate intercession—indeed, of intervention—in the global community. Such a theory envisages a wide range of options ranging from quiet diplomacy through publicity and legal redress to political, economic, and police sanctions. At this time, however, legal machinery and constitutional enforcement for human rights are almost nonexistent or, at best, embryonic.

Prudentially, we continue to struggle to work out a wise calculus of costs and benefits as we struggle to flesh out a theory of legitimate intercession, a most promising prophetic constitutional breakthrough. We struggle with efforts to maximize protection of human rights at minimal costs in life, violence, and freedom itself. We struggle, too, to work out a sensible theory of transition—from where we are now in the battle to secure our human rights more effectively to a time when human rights are constitutionally secure throughout the globe. We struggle to work out wise strategy and tactics: involving the right rate of advance, the proper balancing of equities, the sensible mixture of "carrot and stick," statesmanlike respect for national sensibilities, the sensible development of international law and public opinion, the evolution of constitutional machinery, the cultivation of creative statesmanship. These efforts tax our keenest prudential judgment. But it is not too much to expect the emergence and widespread acceptance of a constitutional theory of legitimate intercession in the years immediately ahead.

THE QUEST FOR ECONOMIC WELL-BEING

Many people consider economic well-being to be a basic human right; but because it is so important, it merits separate treatment.[5] Indeed, it is the case that economic well-being is related not only to human rights but also to peace and ecological balance. The right to income, food, shelter, health care, and education—economic well-being—is adversely affected by war and ecological malaise.

In this section we shall explore some alternative approaches to economic well-being, with particular emphasis on the world's poor, especially those in the developing areas of the Third World, and the even poorer Fourth World. As we do so we do not ignore the pockets of poverty in the First World and particularly the problems of unemployment, inflation, and industrial stagnation that—in varying sectors and at varying times—continue to bedevil the First World of the United States, Western Europe, and their more affluent allies. Given the interrelatedness of the world economy, healthy economies in the First World mean greater opportunities to lift the level of economic well-being in the developing areas of the world. Similarly, we cannot close our eyes to economic performance and social well-being in the Second World, the world of the Soviet Union and its allies in Eastern Europe and elsewhere. The Soviet Union remains a controversial model for nations in the developing world. Our focus on models for development for the poorer developing nations—which are located primarily in the Southern Hemisphere and on such continents as Asia, Africa, and Latin America—is called for by a prophetic concern for the least free.

Liberal Capitalism and Liberal Democracy

Is capitalism enlightened enough to see the need to relate growth and profits to the elimination of poverty and within the framework of liberal democracy? Some believe the answer is yes. They argue that liberal capitalistic and democratic forces can work together—in developing and developed countries—to increase the size of the economic pie and to insist upon a more equitable distribution of wealth and services, a distribution that will ensure the satisfaction of basic human needs. With the right policies, and First World support, the job can be done. Working together, leadership elites, dominant economic forces, and poor people themselves in developing countries can address their key problems. They can develop a stable political organization and crucial administrative and economic skills. They can strike a sensible balance between agricultural and industrial development. And they can deliver on the production of food, health care, housing, and literacy. Richer nations, such as the United States, will see their self-interest served by extending a helping hand. The United States, and other richer nations, will see the value of extending credit and aid to developing nations, of stabilizing commodity prices, of ensuring freer trade, of encouraging abundant and inexpensive food supplies, and of supporting mutually advantageous investment and trade. Moreover, they argue, such peaceful development can occur speedily and with due regard to economic and social justice.

Critics of the model of liberal capitalism and democracy challenge this optimistic answer. They maintain that capitalists are motivated by profits and not by economic and social justice. Capitalists have a vested interest in short-run payoff, not in long-run development. They will be unwilling to adopt those policies necessary to overcome poverty. Adverse critics contend that liberal democratic capitalists are too tied in financially to the dominant system of exploitation to be able to respond to the claims of the least free.

Egalitarian Communism

Is the cost of violent Communist revolution and the fundamental restructuring of life that this entails—especially in terms of lives lost and freedoms violated—justified by hoped-for results of the revolution: the control by working people of their own destiny and the elimination of abject poverty, gross inequities of income, hunger, poor housing, and illiteracy? Those who answer yes maintain that the benefits do, indeed, outweigh the costs. The costs, they point out, are temporary. They argue that lifting the level of economic well-being of the overwhelming majority of people in a developing nation is well worth the loss of freedom to exploiting capitalists and their friends. They also suggest that a more humane communism than that illustrated in the Soviet Union or China is a live possibility.

Those opposed to a Communist pattern of development raise questions not only about the cost of violent revolution but also about the temporary character of the dictatorship of the proletariat, the period between the initial revolution and the ultimate triumph of mature communism. They emphasize the cost of the revolution: bloodshed, rigid one-party rule, social regimentation, bureaucratic centralism, economic inefficiencies, austerity. They do not see the coercive power of the Communist state withering away over time.

Illiberal Capitalism and Right-Wing Authoritarianism

Is it really the case that significant economic growth can only take place under the auspices of a right-wing authoritarian regime that chooses capitalist growth at the expense of political, economic, and social justice? The defenders of this right-wing model are firmly convinced that the economic pie must be increased considerably before the basic human needs of the poor can be satisfactorily met. They see the postponement of political, social, and economic justice as a necessary but temporary sacrifice. They concede that capitalist economic growth may immediately favor the affluent minority, but they emphasize that all benefit a little by larger gross national product and that down the road the less well-off now will benefit much more than they would under communism. They also maintain that right-wing regimes provide a greater opportunity for political liberalization than left-wing regimes.

Those opposed to this model reject the argument that freedom and economic justice must be sacrificed to economic growth, even for a temporary period of time. They see this pattern as perpetuating the rule of an exploiting capitalist class. They see no convincing evidence that the gap between rich and poor is disappearing in countries that follow this model or that political liberalization is really occurring.

Democratic Socialism

Despite good intentions, can democratic socialists achieve economic well-being and still maintain civil liberties? Some answer in the affirmative and argue that this model is the only one that makes sense in the developing countries. They argue that democratic socialism is the only policy that can strike the right balance between liberty and equality and between economic growth and the satisfaction of basic needs. A certain amount of central planning is required to direct the nation's resources, increase its production, and tackle resolutely such problems as hunger, disease, and illiteracy. Moreover, only a government truly respectful of a people's liberties and needs can enlist their energies in a successful program of development.

Those skeptical of the democratic socialist alternative stress the enormous difficulties that face even the best-intentioned democratic socialist government: poverty, populations out of balance with resources, erratic commodity prices, the high price of imported oil, the lack of requisite skills and institutions. They fear that even moderate socialism (especially the nationalization of key industries) will kill the goose (of capitalism) that lays the golden egg (a bigger economic pie for all). Because of its extravagant expectations and inadequate resources, democratic socialist governments may not be able to deliver on even their modest promises; such governments may succumb to enemies on the far Left or Right.

A New World Order

Is a new world order that challenges some of the key premises of the sovereign nation-state system and of the economic systems of either capitalism or communism really desirable and feasible? The advocates of a new world order are themselves convinced that we cannot make progress in the struggle for global economic well-being unless we adopt a global perspective. That perspective, they insist, although it builds on some national and regional endeavors, also requires a number of global initiatives that transcend the selfish interests of nation-states. These global initiatives, for example, call for a better price deal on commodities produced in the developing countries, aid to spur production and development in those countries, and other measures to attack poverty. They frankly see these initiatives as involving a redistribution of global income to overcome the gross inequalities that are evident between affluent and poverty-stricken countries and within all nations.

Those opposed to world order scenarios as utopian point out that such scenarios provide no realistic theory of transition: no clear, practical explanation of how we get from where we are now to that level of economic well-being the world order people would like to attain. They reject as unfeasible such ideas as a global progressive income tax to be used to overcome dire poverty. They doubt whether nations can move to that kind of steady-state economy that would give priority to the satisfaction of human needs and that would avoid wasteful and destructive growth. They scoff at the idea that the rich nations of the world, for example, would accept, instead of the current 12:1 ratio in wealth (of rich nations to poor nations), a ratio of 10:1—let alone the 7:1 ratio proposed by economist Wassily Leontiev or the even more radical 3:1 ratio advocated by economist Jan Tinbergen. They question the world order policies that would eliminate poverty, reduce gross disparities of income, overcome exploitation, and minimize wasteful use of resources.

Conclusion

The need for a creative breakthrough to greater economic well-being, particularly for the world's poor, is clear and present. The persistence of poverty, unemployment, hunger, bad health, illiteracy, poor housing, inequality, is well documented. What is not clear is how to overcome these agonizing problems and how to deal with the troublesome task of balancing costs and benefits in proposed policies. Those in the prophetic tradition would be false economic and political prophets if they pretended that there were quick, easy, miraculous breakthroughs available. The difficulties must be honestly faced, and proposed alternative breakthroughs must be critically appraised.

A number of difficulties handicap the poor themselves and most developing nations. Most developing nations lack the prerequisites for significant and humane development. They often lack a democratic and constitutional consensus. They do not have political stability. They are short on effective party and administrative organization, trained personnel, good transportation and schools. They face enormous obstacles in the very evils they seek to overcome: low incomes, malnutrition, disease, illiteracy, inadequate housing. All these social evils are complicated by burgeoning population, sometimes wildly in excess of resources.

Moreover, it is not clear whether the richer nations of the developed world have the foresight or the will to assist the poorer developing nations to move toward greater economic well-being speedily enough or at a price that humane and freedom-loving people would want to pay. Here, neither the United States nor the Soviet Union hold out, at the moment, attractive models for economic well-being for the poorer developing nations of the world.

Furthermore, models for the Third World based on China or Brazil—that is, models based either on the Chinese Communist model or the Brazilian illiberal capitalist, right-wing authoritarian model—are not attractive either. Minimal economic well-being in a semitotalitarian state is not appealing. Nor is lopsided and unjust economic growth in a right-wing authoritarian regime. Both call for present sacrifices. I do not here equate these two models. I merely emphasize that both require agonizing sacrifices now in order to achieve gains in the distant future.

A democratic socialist model and a more genuinely liberal capitalist and democratic option are more attractive, as is the world order option. But are they fully attractive? And if attractive, how feasible are they?

So, ethically, we recognize the need for sane and humane policies to deal with the empirical realities of economic malaise; but we encounter difficulties in coming up with prudent decisions that would permit us to balance acceptable costs and clearcut benefits on the road to greater economic well-being. Ethically, our consciences compel us to search for creative breakthroughs. Empirically, we appreciate the difficulties of achieving greater economic well-being, particularly for the world's poor. But we have not yet come up with empirical explanations of economic malaise, which would assist us, prudentially, in overcoming such malaise in speedy and satisfactory ways.

My own judgment is that the immediate prophetic creative breakthroughs in this area of concern will be modest and plural; that is, a new global economic order will not immediately emerge through the auspices of a new global organization. But a number of steps will profitably be taken—by rich and poor countries in their own self-interest and by regional and global organizations in the interest of larger conceptions of the common good—to reduce the incidence and pain of poverty and its consequences significantly. A modest national, regional, and global income tax to combat poverty is an idea whose time has come. Resources made available can wisely be used to help citizens, groups, and nations to help themselves. A plurality of programs, compatible with freedom, and compatible too with a wide variety of circumstances, will unquestionably be worked out. To look for a single solution—whether in liberal capitalism, democratic socialism, or a more humane communism—would be illusory. The great unmet human needs in the world, combined with the tremendous energy and resourcefulness of the world's peoples, suggest opportunities for immensely fruitful pluralistic experimentation within the framework of freedom.

THE QUEST FOR ECOLOGICAL BALANCE

Concerning the problem of ecological balance, I will present, and assess, five alternatives.[6] To achieve better focus, these alternatives are presented to an audience of U.S. citizens. The problem of ecological balance is, however, a global problem.

Ecological malaise, at its worst, poses a threat to humankind's biological existence. It threatens both developed and developing nations. The depletion and waste of resources; population growth wildly in excess of food, land, water and, energy; pollution—these are real threats in the modern world.

They threaten the way of life of liberal democratic, democratic socialist, and Communist nations. They threaten hopes for a better tomorrow. These ecological dangers particularly threaten to prevent developing nations from overcoming poverty and from lifting their level of economic and social well-being.

In examining the imperative of ecological health, we see, again, the linkage between (1) the values of peace, human rights, and economic well-being, and (2) ecological balance. For example, war not only destroys human beings; it also destroys the countryside, poisons the air, and wastes vital resources. Economic well-being is vitally related to stable population, adequate resources, and clean air and water. Human rights are violated if people starve to death because the population outruns food supply or if our right to breathe clean air or drink clean water is jeopardized.

Threats to ecological health are thus challenges to political actors and to politics as a civilizing enterprise. In the interest of biological existence, societal growth and development, and cultural quality of life, political actors have an obligation to understand and attempt to respond to threats to ecological health.

We must also stress that ecological problems cannot be considered apart from political philosophy and practical politics. The political philosophies of liberal democracy, democratic socialism, and communism need to be reexamined because they are based on ideas—of growth and abundance—that are intimately related to our ecological difficulties. Consequently, the ecological challenge is also a challenge to prominent political philosophies in the world and to the ideas and institutions that stem from them. In brief, the ecological crisis suggests (at least to some critics) that both capitalism and communism may be fatally flawed in some respects. Liberal democracy and democratic socialism may also be in trouble because some of their key ideas—whether individualism or freedom or social justice—may be placed in jeopardy by the ecological crisis and our responses to it. Thus, a number of problems in politics may have to be rethought as we examine and respond to the ecological crisis.

The Machiavellian pursuit of the vital interests of the nation-state may turn out to be as self-defeating in the ecological domain as in the domains of peace, human rights, and economic well-being. The utopian pursuit of perfect ecological harmony may prove illusory. And the liberal democratic attempt to strike a balance may be an ill-advised compromise.

But let us now examine some of the alternatives to see which one, or what combination, makes sense.

Liberal Conservation, Family Planning, and Environmental Protection

Are liberal democratic policymakers really tuned into the severity of the ecological crisis as a global crisis; and are they prepared to adopt those more radical measures and accept those costs required to restore ecological health? Those who support this alternative in the United States argue that liberal democrats have become aware of the ecological crisis as a result, for example, of the Organization of Petroleum Exporting Countries (OPEC) oil crisis of 1973 and of ecological disasters; and that they are taking important steps not only to make the United States self-reliant in the energy field but also to protect the environment through such agencies as the Environmental Protection Agency (EPA). They also underscore the ability of a nation, such as the United States, to keep its population growth under reasonable control. They also point to U.S. efforts to feed hungry people in the world at the same time that the United States seeks to help developing nations to do a better job of feeding themselves and striking a better balance between population and resources.

Those who are skeptical of this alternative seriously doubt that any nation committed to democracy and capitalism can take effective action to cope with the problem of growing ecological scarcity. The people of the United States—and especially such affected parties as industrial polluters, speedy drivers, and wasteful consumers—are simply not prepared to make those trade-offs (in terms of profits, jobs, convenience) to get clean air and pure water and to conserve scarce resources. The United

States itself may be successful in keeping population and resources in balance—largely because more affluent nations tend to have smaller families and because the United States produces great quantities of food. But our efforts in helping to stabilize population growth in South Asia, Africa, and Latin America have had little impact in those countries. Given the commitment of capitalism to blind growth, and of democracy to satisfaction of the claims of the instant generation, these critics claim that countries such as the United States are unable to make those radical changes now, and on behalf of posterity, that are necessary to secure long-range ecological health.

Scientific and Technological Advance and Sound Political Management

Can science and technology combined with sound political management save us? On one hand, those confident about our scientific and political ability to save ourselves argue that we can cope with short-term ecological troubles while waiting for the future world of prosperity and plenty to be ushered in by science and technology. They maintain that scientific analysis informs us that there are clear signs that population growth is leveling off. Using our brains and our pocketbooks, we can bring pollution under control.

On the other hand, those adversely critical of the guarded optimists contend that the guarded optimists overstate the ability of science to save us. There is a limit to science's ability to feed our enormous appetite for resources. They maintain that it is premature to assert confidently that population growth is leveling off. And they do not see the people or the leadership of nations willing to act resolutely to bring pollution under control. They seriously doubt that the odds are really 5:1 in favor of the scenario of the guarded optimists. This reliance upon science and technology—and the political sense to use them well—serves only to salve the consciences of the affluent while the poor continue to suffer. This approach lulls us into a false sense of security when it is urgent that we act now to protect the planet.

A Steady-State Philosophy

Is ecological scarcity an inevitable reality calling unmistakably for limits to cancerous growth and the ushering in now of a frugal steady-state society? Those who believe that the answer is yes point to what they contend are the ecological facts of life. Certain resources are finite (oil is perhaps the best example); and once they are gone, they are gone forever. Population has in fact been growing at a precipitous rate for the last 200 years. And we are currently guilty of enormous waste and pollution. We are, they maintain, confronted with unique global developments that call for a major shift in our approach to the globe. That shift calls imperatively for the adoption of a frugal steady-state philosophy.

The critics of the steady-state philosophy counter by arguing that this perspective is the nightmare of frightened neo-Malthusians who wrongly perceive that we shall soon exceed the carrying capacity of the planet earth. Even those who are sympathetic to the factual arguments of proponents of the steady-state doubt that either the rich or the poor nations of the world will buy the policies called for by a steady-state society. They emphasize that the rich will not give up their high standards of living and that the poor will not abandon their hopes for a comparable standard. They see troubles ahead for liberal democratic, democratic socialist, and Communist countries—countries whose philosophies have all been premised on economic growth and abundance. But they do not see a steady-state philosophy emerging triumphant from this time of troubles.

Benevolent Authoritarianism

It is really necessary that we sacrifice democratic and constitutional government in order to ensure ecological survival? Those who respond affirmatively to this question maintain that certain democratic freedoms may have to be abandoned if we are to respond to the ecological crisis. We may have to institute a kind of ecological constitutional dictatorship to tide us over during the forthcoming period of great peril. We may have to take strong measures to curb population growth, curtail the reckless use of resources, and develop a new set of ecological habits. The alternative may be mass starvation, an increasing gulf between the rich and the poor, and other social explosions.

Critics of this response do not believe that we are in such bad ecological health that we have to abandon democratic government for a regime of benevolent authoritarianism. Moreover, they have either grave doubts about our ability to identify, or persuasive reasons for mistrusting, such authoritarian rulers. They contend that this authoritarian medicine is worse than the disease it seeks to cure.

A New World Order

Does the ecological crisis really call for significant changes in the nation-state system and, consequently, movement toward global guidance in crucial ecological matters? Some maintain that the problem of ecological health (and the related problems of peace, economic well-being, and human rights) are genuinely inseparable and only capable of solution through a new approach to world order. Such an approach is based on the premise that problems of population, resources, and pollution are global and can only be dealt with by a worldwide organization. The planet must be perceived as a single ecological entity, and in matters that affect all peoples global policies must deal with such matters. Such policies do not, of course, preclude national, regional, and global organizations from working together.

Those critical of a new world order, able to handle problems of ecological malaise, doubt that the policies and institutions of a sane ecological world can be put into place. They argue that it is not possible to bring an enlightened national self-interest into harmony with a wise global interest. It is premature to believe that national, regional, and global agencies can work together to control population growth, ensure adequate resources, and improve environmental quality.

Conclusion

Few deny the imperative of ecological health. But, as we

have seen, there are serious disagreements on the urgency of our near-term problems and on the accuracy of long-term developments. Some of the disagreements may fade as the future confirms or denies trends, forecasts, scenarios. There can be little doubt, however, that care is required if we are to preserve the home—the planet earth—on which we all live. The character of this care is what provides the ingredients of political dispute and challenges our capacity to achieve prophetic constitutional breakthroughs. As we have seen, our ecological response is also a momentous political response that taxes our capacity for wise judgment. We see clearly that in responding to the imperative of ecological health we have to rethink our political values, probe the empirical realities of ecology, economics, and politics more deeply, consider alternatives and their costs and benefits, and ultimately reach a prudent judgment on a wise course of action.

My own judgment is that we need—in the United States and other nations, and regionally, and globally—a prophetic constitutional breakthrough to an Ecological Protection Agency, building on the concept of the EPA but with a broader mandate that would go beyond protecting the environment and that would include protection of resources and, as necessary, stabilization of population. The concept of an Environmental Protection Agency is a good beginning in one important area; but the concept must be broadened to include a larger ecological philosophy of husbandry to guide citizens and corporations, as well as governments, and must be translated into effective operational reality. Pollution, resources, and population are interrelated problems and must be treated together.

An Ecological Protection Agency can only spearhead the attack on ecological malaise. Its effectiveness will depend on the power it is granted and the popular support it receives. To be effective it will have to move beyond a good deal of the laissez-faire thinking of liberal democracy and beyond the thoughtless preoccupation with growth and reckless exploitation of resources that has characterized both capitalism and socialism. Popular support must rest on the recognition that there are limits to the extent to which science and technology can solve the problems of depletion of valuable nonrenewable resources and the waste and imprudent use of renewable resources. We may not be able to overcome all pollution, but we can unquestionably reduce the incidence of the worst pollution. Finally, if and when we can make a dent in world poverty, we may be able to bring population and resources into balance in nonauthoritarian ways. Incremental steps in nation-states can, in turn, prepare for ecological action regionally and globally.

CONCLUSION

This exploration of breakthroughs will not satisfy those critics who expect perfect solutions to difficult problems. At best this exploration can only identify areas of concern that call for our creative attention, present and assess key alternatives, and, modestly, indicate those breakthroughs that are prudent and feasible. It should now be clear that it is one thing to present a *desirable* alternative and another to present a *cogent* argument on behalf of its feasibility. Ethically, I am convinced that the perspective of those whom I have called the *political futurists* —those who share a global, constitutional, democratic perspective—is sound. I also believe that their empirical analysis—which highlights the dangers of nuclear war, gross and persistent violations of human rights, poverty, and ecological imbalance—is fundamentally correct. But I am not persuaded that they have yet articulated a cogent theory of transition from the present world to that future global order that is their goal. Here is where the most difficult and creative work has to be done.

However, the reduction of the risks of nuclear war should be the number-one priority on everyone's agenda. And important, if modest, steps can be taken to accomplish this objective. This priority is, however, but the beginning of those additional steps that must be taken to control, and eventually eliminate, nuclear weapons. This task is intimately related to stabilizing the relations between powerful nation-states armed with nuclear weapons. Mutual self-interest dictates such stabilization. Such stabilization will rest, initially, upon a mutually agreed upon military standoff, preferably at lower levels of armaments; second, upon economic, scientific, and cultural cooperation in areas of mutual benefit; and third, upon the transfer of competition from the military domain to the political, economic, social, and ideological domains. Modest progress along these three fronts—building on a reduction of the risks of nuclear war and looking toward a significant reduction of nuclear weapons—can also encourage the reduction of conventional weapons and the utilization of currently huge expenditures for arms for peaceful domestic and international purposes.

Although the outlook for genuinely effective national, regional, and global machinery to prevent, and remedy, gross and persistent violations of human rights is not presently bright, work must, nonetheless, go forward toward putting such machinery into place. The creation of effective constitutional processes within each political community can follow the lead of liberal democratic and democratic socialist political communities over the last 200 years. In addition, however, concerned political actors—the least free themselves; NGOs; and national, regional, and international organizations—must press for the emergence of a constitutional doctrine of legitimate intercession, under appropriate safeguards, to ensure that there is a remedy for gross and persistent violations of human rights when nation-states fail to protect such rights. The very existence of such a constitutional theory of legitimate intercession, and of the machinery to make it effective, will itself strengthen constitutional forces within existing national communities and within existing regional organizations. The development of such theory and machinery, although slow, halting, and subject to setbacks, seems to be a feasible course of development in the field of human rights in the next couple of decades and in the twenty-first century.

The elimination of the worst aspects of poverty in the world is feasible. We now produce, or can produce, the wealth that—properly shared—can eliminate persistent, oppressive poverty. The scaling down of military expenditures all over the globe, coupled with a commitment to the protection of human rights (including economic human rights), can point the way toward success in the battle against poverty. To say this is to say that a breakthrough in the battle against poverty will rest initially upon the establishment of the right priorities for political actors and political communities. To ease fears of military aggression is to make it easier to produce butter rather than guns: to make production for the sake of satisfying peaceful human needs our number-one priority. Problems of equitable sharing and feasible distribution will not be solved overnight; but they are political, economic, and technological problems that can be feasibly addressed.

A host of forces will need to operate in any successful attack on gross and persistent poverty—including developing and developed nations, capitalist and socialist forces, regional and international organizations. No one should pretend that this battle will be easily won. But if even a modest percentage of current resources being devoted to armaments can be shifted to production for the satisfaction of legitimate human needs, and if concern for the constitutional protection of human rights can emerge as a dominant ethos all over the globe, it will be relatively easy to find a proximate solution to the political, economic, and technological problem of the production and equitable distribution of wealth. These proximate solutions will unquestionably be pluralistic in character; that is, there may be differing proximate solutions to the problem of poverty all over the globe. For example, liberal capitalist and democratic socialist approaches may be successful in some instances and unsuccessful in others. And in many instances, combinations of liberal capitalist and democratic socialist approaches may prove the most successful. Self-sustaining prosperity in every political community is a primary target here; but a host of regional, international, and global organizations may still have to stand by for temporary help in periods of genuine emergency.

Despite the progress of modern science, and its usefulness in helping us to address problems of scarcity, population, and pollution, it is the case that all political actors and all political communities will be required to adopt a philosophy of ecological caring and concern. We do need to be more caring of our global resources, especially those that once expended are gone forever. We do need to strike a sensible balance between population and resources. And although we cannot eliminate all pollution, we do need to take vigorous measures to eliminate the most deadly dangers, to reduce other serious dangers, and to balance costs and benefits more prudently. Action is called for at all levels—national, regional, and global. The limited breakthroughs achieved by such agencies as the EPA in the United States (under a sympathetic administration) indicate what can be done. It is important to ensure a sympathetic administration and to extend the protective powers of the agency. However, regional and global action—difficult as it may be—is essential if gains in one political community are not to be undermined by carelessness elsewhere.

We cannot be sure about which modest breakthroughs in all of these four areas of concern will lead to fuller breakthroughs. But social and other scientists can certainly pay more attention to the subject of creative breakthroughs in politics than they have in the past. That is a prophetic commandment.

9 : Continuous Prophetic Scrutiny and Futuristic Projection

INTRODUCTION

The line between prophetic constitutionalism *and* continuous prophetic scrutiny and futuristic projection (the fourth main commitment of prophetic politics) may not always be clear. This is the case because immediate problems are also future problems and because breakthroughs that we hope to achieve today or tomorrow may take 10 or 25 years or more. The scrutiny of today's or tomorrow's alternatives sometimes merges imperceptibly into scrutiny of futuristic scenarios. We act today, but success may come only in a distant tomorrow. Nonetheless, the immediate problems that face leaders of state concerned with prophetic constitutional breakthroughs today and tomorrow are not the only ones on society's horizons. We must have in society individuals concerned with a longer look ahead. Clearly, the work of prophetic politicians is not done even after they have been successful in constitutionalizing a better world pursuant to fearless criticism and in accord with the prophetic paradigm. Continuous prophetic scrutiny in the future will still remain as an ongoing task. Concern for the prudent calculation of risks, and for a humane and scientific calculus of costs, never ceases. The need for attention to theories of transition persists. So does the need to explore the known and unknown dimensions of politics in a more ideal present and in an always-changing and challenging future.

THE NEED FOR CONTINUOUS
PROPHETIC SCRUTINY

The need for continuous prophetic scrutiny has already been established by some of the basic premises of prophetic politics. These premises, I have argued, also serve to distinguish prophetic politics from utopian and liberal democratic politics and to refute the argument that prophetic politics is really utopian, or is really an endorsement of liberal democratic politics, or does not adequately do justice to the persistence of Machiavellian politics.

Prophetic politics is premised on the proposition that there is not now, and never can be, an earthly paradise. No matter how successful prophetic politicians are, they know that there exists no earthly Eden, no Shangri-la, no perfectly harmonious, blissful resting place. They know that even the best political order is only best relatively. Given the limitations of people and society, as measured against a superior standard, any human achievement is imperfect. Greater excellence is always possible. They know, too, that changing circumstances always produce difficulties; reveal weaknesses; lead to the neglect of responsibilities or, worse, to the abuse of power by the best of people—functioning with the best of intentions, under the best of circumstances. Consequently, there is a need for continuing scrutiny and analysis in order to guard against relapses in even the best human order (and, one hopes, before they occur), to raise questions about even better performance, to reexamine functioning premises, and thus to explore the possibilities of pushing the boundaries of political achievement closer to the ideal borders of the prophetic paradigm. Given this posture, the prophetic politician is sensitized to the weaknesses and dangers of utopian politics and is commanded to act, via continuous prophetic scrutiny, to avoid utopian pride.

A second premise of prophetic politics also illuminates the need for continuous prophetic scrutiny and, simultaneously, seeks to guard against the complacency of liberal democratic politics. Prophetic politics is premised on the importance of recognizing and yet seeking to diminish (since it is not possible to overcome completely) the tension between what ought to be and what is, between the prophetic paradigm and the best (even the very best) actual constitutional order. This itself underscores the need for continuing critical scrutiny. For how else can we deal with the prophetic tension without such scrutiny? This tension is in fact present in the constitutional order because it is a human order. In better constitutional orders we sometimes—nay, frequently—tend to ignore this tension. In brief, we tend to become complacent about our relative constitutional success in balancing liberty and authority, justice and power, and other cardinal values. We tend to ignore the least free who are so often invisible. We tend to be blind to new possibilities, to political becoming. Hence, there is a need always—even in the very best constitutional system—to call attention to the real gulf between what ought to be and what is. This requires continuous critical scrutiny, which alone can remind us of the prophetic tension and the mandate to make greater efforts to bridge the gulf. In this fashion continuous prophetic scrutiny seeks to overcome the weakness—the complacency—of liberal democratic politics.

Finally, we must recall that prophetic politics is premised on a continuing battle against nationalist idolatry—but not against the protection of genuinely vital community interests. Prophetic politicians quarrel with Machiavellian politics because they are not convinced that the vital interests of people and communities can be adequately protected by the current sovereign nation-state system. Only when the vital interests of the nation-state or political community are in accord with the higher standard of prophetic politics can the prophetic politician be content. And, unfortunately, the commitment to success of the nation-state, narrowly conceived, inevitably produces dangers of abuse of power, of constitutional relapses, of questionable performance, of violations of the prophetic order. Hence, again, there is need for continuous critical scrutiny of the functioning of the nation-state (or of any other political community) to check on idolatrous predilections of political actors and political communities. In this way prophetic politicians seek to minimize the idolatrous dangers of Machiavellian politics, dangers that will probably remain with us until the end of time.

It should also now be clear how futuristic projection (which rests upon continuous prophetic scrutiny in the tradition of prophetic politics) differs from utopian futuristics. The prophetic understanding of futuristic projection still operates within that constitutional framework that rejects the utopian belief in the completely harmonious society. The prophetic view is thus one that can better cope with an imagined better future and with the real people, contending interests, and real problems of such a future. The prophetic view of the future is dynamic, not static. Change and conflicts will not cease in the future. Difficulties will not disappear. And there will still be a need for constitutional accommodation—and hard choices—in the future. Alienation will not be abolished. Continuing prophetic criticism is a necessary safeguard against utopian hubris. The prophetic politician must continue to develop the superior constitutional principles that will guide the prophetic future.

But how? The prophetic future, we may be sure, cannot be left to shape itself automatically. But how do we proceed to face up to the future? How can we move beyond the immediate problems that face us, and already tax our capacity for creative breakthroughs, to anticipated future problems, and even to currently unforeseen problems? Here we have to face up to the task of constructing scenarios of intermediate range (25 or 50 or 100 years) and of even longer range (200 or 500 or 1,000 years). The objective is to utilize these scenarios, as best we can, to anticipate future changes, problems, dangers, opportunities. This can be attempted with the help of both "negative" and "positive" scenarios that outline evil as well as good possibilities.

FUTURISTIC SCENARIOS

Futuristic scenarios are made necessary by our heightened prophetic consciousness, by the impact of developments in science and technology, and by the inevitable need to recalculate the risks of the human enterprise on a regular and sustaining basis.[1] A world without war, tyranny, poverty, or ecological malaise is a world that the prophetic consciousness can envision. But so, too, can we imagine a nuclear holocaust; the worldwide spread, or even triumph, of authoritarian governments; a world sorely divided between the affluent and the poor; and an overpopulated, polluted, and resource-hungry globe.

The fuller shape of such a world remains to be explored. Science and technology promise to lengthen and improve our lives, to enhance our benevolent power over nature, to reduce drudgery on earth, to explore the mysteries of the solar system, to heighten our cultural appreciation. But science and technology also threaten to destroy the globe, poison our lives, rape nature, substitute dull electronic routines for pleasant physical labor, perpetuate earthly pride in the larger universe, and prostitute mind and heart.

The recalculation of risks confronts us with both attractive and unattractive possibilities. The balance of terror may preserve the peace, or it may lead to the greatest catastrophe we can imagine: total nuclear war and the destruction of all human life on earth. Constitutional government may spread its civilizing influence, or it may degenerate and be replaced by gross or petty tyrannies. We may learn to solve the riddle of persistent, debilitating unemployment, or we may continue to be plagued by willing and able workers unable to find jobs. The superpowers may work out successful patterns of genuine accommodation, or aggravating rivalries may persist and continuously threaten to erupt into political, economic, and military conflict. We may or may not succeed in striking a prudent balance between population and resources, between jobs and profits (on one hand) and pollution (on the other), and between our seemingly insatiable and immediate hunger for resources and a thoughtful concern for posterity. And so on!

Although one risks disagreement in sketching such scenarios, the format for this operation is reasonably clear. Let me first sketch the format for the positive scenarios.

1. We must select the problems to be investigated or the topics to be explored;
2. We must examine several responsive scenarios, sketch their major characteristics, criticize alternative possibilities, and, tentatively, choose the most attractive, plausible one;
3. We must flesh out the chosen futuristic scenario, more fully developing premises, principles, institutions, behavior patterns, interrelationships, problems, and consequences;
4. We must criticize the constructed scenario and amend it as necessary; and
5. We must prepare the more fully constructed and more adequately criticized futuristic scenario for ultimate prophetic constitutionalization.

In this fashion we can choose among alternative scenarios, deliberately building into our process ways of avoiding dangerous scenarios and of minimizing the harmful consequences of our future choices. In this fashion, too, we seek to remain open to bold, promising, and fruitful futures while still guarding against the dangers of hubris. It may be utopian to attempt to spell out all the details of such futuristic scenarios, but it is prophetic to look to areas of concern and attempt to identify problems, alternatives, and consequences. A comparable format would be employed for negative scenarios, only here we would be concerned with highlighting values, principles, institutions, behavior, and policies that we would like to avoid through imaginative anticipation.

To illustrate my argument, let me now set forth in abbreviated fashion some futuristic scenarios.[2] I will begin with a negative scenario—but the least objectionable of the negative scenarios that will follow. I will then contrast these grim scenarios with a more prophetic scenario.

One scenario would be a perpetuation and intensification of the status quo. This would mean a world dominated by sovereign nation-states, the rivalry of the superpowers, an ongoing arms race, and nuclear proliferation. Also prominent in such a world would be dreadful struggles by people in the Third and Fourth

Worlds to overcome poverty and to address the widening gap between the rich and the poor. This scenario would also be characterized by widespread violations of human rights and by disturbing ecological conditions. Currently, the odds are high that this is the future we will in fact face in the twenty-first century. We are challenged to ask whether muddling through will get us safely through the twenty-first century, as it has seen us through most of the second half of the twentieth century, or whether we have to make significant changes in this status quo scenario.

It is also possible that one or more dreadful catastrophes—for example, nuclear war or ecological disaster—might dominate the politics of the twenty-first century.[3] Nation-states might then be seeking to recover from dreadful wounds. We need to speculate on whether they can do so within the framework of liberal democracy of communism or democratic socialism. We need to reflect on whether or not modern civilization—politically, economically, socially, culturally—can survive. We have to face up frankly to several grim alternatives. One of these alternatives is *anarchy*, understood here as lawlessness, the absence of effective government, the prevalence of a brutal dog-eat-dog attitude among survivors. Another alternative would be authoritarianism (either benevolent or malevolent) in which the powerful offer protection to the weak at the sacrifice of liberty. This alternative assumes that the demand for security would be so great in a devastated world that survivors would willingly accept strong authoritarian, "law-and-order" rule in the interest of continued survival. A third alternative here would be retrogression, that is, a reversion to a more primitive level of preindustrial, agricultural, feudal living. Our human powers of recovery and adjustment are great, but they have never been put to the truly awful test of a really dreadful catastrophe such as all-out nuclear war. After such a test, only the bravest optimist could say that civilization as we have known it could easily survive. We tend to forget that democratic and constitutional government, in the history of civilization, is very young and has evolved under relatively favorable circumstances. In the event of an all-out nuclear war the likelihood is that the blows to security, liberty, justice, and welfare would be devastating. This scenario also challenges political scientists to exert themselves to avert the outcomes foreseen. Although the odds are probably against an all-out nuclear war in the twenty-first century, the possibility of small-scale nuclear wars is greater. And such wars, if not the most fearful apocalypse, could trigger comparable pressures toward anarchy, authoritarianism, or retrogression.

Other authoritarian or semitotalitarian dangers also loom in the future. Here we come to a third scenario. It is also possible to envisage a twenty-first century in which authoritarian or totalitarian forces of the Right or Left would grow stronger and exert great pressures against the vital center of liberal democracy and democratic socialism.[4] It is possible that liberal democracy and democratic socialism might not survive such a squeeze play. The world might then face the prospect of a world divided between Left and Right or an ultimate conflict between these forces. Clearly, this scenario also poses ominous prospects for democratic and constitutional government and the values upon which these governments rest. We are, consequently, challenged to ask: What can be done to avoid this scenario?

Still another authoritarian scenario is possible in the twenty-first century: benevolent authoritarianism called into being (prior to a dreadful catastrophe) to cope with the building pressures for security, justice, and welfare—but at the price of liberty.[5] The call for strong law-and-order government might arise from crime in our cities; but it might also arise from the cry for an end to war, to violations of human rights, to poverty, and to ecological malaise. If conditions rapidly deteriorated around the globe, it is possible that the cry might go out for a benevolent dictatorship to take charge and save us from ourselves. Such a development might be rationalized through the argument on behalf of a constitutional dictatorship, an institution not unknown in the history of politics when a people's survival is at stake. It is not likely that liberal democracy or democratic socialism could survive under the continued existence of such a benevolent authoritarian regime. It is more likely that communism and that variant of "democracy" that has emerged in the new developing states of the Third World would fare better under such regimes—given their predilections, respectively, for the dictatorship of the proletariat and some form of "guided democracy." Again, we are challenged to act to prevent the buildup of those pressures that might lead to benevolent authoritarianism as a way to avert even greater disasters.

However, these grim—negative—scenarios are not the only ones that we can envision. As I have argued, they are important because they put before us plausible, anticipated worlds that we would then strive to avoid. By envisioning these possibilities, we might be stimulated to take steps to avert their coming into being. But, as we might seek to anticipate and avoid these grim scenarios, so, too, we might be encouraged to construct and fulfill a more positive, hopeful scenario. Thus, it is also possible to envision a transition to a twenty-first century characterized by a planetary prophetic politics. Here we come to the greatest challenge facing humankind as we face the future. Can we begin to use our ethical, scientific, and prudential resources now to help usher in a world without catastrophic war, without flagrant violations of human rights, without egregious poverty, and without deadly ecological malaise? A prophetic scenario envisions an affirmative answer.

A prophetic scenario envisions a world in which conflicts exist but are handled in a democratic and constitutional way; in which there are political and legal remedies for violations of human rights; in which peoples and communities work together to achieve economic well-being; and in which we have taken those steps necessary to ensure ecological health. It envisions a world in which national, regional, functional, and global communities work cooperatively to achieve these same goals. The steps necessary to move toward these goals call for a number of creative breakthroughs in our future politics. And as such futuristic breakthroughs to a more prophetic politics occur, human beings all over the globe can increasingly turn their attention to the cultivation of that excellent quality of life that is the supreme mark of politics as a civilizing enterprise.

These brief sketches of futuristic scenarios—negative and positive—may suggest that it is not utopian and it is not foolish to begin thinking now about the fulfillment of the task of continuous prophetic scrutiny and futuristic projection. Of course, there are difficulties in attending to these tasks. But, appreciative of Marx's warning about futuristic blueprints and about the need to appreciate that the future will emerge out of present conflicts, we can seek to attend to the future more sagaciously than did Marx. Futuristic projection is not a foolishly utopian "blue sky" enterprise; rather, futuristic projection calls not only for prophetic imagination but also for continuous prophetic scrutiny. So in following the format outlined earlier, we have built into this fourth task of prophetic politics some crucial safeguards.

In selecting problems—whether of war and peace, freedom and tyranny, prosperity and poverty, ecological balance and ecological malaise—it is important to appreciate their interrelationship within a prophetic perspective. Within that perspective it is possible to focus on any one of these problems and, indeed, to limit the problem to a given area or political community. If those with a prophetic perspective focus on peace among the superpowers, it is because of their recognition that concern about a nuclear war between these powers should be our number-one concern. Moreover, any futuristic scenario directed to global peace almost inevitably is compelled to address other vital global concerns.

One futuristic scenario addressed to global peace and other vital global concerns envisages the evolution of a more effective democratic, constitutional, federal, global order. There may be many paths to such a global order. But almost all futuristic scenarios envisage the emergence of a world community able to deal with limited but important global problems—war, basic economic justice, fundamental human rights, ecological malaise—that currently go beyond the capacity of the present sovereign nation-state system to handle. One scenario envisages the present United Nations emerging into that more effective global order. Another envisages the bold evolution of international law as the sensible way to achieve the desired goal. Still another scenario calls for a new world organization built upon principles more sympathetic to global peoples and less sympathetic to present sovereign nation-states.

Each of these futuristic scenarios could be sketched more fully. Richard A. Falk, for example, has done so on behalf of a new world order approach in *A Study of Future Worlds* (1975).[6] And other scholars have done so for the present United Nations and for international law. Here we can use Falk's book to illustrate what fleshing out a futuristic scenario involves. Falk opts for a strategy of "drastic gradualism" in order to move toward his preferred world order. He would work toward world order gradually, by stages: building on enhanced domestic consciousness for such an order in stage one, building on regional world order experiments in stage two, and coming to the construction of a central guidance mechanism only in stage three.

Falk calls his central guidance system "the World Polity Association." Its principal policy-making organ would be a World Assembly that "will set world standards and render binding decisions by achieving a four-fifths majority vote within each of its three chambers"—an Assembly of Governments, an Assembly of Peoples, and an Assembly of Organization and Association.[7] The World Assembly could also make recommendations by a two thirds vote of its three chambers. A Council of Principals would function as the main executive body of the World Polity Association. A World Security System would focus on minimizing large-scale violence. A Central Committee of the World Security System—composed of the directors of the World Security Forces, the World Disarmament Service, and the World Grievance System—would coordinate activities directly related to war prevention.

Thus, the World Security Forces would maintain international peace under all possible circumstances. This organization would operate as a police force rather than as an army. It would place great emphasis of nonviolent strategies of policing and regard recourse to violence as a last resort. It would work closely with regional security forces, would utilize early warning procedures against violators of the peace, and would use minimum-violence weaponry and tactics. The "permanent constabulary" of the World Security Forces—according to Falk's scenario—"might be a police force of 200,000, or even less, supplemented by regional constabulary establishments of 50,000 to 75,000 and by much larger standby militia forces specially trained under national auspices for emergency international services." The constabulary "might undertake most, if not all, of its functions without benefit of arms."[8]

A World Disarmament Service would "supervise the agreed-upon process of disarmament . . . report violations immediately to the World Security Forces and the Council of Principles, and . . . verify compliance with the terms of the disarmament arrangement so as to maintain confidence." The "goal of disarmament will be to eliminate national military establishments." In its actions in handling violations, actual or potential, the World Disarmament Service would stress nonviolent, conciliatory resolution of disputes.[9]

A World Grievance System would rely strongly on "mediational procedures and flexible solutions" and on regional, decentralized approaches. The Central Commission of the World Grievance System would review grievances, through hearings and fact finding, and recommend a mode of settlement via private or public (global) conciliation or mediation. Implementation would be left to the Implementing Board and the World Security Forces. Again, voluntary, noncoercive resolution would be stressed.[10]

Writing in 1975, Falk anticipated "notable progress toward minimizing collective violence" during stage one of his scenario. But he did "not expect any dramatic transfers of police and peacemaking capabilities" to occur in this first stage. He did not expect an end to regional wars. Arms development, he anticipated, will still be troubling, especially significant nuclear capabilities. But, although the "objective status of the war system" would not change in this period, a new mood would make possible progress in dismantling the war system at later stages. Even in stage two, the war system would not yet be dismantled; but governments would be less disposed to use "military capabilities to solve national problems." The war system would continue to erode. The dismantling of the war system would finally occur in stage three—in the early years of the twenty-first century.[11]

Falk's global order scenario also envisages worldwide protection of human rights, efforts to improve economic well-being, and a program to achieve ecological balance. Thus, his Central Guidance System would include a World Commission and Court on Human Rights (as part of his World System for Human Development) with effective power to investigate and deal with complaints unresolved at national and regional levels. His World Economic System would address the problem of economic need —income, food, shelter, health, clothing, education—and seek to enhance the quality of life. When nations fail it is both desirable and feasible to shift control over economic policy to regional and global actors. Falk's World Economic System would encourage a favorable adjustment in the terms of trade to help producers of primary products in the developing countries; subsidies for capital development; favorable terms in the world money market; a minimum-need threshold throughout the world; a 10:1 ratio between rich and poor nations. A World System for Ecological Balance would address global environmental, resources, and population problems, including problems of trade-offs between ecological balance and economic well-being. These tasks would be addressed by specific institutions: a World Environment Authority; a World Forum on Ecological Balance; and a World Agency of Resources, Conservation, and Development Policy.

Scenarios must also be criticized—and amended—as necessary. Here, again, we can only briefly illustrate the format. We will attempt to do so by raising some criticisms of a new world order scenario, with particular attention to the political aspects of futuristic projection. For example, apropos Falk's world order scenario:

1. Is Falk's world order scenario really desirable? (Is it really a good idea to alter our present sovereign nation-state system?)

2. If desirable, is it really feasible—or is it a foolishly utopian dream, incapable of fulfillment in a world of jealous, protective, sovereign nation-states?

3. Does this world order approach inadvertently create the possibility of world tyranny as it either consolidates its powers or absorbs new powers not originally granted?

4. Would such a world order, while theoretically maintaining peace among sovereign nation-states, conceal disastrous civil war between the member units of the world order system?

5. How will members of the world order system continue to face up to the sacrifices that they have been, or will be, called upon to make to sustain such a world order system—sacrifices, for example, involving wealthy and modernized nations that might be called upon to share at least part of their wealth (and reduce their life-styles or incomes, however modestly) in order to achieve minimum standards of decency in poorer, undeveloped, and developing countries?

6. Will it turn out to be the case that such a world order system is in fact a cover for the repression, or oppression, of the poor and developing peoples and lands by the richer and more fully developed countries and peoples—or, if this is not too bizarre, vice versa?

7. How will countries with more authoritarian and more democratic governments, as well as those with capitalist and those with Communist economies, interact politically and economically in a new world order system; and what will be the consequences of this interaction on their domestic regimes?

8. What will be the ongoing consequences for human freedom of the inclusion in such a world order system of a truly effective global Bill of Rights?

9. Can a new world order system function both to increase the size of a worldwide "pie" and to ensure the pie's more equitable distribution in accord with a global Economic Bill of Rights—and how?

10. And perhaps most important of all, assuming feasibility, *how* (with the help of what forces and according to what strategy)

can we move from our present sovereign nation-state system to a constitutional, democratic, federal world order system?[12]

This list of questions is by no means exhaustive. A host of other critical questions could also be raised. These questions are, however, designed to illustrate the kind of probing criticism that any futuristic scenario must be subjected to in the interest of fuller understanding of opportunities and dangers. These questions are not intended to destroy hope and faith in a better way of handling vital global problems. They are meant to emphasize that continuous prophetic scrutiny calls for critical examination of futuristic scenarios at an early stage as well as for critical appraisal of actual breakthroughs now and in the future. Only in this way can political philosophers and political scientists guard, simultaneously, against the weaknesses of both liberal democratic politics and utopian politics.

A comparable format can be employed with regard to other futuristic scenarios—involving, for example, healthy domestic political communities and the pursuit of excellence. Fleshing out these scenarios—instead of being a vain utopian enterprise—can be a most stimulating intellectual experiment. Such fleshing out, again, calls for the raising of critical questions—questions that speak to the *who*, the *how*, and the *what* of our futuristic scenarios. These are crucial questions (old and new) about the identity of crucial political actors and their values, about alleged superior patterns of constitutional accommodation, about supposed wise substantive policies.

As we struggle to eliminate war, we will continue to struggle with the old/new issues of the control of power and the uses of law. As we struggle to overcome poverty, racism, sexism, alienation, we will continue to grapple with the old/new issue of the meaning of equality—and of freedom. As we struggle with new troublesome problems posed by scientific and medical advances (problems involving human genetics, prospects of increased longevity, test-tube production of human life, human transplants, cloning, and so on), we will continue to confront the old/new problem of the definition of humanity—and the thorny (but unavoidable) problem of priorities. As we struggle with problems produced by technological advances (problems involving the uses of increased leisure, the impact of the mass media, information-gathering systems, the relation of people to machines), we will continue to be confronted by old/new questions of human ends, human excellence, human privacy, human character. As we investigate problems occasioned by our exploration of outer space, and by our inquiry into more fruitful and humane life-styles in our earthly space, we will still have to struggle with working out the sane and workable rules of the political (and economic and social) game, with the use and abuse of power, with interests and their accommodation, and with choices among priorities.

So although our prophetic imaginations may open up new dimensions, we err if we think that we will be able to shape a new person in a new society entirely. This recognition helps to guard our futuristic projections from becoming wild and irresponsible utopian fantasies. On the other hand, we are strongly encouraged to move considerably beyond the bounds and constraints of both Machiavellian politics and liberal democratic politics. As we do so, however, we have to be aware—in the spirit of continuous prophetic scrutiny—of the strengths and weaknesses of prophetic politics.

THE STRENGTHS AND WEAKNESSES
OF PROPHETIC POLITICS

Let me attempt now to summarize the strengths and weaknesses of prophetic politics. This summary will also serve to recapitulate the argument I have been making in this book up to this point. I will reserve for my concluding chapter a final assessment of the probability of the possibility of a more prophetic politics.

The Strengths of Prophetic Politics

Prophetic politics commands us to raise, not lower, our sights. Consciously, then, it takes a stand on this point against

Machiavellian politics. It insists on efforts to dispense with brutal force or cunning deception. It looks beyond the nation-state to the global community. It insists that we distinguish between prudence and mere cleverness. It holds open new possibilities in political affairs. It does so, however, without prejudice to the protection of the legitimate interests of the political community. It does so while stressing human ability—the creative artist's ability—to shape a better community. It demands both imaginative and sensible strategies in public affairs, strategies in tune with the deeper, truer, fuller realities of power as they are or as they can wisely become. In these ways, while avoiding the weaknesses, and yet incorporating the strengths, of Machiavellian politics, prophetic politics is addressing the dangers of civilized survival.

Prophetic politics is also protected against hubris and heresy. It never forgets human limitations. Prophetic politics is not naive about power and change. It is always conscious of the sin of Procrustes. Knowing the depth of human evil, it is immune to cynicism. Not expecting an earthly paradise, it cannot become bored at the prospect, or presumed reality, of earthly salvation. These responses make clear how prophetic politics can avoid the dangers of utopian politics. Yet, while avoiding these dangers, prophetic politics keeps alive a bold vision of a better world. It is nourished by an inspiring image about the future. It can thus stimulate imaginative undertakings of how things can be. It can vigorously criticize ideas, institutions, and behaviors that destroy, cripple, or harm people and their legitimate needs and aspirations. It retains the pragmatic ability to translate ideal into reality. These are the ideals that nourish the civilizing enterprise.

Prophetic politics is not complacent, blind, timid. It possesses a broad and illuminating ethical vision. Its vision is, moreover, not a single vision, either ethically or empirically or prudentially. Its empirical understanding incorporates a wise range of human experience. It is open to potentiality as well as to actuality. And, consequently, its prudential assessments are bold and creative. It possesses a genuinely sound radical sensitivity that operates against a stodgy conservatism, the inertia of the existing Establishment, the cozy balance of equilibrium politics. In these many ways, then, prophetic politics avoids the weaknesses of liberal democratic politics. But it retains the mandate to constitutionalize efforts to overcome needless war, death, and destruction; to continue to develop superior constitutional rules of the game in the interest of protecting human rights and striking the difficult, and changing, balance between liberty and authority; to diminish the domain of poverty; and to achieve a prudent ecological balance. By linking certain ideals to constitutional construction, the prophetic politician can move imaginatively into the future without losing touch with an evolving reality and sane judgment.

All of this is to say that the great strength of prophetic politics lies in its superior ethical vision, its more generous and realistic understanding of political reality, and its bolder and more farsighted sense of political becoming. And these are the qualities that contribute to its ability to facilitate a more humane and decent life, vigorous growth, and excellent achievement in all fields of human endeavor.

But is this account of the strengths of prophetic politics an accurate and convincing one? And what of the adverse criticism that might be made of this model—and its perhaps extravagant claims?

The Weaknesses of Prophetic Politics

Continous prophetic scrutiny requires one to focus on the weaknesses, as well as the strengths, of prophetic politics. And awareness of the weaknesses of prophetic politics serves to puncture a naive optimism and to challenge the easy triumph of prophetic scenarios. These weaknesses can be put in the form of the nagging questions we raised at the end of Chapter 1, exceedingly troublesome questions that plague students (and practitioners) of prophetic politics and challenge their most creative responses. These five disturbing questions force us to recognize the disagreement, in theory and practice, about prophetic values—

summarized in such seemingly simple, but actually complex, words as *peace, freedom, justice, well-being, health,* and the like. They force us, too, to recognize that prophetic criticism has not advanced very far in exploring the necessary and sufficient conditions of civilized life, healthy growth, and creative fulfillment and in working out a clear-cut prophetic diagnosis and remedy for our present ills—comparable in scope, substance, and practical application (if not in actual content) to a Marxist philosophy. They also make us recognize that although modest constitutional breakthroughs have been possible, the pace of creative breakthroughs has been agonizingly slow, and that today we often lack the faith and the patience to persist in our search for such creative breakthroughs.

These questions also make us painfully aware of the difficulties of futuristic projection. They make us wonder whether this task is not (despite disclaimers by partisans of prophetic politics) a utopian pastime designed to blind bourgeois liberals to the enormities of present oppression. The fifth question underscores the adverse argument that prophetic politics is either a fancy reformulation of liberal democratic politics (as practiced, for example, in the United States) or, again, a not-very-clever disguise for an illusory utopian politics. We must address these questions—and comments. Difficult and complex answers await the attack of a new generation of thinkers who have moved beyond the old and stale patterns of politics.

Initially, a serious question confronts the advocates of prophetic politics. Can they state and get workable agreement on the meaning of the prophetic paradigm among the diverse forces of the modern world—religious, philosophical, political, and scientific? And especially among the powerful political forces in powerful political communities? Clearly, without at least minimal consensus, the entire effort to move toward a more prophetic politics will flounder. Currently, there is certainly no unanimity on the meaning of the prophetic paradigm, and nothing approaching a workable consensus exists in the religious, philosophical, political, or scientific domains—so this argument runs. In the religious domain, these critics note, God is dead for too many people. And even if God is held to be alive for some, there is no agreement on the meaning of divinity or on what divinity demands of us. And neither philosophy nor science nor social science provides us with a model of a superior universal order commanding worldwide assent, or even majority assent. And certainly in politics—in international affairs as in domestic affairs—we work at cross-purposes, as war and rebellion and other forms of strife make abundantly clear. There is no universal agreement on the prophetic values of peace, freedom, justice, truth, well-being—and love. Rhetorically, of course, they are all honored; in reality, they are mocked and denied.

We also have trouble on other matters. We have trouble distinguishing true and false prophets—and even within the Judaic-Christian–Islamic traditions. Atheists and agnostics challenge the concept of a living God whose commands constitute standards that all people are to follow. Even those within a given religious tradition fight over the meaning of divine commands. Other critics challenge the validity of a higher law, or a natural law, which we are led to by philosophic "right reason" and which supposedly commands us to behave in accord with the precepts of the prophetic paradigm. The very belief in the possibility of a superior standard is in doubt among logical positivists and ethical relativists. There are also doubts among advocates of situational ethics about absolute standards absolutely applied. Their argument is that no ethical system can be convincingly demonstrated to be superior. Scientists may agree on certain dangers to the globe, but they are by no means agreed on prophetic values or on what standard is to be utilized in the domain of politics or on what practical measures are to be adopted in order to move toward those goals about which they may be in agreement.

If, then, a rational, convincing case for the higher standard of prophetic politics is in doubt, prophetic politics is weakened at its root. If there is no clear, precise, true, acceptable, operational, efficacious concept of a prophetic paradigm, then, it would seem, the entire argument on behalf of prophetic politics is vitiated. And, if this is the case, fearless criticism, constitutional breakthroughs, and futuristic projection must all fail because there is no standard in the light of which one can criticize, break through, and project. Given the absence of a working consensus, must we then abandon—as impossible, futile, self-defeating—the effort to employ a prophetic model of a superior universal order? Must we concede diversity and inevitable disagreement on ultimate values and modestly opt for a policy of peaceful coexistence—even if this means coexisting (reluctantly) with war, tyranny, injustice, poverty, falsehood, and hate?

However, even assuming for the sake of argument that one could state and get workable agreement on the meaning of the prophetic paradigm, troublesome questions remain. Here a second question arises: What does fearless criticism of the existing order consist of, and how does it proceed? And, additionally: Can we move beyond simple moral condemnation of war, injustice, poverty, and other evils? And can we really develop a more ethically sophisticated and more scientific theory of criticism? Who will the prophetic critics be? How do they come to be such critics? Are they appointed by God? Are they self-appointed and self-annointed? Is it not the case that conscionable, reasonable, and humane people will differ in their criticism? Are not critical conflicts inevitable, especially because criticism will almost invariably involve differing judgments on the meaning of peace, justice, freedom, order, and prosperity and differing judgments on the balancing of such complex equities as peace and defense, freedom and order, liberty and equality, the one and the many, the center and the circumference, and so on?

The task of developing a more ethically sophisticated and powerfully scientific theory of criticism is particularly difficult. Can we, with the help of appropriate social indicators, operationalize the meaning of our standards—peace, justice, freedom, prosperity? Or is this a methodologically utopian dream? Are we, therefore, defeated in our efforts to ascertain our political health more scientifically? And is it not too much to expect that we can work out norms for evaluation that will enable us as critics to say that the state of peace, justice, freedom, prosperity, is, as the case may be, excellent or good or fair or poor? And is it possible to work toward a scientific theory that would account for our political health and that might point toward public policy alternatives whose implementation might narrow the gap between the existential reality and the prophetic standard? The skeptics here also hold this hope to be utopian. Still another adverse criticism is that which comes from those who worry lest fearless criticism lead to an erosion of support for a decent constitutional prescriptive order. They are concerned about criticism gone wild: criticism that can lead to the solid virtues of a liberal, constitutional order being thrown out along with the vices of that order. They are disturbed because they fear that wide-open criticism, however well intentioned, can destroy the fundamental pillars of the political community.

Here, then, are some of the troublesome questions and points that are raised and that challenge the meaningfulness of this second distinguishing charateristic of prophetic politics. These questions are perhaps not as fundamentally disturbing as the attack on the prophetic paradigm, but they still demand a more substantial response than that given so far.

Important practical difficulties confront the proponents of prophetic politics when one asks a third major question: Can prophetic politics successfully express itself in a superior constitutional order—be made to work here on earth, amidst the conflicts of real political interests and actors in real political communities—without being idolatrous, perfectionist, or complacent? Without itself becoming prey to the weaknesses of Machiavellian, utopian, or liberal democratic politics? In brief, are creative breakthroughs in politics really possible? Breakthroughs in political science—in our scientific understanding of political problems? Breakthroughs in wise statesmanship—in our ability to arrive at prudent judgments that enable us to cope successfully with the practical issues of peace and war, justice and injustice, prosperity and poverty—judgments that really enable us to beat swords into plowshares, to let the oppressed go free, to feed the hungry?

Are creative, constitutional breakthroughs really possible in today's world? For example, given the existence and persistence of conflicts among, or within, sovereign nation-states, can we succeed in establishing a world order that eliminates at least nuclear wars between nations and catastrophic civil wars within nations? For example, given the existence and persistence of tyranny and injustice, can we succeed in ending persistent, gross, and unpunished violations of human freedom and human rights? For example, given the existence and persistence of the maldistribution of resources, can we succeed in eliminating poverty? And so on, for the other complicated ills that afflict mankind. Skeptics and "hardheaded" realists will respond in the negative. They will emphasize the obstacles to successful constitutionalization of a better order (for example, those outlined in Chapter 6) and conclude that it is utopian to believe that these obstacles can be removed in any major way. War is a fact of life and here to stay! Ditto tyranny, poverty, and ecological malaise! These critics will also caution about the dangers of attempting to remove such obstacles, the dangers of even seeking alleged breakthroughs. They will emphasize the danger of succumbing to the Leninist argument that, alas, it is necessary to break some eggs in order to make an omelet. Here they underscore the dangers of the costs of "success."

So it is, then, that adverse critics may hold that constitutionalization of a better order may not be possible and that the effort to achieve success may result in a cost higher than the benefits of the alleged success. Here again, they maintain that those who advocate prophetic politics are really utopians in disguise.

Skeptics also have doubts about the fourth distinguishing characteristic of prophetic politics and are prompted to raise a fourth major question: Is continuous futuristic scrutiny and furturistic projection really possible and genuinely fruitful? Or are these tasks vain illusions? And beyond the creative possibilities of limited, fallible, myopic, perverse, sinful humanity? Is futuristic projection, for example, a crazy science fiction dream? Is it really possible to imagine a peaceful world community in which a democratic, constitutional, and federal world order system functions (when local, national, and regional communities fail) to uphold a global Bill of Rights and the global rule of law, to ensure economic justice, and to encourage common global action against common global enemies (such as famine and disease and pollution) and on behalf of the fulfillment of basic human needs? Is it impossible to imagine the end of sexism and racism and pervasive alienation in human work? Is it impossible to imagine a worldwide renaissance of culture embracing the masses as well as the classes? Can we now, by anticipating the problems of the future, safeguard the future for a healthy and flourishing civilization? Can we, given the complexity, resistance, stubbornness of politics, and given human fallibility, maintain the prophetic posture in politics? Can we really anticipate the future and its problems and, beyond that, translate our anticipations into sensible, practical policy?

Here the responses of the skeptics are negative. Their argument is, again, that upon closer examination the advocates of prophetic politics are utopians and betray all the weaknesses of utopian politics. Moreover, the skeptic adds, the prophetic politicians have really lost touch with that sense of reality about the truly vital interests of the nation-state, vital interests that we have earlier identified as a strength of Machiavellian politics. And finally, the skeptic might conclude, the advocates of prophetic politics, by attempting to get beyond liberal democratic politics, have lost a true sense of constitutional balance. Here, then, the skeptic is charging that the claim that might be made on behalf of prophetic politics that it has avoided the weaknesses of utopian politics is unfounded, as is the claim that prophetic politics has successfully incorporated the strengths, and avoided the weaknesses, of Machiavellian and liberal democratic politics.

These four disturbing questions could be further developed and others could be added. Here we can only summarize a few additional critical questions to underscore weaknesses in the theory of prophetic politics. For example, how do we move from where we are now to the prophetic future? What theory of social change will guide prophetic change? How does the proponent of prophetic politics propose to distinguish between the true prophetic politician and the false prophetic politician? What, more fully, is the relation of prophetic politics to the going political order—including a more prophetic political order? Before change? After change in a prophetic direction? What, more specifically, is the position of prophetic politics on reform and revolution in a constitutional order? In an authoritarian order? Is prophetic politics possible only in an advanced constitutional order—and one significantly influenced by the Judaic-Christian-Islamic religious tradition? When prophetic politicians are themselves in power can they remain immune from the evils and weaknesses that they have identified in the other patterns of politics? And still remain effective? What must prophetic politics accept of the past and the present? And what must it reject? How does prophetic politics deal with "heartbreak"—the inability to overcome here on earth, completely, or even significantly, the evils of war, injustice, and poverty? These queries serve to give meaning to the fifth disturbing question posed in our introductory chapter: Is it the paradoxical case that prophetic politics is necessary but impossible?

The tough questions that point toward the weaknesses—the difficulties—of prophetic politics seem to lead, initially, to a very sobering and paradoxical conclusion: that prophetic politics may be ethically necessary but is, alas, impossible of fulfillment, and may, if attempted in practice, be catastrophic! It is easier to argue that we must move up to a higher level of politics, in the interest of civilized survival, than it is to spell out more precisely the successful operationalization of prophetic politics. It is also easier to identify the strengths and weaknesses of Machiavellian, utopian, and liberal democratic politics, and to argue that prophetic politics must incorporate these strengths and avoid these weaknesses, than it is to state more precisely how this can be done. So, necessary but impossible; and if attempted, dangerous!

CONCLUSION

Prophetic politics seems to be a most attractive pattern of politics. But what of its seeming weaknesses? Continuous prophetic scrutiny, by calling our attention to these weaknesses, seems to have undermined the possibility of prophetic politics. But what fuller response can be made to those who have called our attention to these weaknesses? To that question I now turn in the following—and concluding—chapter of this book. More specifically, I will address the challenging question: What is the probability of the possibility of a more prophetic politics?

IV : Conclusion

10 : The Probability of the Possibility of a More Prophetic Politics

INTRODUCTION

Before turning directly to an examination of and response to the troubling questions highlighted by our summary of the weaknesses of prophetic politics in Chapter 9, let me recapitulate the argument on behalf of prophetic politics that I have made in this book to this point. This recapitulation will put the whole argument before us again, in a final summary, and also enable us to appreciate the force of those troubling questions examined in the preceding chapter.

By *prophetic politics,* I have argued, I mean a pattern of politics characterized by four commitments. There is, initially, a commitment to prophetic values: life, peace, human rights and social justice, economic well-being, ecological health, and human excellence. Second, there is a commitment to fearless criticism of all existing orders in the light of the prophetic paradigm. Third, there is a commitment to prophetic constitutional breakthroughs in order to narrow the gap between ideal and reality. And finally, there is a commitment to futuristic scrutiny and projection (via imaginative scenarios, positive and negative) to illuminate future problems and prepare us, in advance, to deal with them.

For the political theorist, I have also argued, these commitments translate into a set of values and norms for judging goals, principles, and behavior in politics and society; into scientific investigation and criticism of existing communities in the light of those values and norms; into creative breakthroughs (bold but prudent public policy proposals and constitutional action) to narrow the gap between ethical ideals and existing reality; and into sane and humane imaginative efforts to deal with future problems. A more prophetic politics would, consequently, attempt to fulfill prophetic values universally; would study the politics of all political communities with an eye to reasons for fulfillment, or nonfulfillment, of those values; would seek to articulate and implement those policies that might prudently narrow the gap between prophetic promise and actual political performance; and would seek to anticipate both difficulties and opportunities in the future.

It is important to emphasize, I have contended, that the model of prophetic politics seeks to avoid the vices of competing models—for example, Machiavellian, utopian, or liberal democratic politics—while incorporating their virtues. Since the case for a more prophetic politics can better be understood in terms of the dialogic relationship of prophetic to Machiavellian, utopian, and liberal democratic politics, I have attempted to examine that relationship. My purpose in exploring that relationship was to clarify the principles of prophetic politics—and, particularly, to stress what I held to be its superior ethical vision, its more generous and realistic understanding of political reality, its more farsighted sense of political becoming, and its sanely imaginative view of the future.

Thus, I emphasized my reasoned conviction that prophetic politics is characterized by a superior ethical vision. This vision, I maintained, is universal and applicable to all people. Unlike Machiavellian politics, prophetic politics does not stop with the protection of the vital interests of the sovereign nation-state. Unlike utopian politics, the model of prophetic politics is not premised on earthly perfection, harmony, and salvation. Unlike liberal democratic politics, moreover, prophetic politics does not use its understanding of human and social limitations as an excuse for not continuing the battle on behalf of peace, freedom, justice, and excellence. Those faithful to the model of prophetic politics recognize vital interests, but they see such vital interests as the vital interests of all peoples and all political communities—not simply as those of the powerful, of whites, of men, of the United States or the Soviet Union. Those in the tradition of prophetic politics see the vital interests of all people being secured best within a framework of global and national limitations wisely accepted by fallible human beings capable of working out the more detailed rules of a superior constitutional order to ensure civilized life, healthy growth, and creative fulfillment.

Prophetic politics, I also argued, is characterized by a more generous and yet more realistic understanding of political reality. Perfect earthly salvation is impossible. But a more prophetic world nourished by realistic prophetic endeavors is not. An earthly hell is quite possible; consequently, effort is required to avoid the dreadful and massive violations of human rights. Conflict may not be eradicable, but success in overcoming the most disastrous warfare is possible. Superior levels of accommodation among inevitably contending interests can be achieved. And a prophetic sensitivity to the least free requires criticism of all political orders (whether democratic, socialist, capitalist, Communist, West or East, North or South, "developed" or "developing," white or black or brown) in which the least free are struggling for emancipation and fulfillment. Prophetic standards sensitize us, ethically, to what to look for as social scientists: the necessary and sufficient conditions of peace, freedom, justice, prosperity, and excellence. The tools of social science make possible a more penetrating assessment—a more accurate appraisal—of the gap between prophetic standards and contemporary reality. Thus, I argued, the tension between "what ought to be" and "what is," is maintained, and the complacency of liberal democratic politics is avoided.

In my argument I also maintained that those committed to prophetic politics possess a more farsighted sense of political becoming than that possessed by those practicing Machiavellian, utopian, or liberal democratic politics. Action is commanded. Long before Marx wrote Thesis 11 on Feuerbach, I noted, the Biblical prophets demanded action to change the world, action based on an ethical commitment to prophetic values—but action that could only be justified and safe within a framework of constitutional limits. Such actions, then, had to be creative, sane, and superior constitutional actions. Those in the prophetic tradition are buoyed by the hope that creative breakthroughs in this spirit are possible. They affirm that it is possible to move beyond the frequently timid constitutional conservatism of liberal democratic politics.

Moreover, I argued, given the commitment to futuristic projection, we can do more than simply picture a more messianic age, where swords will be beaten into plowshares. We can begin to do what in the past we have only rarely done: project the scenarios (positive and negative) of the world we would like to create (or avoid) and (by anticipating problems) work through differences we now foresee—and perhap even uncover some not currently in sight. This fourth commitment, I emphasized, underscores the importance of an open and self-correcting political system.

In this fashion, then, I maintained, those committed to the model of prophetic politics can protect genuine vital interests and harness the struggle for power while avoiding idolatrous worship of the nation-state and the worst uses of force and craft. In this fashion, too, I held, prophetic politicians can again provide us with an inspiring image of a future world, a fruitful and powerful image that can enlighten the past, orient the present, and illuminate the future while avoiding the sin of hubris. Prophetic politics may also assist us, in our national political communities, to move more generously toward the more nearly perfect Union, pursuant to notions of limited, representative, responsible, and welfare-oriented government and in accord with a mandate to balance human equities while avoiding the limited vision, deficient understanding, and timid assessments of liberal democratic politics.

So much, then, for the argument on behalf of prophetic politics. But is such a politics possible? Probable? I use the circumlocution *probability of the possibility* to emphasize two key points that are crucial to my argument: (1) that a more prophetic politics is not impossible (because we can conceive it and because we have some evidence, however limited, of its operational reality); and (2) that the key question is: How probable? Let me now return to the troubling questions that call for a fuller response. These questions provide the critical framework for exploring the probability of the possibility of a more prophetic politics.

1. What conception of prophetic values can command the support of the diverse forces of the modern world—religious, philosophical, political, economic, scientific? Here we are confronted with the difficulty of stating, defending, and achieving workable agreement on the cardinal values that illuminate prophetic politics.
2. Can we develop a more ethically sophisticated and more powerful scientific theory of criticism? Here we need to demonstrate how fearless criticism, informed by both the prophetic tradition and modern social science, can go forward.
3. If prophetic values, principles, institutions, and policies are theoretically sound, and if an ominous gap exists between prophetic standards and existential reality, can we creatively break through to a superior constitutional political order that will work in the real world of politics and that will not itself become idolatrous, perfectionist, or complacent? Here we seek to ascertain whether such creative breakthroughs in a political world of clashing actors and interests can occur.
4. Is a prophetic variety of futurist scrutiny and projection really possible and genuinely fruitful? Here we need to find out whether such futurist scrutiny and projection make prophetic sense and not utopian nonsense.
5. Our last question recapitulates the first four questions and focuses sharply on the probability of the possibility: Is it the paradoxical case that prophetic politics is ethically necessary but politically impossible, or, if possible, highly improbable? Here we will explore some striking parallels between the prophetic politician and the creative artist.

To some adverse critics these questions suggest that prophetic politics is a contradiction in terms; others suggest that the model, on closer examination, turns out to be either a variety of utopian politics or a variety of liberal democratic politics. In this concluding chapter, I shall argue, on the contrary, that a fuller response to the five troubling questions points toward the reality of a distinct prophetic politics and toward the probability of the possibility of its modest theoretical and practical success.

As my earlier comments in Chapter 7 have suggested, I am encouraged in affirming my thesis about prophetic politics—and in developing an argument to support it—by my understanding of the prophetic American generation of 1776–87. Those in this generation demonstrated a variety of prophetic politics at the very beginning of the American nation's history. We are foolish and unduly cynical if we do not take heart from their great, if sometimes flawed, achievements and, building on their endeavors, at least hold open the option of a more prophetic politics today.[1]

That the generation of 1776–87 saw themselves as attempting to create a superior constitutional order (what I would call *a more prophetic politics*) is, in my judgment, unmistakable. Unmistakable, too, is their conviction that the superior constitutional order is rooted in superior religious, philosophical, and historical principles and practices—tested, enduring, prescriptive. Unmistakable also is their commitment to bold and radical action to fulfill a vision of superior constitutional values. They saw themselves as engaged in a great republican and constitutional experiment extending the Empire of Liberty. Such an experiment rested upon keen criticism of violations of a superior constitutional order and upon creative breakthroughs in republican theory and practice in the building of a superior political community. Finally, they projected an image of the future—of its great opportunities, of its real dangers—and sought to safeguard it. Those in the prophetic generation of 1776–87 encourage us because we see today that they did, indeed, demonstrate the probability of the possibility of a more prophetic politics.

Past successes do not, of course, guarantee future ones. But they may, at least, encourage us to face up to the troubling questions of today—questions of the unhappy democratic consciousness—more resolutely and to explore, with greater nerve, imagination, and creativity, the prophetic tasks we face today and will unquestionably face in the future. In doing so, we need not contend—indeed, how could we?—that the prophetic leaders of 1776–87 were successful in all their endeavors or that their prophetic imagination was unfailing. As we have already suggested, on a number of issues—and from today's perspective—their record (for example, their understanding and treatment of blacks, native Americans, women, the poor) is far from admirable. Nonetheless, in significant ways they succeeded in theory and practice in moving toward a superior—a more prophetic—constitutional order. And they did so with minimum defections to the nation-state idolatries of Machiavellian politics, to the perfectionism of utopian politics, and to the complacency of liberal democratic politics. For these reasons they stimulate us to hold open the probability of the possibility of a more prophetic politics.

THE PROBLEM OF PROPHETIC VALUES

What conception of prophetic values can, indeed, command the support of the diverse forces of the modern world? And does the generation of 1776–87 help us in our efforts to state, defend, and achieve workable agreement on the cardinal values that illuminate prophetic politics?

The values of the Preamble to the U.S. Constitution of 1787 call attention to an eloquent statement of political values. When these values are understood in a more democratic fashion and illuminate the operational text of the Constitution (and of course guide the political actors who interpret that text), they provide us with inspiring prophetic standards. Of course, the Preamble constitutes only a set of objectives; the Preamble constitutes no grant of constitutional power. Constitutional power is set forth only in the body of the Constitution. Yet the concrete meaning given to the exercise of constitutional powers (say the power to tax and spend) and the concrete meaning given to prohibitions on governmental power (say the prohibitions in the Bill of Rights) serve to clarify both the values inscribed in the operative Constitution and the values and high purposes of government set forth in the Preamble. These values, then, can be identified, justified, and made operational in a democratic community.

Moreover, in examining the generation of 1776–87, we can identify the sources of the Preamble's values and of the operative ideals of the Constitution proper. They drew, pragmatically, upon three sources—historical, philosophical, and religious—in support of their position. Their political values were defended in terms of the tested insights of our basic Judaic-Christian religious heritage, the enduring propositions of selected philosophers, and the enduring prescriptive constitutional principles of free government in the West. In defense of their values, and in their efforts to make their values operational, the rebels of 1776 and the Constitution builders of 1787 may have lacked our philosophical and political sophistication (or did they?); but they were not paralyzed by doubt. They could articulate their constitutional values. They suffered from no loss of nerve. They ably defended their values. Moreover, they were able to build successful coalitions around those "self-evident" propositions that we are so skeptical about today: that human beings are entitled to life, liberty, and the pursuit of happiness; that governments derive their "just powers from the consent of the governed"; that a constitution must include a "bill of rights, providing clearly . . . for freedom of religion, freedom of the press . . . restriction of monopolies . . . habeas corpus laws, and trials by jury"; that government must ensure "equal and exact justice to all men"; that our minds have been created for freedom.[2]

In their successful political efforts to make a revolution and to remodel constitutions, they looked pragmatically to the desirable fruits of their selected principles as one test of their worth. For them, religion and philosophy, history and science, affirmed the sense of their political values. They made the strongest ethical, scientific, and logical case for their political values and then worked heroically to make their normative prophecy a self-fulfilling one. They did not assume unanimity on values, but they did recognize the need for a workable consensus; and they energetically and prudently built such a consensus.

For us to moral should be clear. Instead of waiting vainly until we get unanimity on the truth that ethically good, scientifically informed, and logically trained people *must* accept, let us—building on the best ethical insights, enduring philosophical propositions, and prescriptive constitutional principles—continue to develop the values that nourish the ongoing democratic and constitutional experiment.

We can be encouraged by the generation of 1776–87; but we also need to supplement, as well as endorse, their efforts. In our endeavor to state, defend, and achieve workable agreement on prophetic values, we can count on a number of key, interrelated ideas.

One such key idea is that of *minimum consensus*, that is, consensus on enough fundamentals of the prophetic paradigm to permit global survival, a modest measure of healthy growth, and a decent degree of creative fulfillment. We may not be able to obtain complete agreement on the meaning and operation of life, peace, human rights, social justice, economic well-being, ecological health, and human excellence. But agreement on enough prophetic fundamentals at any particular time may make the limited operational success of prophetic values not only possible but probable.

Confidence in our ability to achieve minimum consensus is reinforced by religious faith, philosophic reason, and historical experience. Some, but not all, will accept the proposition that the superior order is revealed to us by God and that we are commanded to follow God's word. But most will accept the anthropological argument that people in history, influenced by ideas of divinity or natural law or philosophic reason, have employed their human faculties to articulate notions of a superior political order and to utilize them in their lives in the political community. We know that, biologically, we are not incapable of perceiving the worth of a more prophetic politics. We can appreciate that, philosophically and socially, we are capable of grasping the concept of a superior order as a standard that may serve as a basis for judgment in our lives. The specific substantive content of this order—as it may ordain peace and righteousness, truth and justice, love and prosperity—and the specific interpretation of these values in a wide variety of decision-making circumstances will probably always be controversial. But these values can take on quite clear meaning in a given situation, as they have in history, as they do in the fluid present, as they will in the evolving future.

To make this argument is not to deny the reality of opposed values—whether war or tyranny or hate or poverty—or the fact that peace and justice and so on are often understood as requiring quite-opposed courses of action in history. Despite this, it remains the case that the ethical appeal of opposed values is limited. Moreover, the reasons for opposed courses of action designed allegedly to advance the same values may be critically examined to reveal that some of these reasons are genuinely humane, rational, or practical, whereas others are not. The existence of opposed values, or opposed courses of action based allegedly on the same values, does not prevent the achievement of minimum consensus on prophetic values and does not prevent efforts to maximize that consensus by pointing to flaws in opposed values or flaws in courses of action based on faulty interpretations of prophetic values. The critical examination suggested calls attention to a second key idea and requires a little fuller explication.

Given minimum consensus on prophetic values, it is also possible to opt for the acceptance of a *process of critical inquiry* by which we seek to optimize, if we cannot always maximize, agreement. This process involves keeping the door of ethical inquiry open. It involves making, and testing, the commitments of the prophetic paradigm in a sensible way. In this way the prophetic paradigm will be seen as relevant or irrelevant to civilized life, healthy growth, and creative fulfillment. Such testing is one way, moreover, to distinguish between genuinely prophetic and falsely prophetic courses of action. Does the course of action really lead to peace or justice or prosperity? Professions of prophetic values may be similar; but critical analysis of behavior based on values and of consequences that flow from such behavior may help us to distinguish between genuine and spurious prophetic values. This task is not an easy one; judgment about values—especially when several prophetic values are involved as competing equities—remains difficult. Yet one can, utilizing the best social science, look to both genuinely prophetic profession and genuinely prophetic fulfillment in testing the reality and power of prophetic values in the real world, a world that develops out of past but is in the process of becoming. The process of critical inquiry, reinforced as it is by modern science, is a powerful force in the modern world and transcends national and ideological boundaries. Critical inquiry—always, of course, within the framework of life-affirming values—provides a valuable ally for prophetic politics in the modern world.

Critical inquiry itself suggests a more favorable verdict about another key idea crucial to prophetic politics: *the idea of the commandment, or obligation*, to act to fulfill prophetic values. This obligation is moral. We can ignore or reject it. We are not physically compelled to act on behalf of prophetic values. However, historically, it is the case that certain people in certain religions have followed prophetic commandments. Not all people. Not even some all the time. But enough have done so with sufficient regularity so that we can establish a link between their belief in certain religious obligations and their actual behavior. It is certainly the case that religious commandments have made their way into the fabric of institutions—religious, social, and political—and that human beings have in fact been socialized in obedience (thoughtful or thoughtless) to such obligations.

It is also the case that we have, historically, felt commanded to obey cardinal prophetic values and a higher order of which they are a part. We have been persuaded by the sense of certain ethical, political, and scientific arguments as these arguments, for example, rest upon such compelling ethical values as respect for human life, such compelling political considerations as the worth of due process of law, such compelling scientific awareness as appreciation of the nuclear bomb's dangers to human life. Relevant ethical, political, and scientific obligations have also been embodied in such institutions as the school, the church, the state, the university, the labor union, and the corporation and have influenced behavior through the process of socialization. In our preoccupation with what divides religions, groups, and other political actors, we have often ignored those elements, including common obligations, that we share. We have tended to ignore our agreement on the power of many simple commandments: to satisfy—and not to jeopardize—the basic needs of life; to do justice and to be fair and not arbitrary; to use good logic and follow a scientific method in human discourse, research, and problem solving.

To make this argument is not to say that our ethics, law, and politics are invariably based on the same values and result in the same behavior. It is to suggest—and here my argument about commandment links up with my argument about critical process of inquiry and minimum consensus—agreement on enough commandments in the prophetic tradition to make action in the tradition of prophetic politics possible and, indeed, probable.

Let me, as I conclude this brief discussion of the problem of prophetic values, mention one additional idea—*the constitutional idea*—that supports my argument about our ability to state, defend, and achieve workable support for prophetic values. The constitutional idea—itself strongly rooted in the covenantal tradition that mandates obedience to a higher law—is in the world, and it cannot be dismissed easily. Of course, constitutionalism has not triumphed globally; and violations of constitutions occur; and constitutions vary from one political community to the next. Yet it is the case that the sense of the constitutional idea—the sense of known and fair rules for the political game, the sense of effective and regularized restraints on power—will endure because the constitutional idea plays a vital role in meeting human, social, and political needs. It provides opportunities for human beings to grow in freedom. It guards against the abuse of power. It facilitates cooperation, encourages accommodation, and supports the creative resolution of conflicts among contending political actors. By keeping the belief in a higher law alive and by demonstrating its practical utility in coping with the ongoing struggle for power in politics, the constitutional idea rallies support for prophetic values.

There may, then, be enough agreeement on enough fundamentals of the prophetic paradigm to make its operational political success possible. Its ethical and political appeal is considerable. Its testing is not impossible. Minimum agreement can, in time, be replaced by optimum agreement. At the very least, enough minimum agreement is possible now to ensure feasible fearless criticism of the existing order in accord with the prophetic paradigm and to point toward creative breakthroughs in the prophetic constitutional spirit. The strength of the prophetic paradigm rests upon religious, ethical, philosophical, scientific, and political arguments and realities that, if not dominant, are at least too potent to be easily dismissed. These arguments and realities encourage us to believe in the probability of the possibility of stating and defending prophetic values and reaching agreement on the meaning and operation of the prophetic paradigm.

THE PROBLEM OF PROPHETIC CRITICISM

Can we develop a more ethically sophisticated and more powerful scientific theory of criticism? Can we demonstrate how fearless criticism, informed by both the prophetic tradition and modern social science, can go forward? And do the leaders of 1776–87 assist us in this endeavor?

The American rebels and Constitution builders of 1776–87 do not provide us with perfect answers to the nagging questions of prophetic criticism anymore than they provide perfect answers to the disturbing questions about prophetic values. They do, however, provide us with some clues as to the character of sensible criticism.

1. Criticism must be principled: that is, criticism must take place within a framework of ethical and political principles. For the leaders of 1776–87 these principles were republican and constitutional.

2. Criticism must be as realistic as possible: that is, criticism must face up to the realities of human nature, human interests, the struggle for power; it must be unafraid to report the behavior of political actors (whether individuals, groups, rulers, communities) as accurately as possible; and it must not flinch from making judgments about political health and social change.

3. Criticism must look beyond empty moralizing and beyond armchair scientific theorizing to sound political action; criticism must move beyond ethical indictments and beyond empirical generalizations to public policy alternatives whose practical wisdom can be tested in the political laboratory. *The Federalist* remains a superb model of such criticism.

Taking our cues from Jefferson and Madison, and employing a concept such as that of political health, we can develop a mode of criticism that will carry us beyond empty Sunday school sermonizing and beyond the sterility of much modern social science. In developing a prophetic theory of criticism we can be instructed by ethics, science, and statesmanship. We can be instructed about the operational meaning of prophetic values; about relevant and telling social indicators; about norms that make possible meaningful evaluation of the evidence; about testing empirical hypotheses and broader explanatory theory; and about healing public policy alternatives. Such instruction suggests five tasks for prophetic criticism. These are difficult but not impossible tasks. The probability of modest success will depend on the willingness of political scientists to end the separation of ethical, empirical, and prudential investigations and to address themselves forthrightly to the integrating concept of political health. A brief explanation of the concept of political health may appropriately set the stage for summarizing the defense of the five tasks of prophetic criticism that I first outlined in Chapter 6.

The concept of political health, correctly understood, can be vitally helpful in linking the ethical concerns of the prophetic paradigm with the empirical concerns of fearless criticism and with the prudential concerns of prophetic constitutionalization. The concept of political health is, initially, value laden: it assumes that life, growth, and development are worthwhile. It points toward the significant problems that need to be investigated. Second, the concept of political health permits—nay, encourages—scientific investigation of the necessary and sufficient conditions of civilized life, healthy growth, and creative fulfillment. It sensitizes the empirical political scientist to be concerned about the gap between prophetic values and existential political reality and to seek reasons for this gap. Third, the concept of political health is incomplete unless those concerned with political health move on from health standards and scientific diagnosis to prescription. Here political scientists are encouraged to recommend political therapy, to undertake wise action, to pursue prudent public policies that might improve the state of our political well-being.

Let me now recapitulate the five tasks of prophetic criticism and indicate my judgment about the probability of their possibility. My argument has been that fearless criticism of the existing order, in accord with the prophetic paradigm, depends upon the fruitful performance of these tasks.

1. Social scientists must clarify, justify, and make operational the meaning of prophetic standards. They must—helpfully guided by the concept of political health—provide an operational meaning for the triad of civilized life, healthy growth, and creative fulfillment and, thus, for the prophetic values of peace, freedom, justice, prosperity, love, and excellence. This task is one that we have been engaged in, with some modest successes, for several thousand years. In our constitutional history—in our prescriptive historical development in both domestic and international politics—we have been performing this task day in and day out. We have not, of course, reached unanimity on our more precise identification, justification, and clarification of prophetic values, but there exists a modest degree of operational agreement on these values in limited areas. Failures also punctuate this same history, as the record of war, tyranny, and injustice makes clear;

but there exists no theoretical reason that inhibits our ability to move on from minimal agreements and optimal consensus to maximal agreements and broader consensus. Rhetorical agreement is clearly visible, in the global community, in many (but certainly not all) of the pronouncements of the United Nations; what has been lacking in the international community (or within many nation-states with eloquent constitutions) is the translation of the key constitutional values of peace, freedom, justice, and prosperity into operational reality. In attending to this initial task, our success record will never be 100 percent; but, certainly, we can do considerably better than we are now doing.

2. There must occur a more scientific development of political, social, economic, and cultural indicators if there is to be more precise measurement of the political health of our political communities (and I use the concept of political health to summarize the goals of prophetic politics). Theoretically, I see no insuperable difficulties in the performance of this task. Practically, the task is complicated, but it may be enormously speeded up with the use of intelligent programmers and sophisticated computers. This task is rewarding insofar as telling criticism depends upon data that inform us of the state of health of the political community. We already know a great deal about wars (including civil wars), about constitutional and authoritarian regimes, about the enjoyment of human rights, about peaceful elections and change, about governmental responsiveness to human needs, about prosperity and poverty, about ecological problems, and the like. With such knowledge, which will surely grow over the years, especially as political scientists make the study of political health their central concern, criticism of the existing order becomes highly informed and pointedly relevant. Such knowledge thus becomes highly significant. It cannot be ignored easily. So it is bound to have an impact on public policy.

3. There is the task of developing norms to assess the meaning of empirical evidence. The facts themselves permit no evaluations. Norms, together with empirical measurements, make evaluations possible. The articulation and operationalization of prophetic standards may illuminate our values but do

not alone tell us where we rank in the achievement of these values. Norms of excellence (for example, of excellent, good, fair, or poor political health, in general; or of excellent, good, fair, or poor ranking on components of political health such as peace, freedom, justice, and prosperity) have to be formulated and defended and related to social indicators before more precise evaluation is possible. This task has been neglected, but can be judiciously performed, by political and social scientists. The neglect is attributable to the fact that often empirical social scientist have not fully appreciated that this philosophical task is intimately connected to the possibility of assessment of empirical data. Political and social scientists—conscious of the neglect—can ensure that meaningful criticism can go forward as they articulate and refine such norms. Of course, disputes about these norms will arise. Clearly, it will be much easier to reach agreement on norms at either end of the normative scale (for example, the peaceful, free, just, prosperous society, at one pole, or Hobbes's state of war of all against all, at the other pole). Yet debate about norms can, to a modest extent, limit some of the disputes. To some extent the evidence will prevent the affirmation of norms that are contradicted by our common sense. And the debate about norms can be positively healthy insofar as it illuminates how people interpret evidence, and fare, in various political communities. So, the probability of the possibility of this task must be affirmed.

4. There is the task of formulating and testing empirical hypotheses within the framework of a larger scientific and explanatory theory of political health. More precise measurement is only the beginning in empirical political science. Data must not only be obtained but also be put to intelligent use in the formulation and testing of significant empirical hypotheses. What, indeed, makes for political health—or political illness? What makes for peace or war, justice or injustice, freedom or tyranny, prosperity or poverty, and so on? Such scientific understanding must also involve a fuller comprehension of how social and political change has occurred, is occurring, and will occur; and it must lead to a fuller knowledge of political healing. This task—crucial to the

effort to arrive at helpful empirical generalizations and a guiding empirical theory—can be addressed if political and social scientists who have carried on the behavioral revolution will focus their attention of the concept of political health. We should not expect a political science equivalent of $E = mc^2$ to emerge, but modest generalizations are certainly probable; and, in time, an explanatory theory of political health, based on a democratic and constitutional paradigm, will probably emerge.

5. We come to the exploration of wise statesmanship—political healing—in the tradition of prophetic politics. This final task of prophetic criticism is opened up by a fuller scientific theory of political health. This task looks to healing public policy alternatives, policies of wise statesmanship; it looks to the effort to identify, state, and make ready for sound political experiment a wise public policy alternative. This task of political healing is, in fact, a traditional concern of statesmanship and of political philosophy. This task has been carried on for a long time by political philosophers and prudent politicians. What remains to be done, and can successfully be done, is to highlight and maximize the healing character of public policy decisions.

As we put social science to work here in seeking to explain what makes for the political health of the political community, we are ensuring that fearless criticism of the existing order will be most constructive. Such criticism will be addressing itself to significant problems on the basis of significant, abundant, and relevant information; on the basis of defensible norms and meaningful evaluations; on the basis of illuminating hypotheses and explanatory theories; and on the basis of a larger theory of social change that may suggest wise alternatives to the policies and practices of the existing order. Such criticism will, therefore, carry more weight than empty preachment or irrelevant facts. Only when criticism attends to the problems delineated here can it be most rewarding, fruitful, and telling.

In brief, then, fearless criticism of the existing order can proceed in the fashion sketched above. Such a more ethically sophisticated and scientific theory of criticism, although challenging and difficult, is not theoretically impossible. In modest ways such a theory of criticism is already in practice in social science in limited areas and with limited success. Here, too, then, we can see the case for the probability of the possibility of a more prophetic politics.

THE PROBLEM OF CREATIVE CONSTITUTIONAL BREAKTHROUGHS

But can we break through to a superior constitutional political order that will work in the real world of politics and that will not itself become idolatrous, perfectionist, or complacent? Can creative breakthroughs in a political world of clashing actors and interests really occur? And what encouragement do we get from the political actors of 1776–87?

Creative breakthroughs, as we noted in Chapter 7, mean significantly fruitful resolutions of major problems. These problems involve conceptions of the good political life; the necessary and sufficient conditions of political health; wise practical decisions on peace and war, liberty and tyranny, prosperity and poverty, ecological balance and imbalance, human excellence and mediocrity. Ethically, as we have emphasized, a breakthrough involves a superior vision of a people's vital interests. Empirically, a breakthrough involves a keener, deeper, more profound understanding of the struggle for purpose and power, for sane and humane accommodation among conflicting interests. Prudentially, a breakthrough involves wisdom-in-action. The achievements of the great republican and constitutional generation of 1776–87 suggest the reality—not simply the possibility or probability—of creative breakthroughs. Expanded Bills of Rights, religious liberty, a more democratic theory of political obligation, the constitutional convention, the American presidency, a scheme for overcoming colonialism, the federal republic—these were all creative breakthroughs, and they encourage us to seek comparable breakthroughs today and tomorrow. Creative breakthroughs have occurred in the past;

there is no persuasive reason why they cannot occur again, today and in the future.

Moreover, as we also noted in Chapter 7, creative breakthroughs are not limited to the late eighteenth century and to the United States. The expansion of suffrage—a great political breakthrough—occurred throughout the nineteenth century and continued in the twentieth century. In the nineteenth century the Morrill Land Grant Act opened up the doors of higher education to hundreds of thousands of Americans and anticipated other educational breakthroughs such as the G.I. Bill of Rights, which made higher education possible for hundreds of thousands of returning veterans after World War II. And these are only a few additional examples of modest creative breakthroughs—breakthroughs that have opened up doors not only to participation in politics or to higher education but to improved health and housing, business opportunities, and the like.

Moreover, the United States is not unique among nations in enacting prophetic social legislation or in protecting the least free. There are some success stories among nations. For example, the European Common Market demonstrates how historic enemies can overcome national rivalries and advance their common economic, social, and political interests. The European Economic Community (EEC) has encountered setbacks (particularly in periods of economic recession) and has by no means fulfilled the more ambitious dreams of an even more integrated Europe; but its limited successes constitute a breakthrough to cooperative action that would have been deemed impossible prior to World War II. Past breakthroughs do not, I appreciate, guarantee future ones; but they do suggest that attention to creative constitutional breakthroughs is not utopian fantasy. The study of such past breakthroughs should embolden us—aided by critical theory—to explore alternatives, calculate costs and benefits, assess probabilities, and make prudent decisions on "go" or "no go."

The immediate agenda, as I have already argued, should be reasonably clear: the abolition of nuclear war, improved constitutional machinery for the effective protection of human rights, more successful efforts to diminish the dominion of poverty, and a winning campaign to achieve a prudent ecological balance. It is cynical, and, I believe, false, to say that the objectives of this agenda cannot be achieved. If it is true that to attempt too much is to commit hubris, it is also true that to do too little or to act without some larger vision of how smaller breakthroughs can move us toward larger breakthroughs is to invite disaster. The complete and miraculous transformation of peoples and communities is, I am persuaded, a falsely utopian dream; paradise on this earth is an illusory expectation. But small steps in all these areas of concern—in modest disarmament agreements, in the universal prohibition of torture, in an increased and better-distributed food supply, or in population control and protection of resources and environment—are probable. And these modest, measurable achievements can lead to fuller ethical, empirical, and prudential breakthroughs.

There are, of course, a host of factors that constrain our imagination and behavior and inhibit us in our ability to achieve creative breakthroughs. We cannot ignore these limiting factors. Throughout this book I have stressed the perils of Machiavellian and utopian politics as well as the dangers of liberal democratic politics. These perils and dangers must be honestly faced as we seek to develop the prophetic constitutional order. More often than not, narrow self-interest dominates the behavior of most political actors. The temptation to employ cunning deception or brutal force remains strong in politics. So does the temptation to force people to be free and to accept an authoritarian "paradise." There is also the danger that active and successful involvement in constitutional efforts will lead to compromise inconsistent with prophetic politics—and thus to the complacency, myopia, and timidity that sometimes characterize liberal democratic politics. These perils, dangers, and temptations are not always inevitable, but they underscore the realistic constraints facing prophetic politicians as they seek to achieve breakthroughs to a more prophetic constitutional order.

However, we should not forget that the probability of the possibility of creative breakthroughs—say in the United

States—is reinforced by several counterarguments. First, it is probable that we can persuade key forces, pragmatically responsive to evidence (to what works), that neither America's truly vital interests, nor the globe's vital interests, are being adequately protected by current U.S. policy. For example, increased and modernized nuclear arms do not move us away from nuclear war. For example, the invasion of one of the world's smallest nations—Grenada—by the world's preeminent superpower does not point the way toward those peaceful and constitutional policies of genuine reform, which are the only policies that can bring real democracy and prosperity to troubled and distressed Latin American countries.

Second, one can make the persuasive argument that prophetic values constitute a superior realism: that peace, human rights, economic well-being, and ecological balance constitute the more enduring basis for national and foreign policy; and that democratic and constitutional processes, worldwide, can best protect a political community's vital interests. The Marshall Plan of aid to war-torn Europe and the EEC are examples that illustrate the practical success of prophetic values. Efforts of the United States in the 1970s to make human rights a more meaningful and effective part of U.S. foreign policy is a third example. A superior realism can build on these and other such examples.

Third, we can identify and mobilize key forces in support of our truly vital interests. Support would come from a host of forces. Support would come from many religious leaders and rank and file because of their historic commitment to the biblical prophetic tradition. For example, America's Catholic bishops have taken a forthright stand in their opposition to nuclear war. Catholic, Protestant, and Jewish clergy have also been in the front ranks of those seeking enhanced protection for human rights and relief for the hungry. Support would also come from Enlightenment intellectuals and their allies because of their ongoing commitment to a secular tradition of prophetic politics. These forces are prominent in the peace movement and in the battle for human rights. Amnesty International illustrates only one of the many groups dedicated to prophetic values. The roster of such groups—in the varying domains of peace, human rights, social and economic justice, a healthy ecology—is impressive.

Support would also come from scientists and educators. Support would come from scientists—physicists, biologists, ecologists, doctors—because of their keen awareness of the dangers of radiation and pollution. Concerned scientists have already done a major job in alerting the American public to the consequences of nuclear war. Support would come, too, from educators because the true name of their "game" is prophetic evaluation, criticism, and judgment. It is hard to assess the influence of prophetic educators; but we would be foolish to underestimate the role of prophetic education in shaping an agenda for debate and in influencing American public opinion.

Television, newspapers, radio too, can play an important role because they help to dramatize the gap between prophetic values and existential reality. For example, the media's reporting on war, violations of human rights, poverty, and ecological disaster has had a profound effect on American public opinion. The media have helped to dramatize the ugly realities of nation-state behavior and the frequent gulf between profession and practice.

The least free themselves can also be mobilized to support prophetic values that constitute our truly vital interests. Blacks, other maltreated ethnic groups, the poor, women, can be mobilized because they are already sensitized to violations of human rights, social justice, and economic well-being and thus constitute a natural constituency for a more prophetic politics. Workers, too, can be mobilized because they can sympathize with the exploitation of fellow workers and because their jobs are intimately related to a larger global prosperity. Organized labor has a long-range vested interest in lifting the level of well-being of all workers. The support of farmers can also be tapped because they can see the tie between the food they produce and would like to sell and the hunger in the world that bespeaks an untapped market—and income. There can be nothing unethical about linking legitimate self-interest to the battle for peace and against hunger.

Similarly, enlightened industrialists and business people can be enlisted to support prophetic values that are also vital interests. Enlightened industrialists and business people can see that a growing demand for peaceful products from people in a world considerably below minimum standards of human need will unquestionably enhance profits and advance a prosperous global community. As people move out of poverty, they will seek greater economic enjoyment of the goods of this world that make human life more commodious and fulfilling. Profits from production, trade, and commerce that flow from the fuller satisfaction of human needs and aspirations need not be rejected; they can be seen as legitimate incentives to involve the industrial and commercial community in the fulfillment of prophetic values.

Lastly, I come to political leaders. They have two responsibilities that some, but not all, have met. They have a responsibility to provide prophetic leadership; and they have a responsibility, in a democratic and constitutional society, to respond to an increasingly prophetic electorate. Some political leaders have cheapened prophetic rhetoric by their failure to move beyond rhetoric to prophetic action. On the other hand, a number of prophetic voices have emerged in American politics; and not only are they speaking out, but they are also seeking to translate prophetic values into practical prophetic policies. Modest progress can be discerned in the field of nuclear arms: for example, nuclear explosions have been banned in the atmosphere; a human rights foreign policy was articulated and partially put into practice in the 1970s; the United States has been generous in using its copious food stocks to aid in the relief of famine; and an important step was taken with the passage of the Environmental Protection Act. These are signs that political leaders can, in limited areas, lead and respond. It remains to increase the ranks of prophetic politics leadership and broaden the base of prophetic legislation and action.

These counterarguments—directed at those skeptical of overcoming the perils, temptations, and dangers of the real world of politics—do not achieve an instant victory for those seeking creative breakthroughs. But, in conjunction with the reality of past creative breakthroughs, they reinforce the conviction of the probability of the possibility of a more prophetic politics. A more democratic, constitutional, peaceful, just, prosperous global order has already been envisaged; and some political actors have been mobilized on its behalf. It remains now for creative leaders to respond more fully and, in Tocqueville's spirit, "to educate democracy, to reawaken . . . its religious beliefs; to purify its morals; to mold its action; to substitute a knowledge of statecraft for its inexperience, and an awareness of its true interest for its blind instincts, to adapt its government to time and place, and modify it according to men and to conditions."[3]

THE PROBABILITY OF FUTURISTIC
SCRUTINY AND PROJECTION

Is a prophetic variety of futurist scrutiny and projection really possible and genuinely fruitful? Does such scrutiny and projection make prophetic sense and not utopian nonsense? And do the leaders of 1776–87 encourage us in the performance of this task?

Jefferson and Madison were able to project the democratic Experiment into the future, to suggest the principles that must guide the future, and to warn of the dangers that threatened the democratic future.

The generation of Jefferson and Madison had a great dream of a democratic Empire of Liberty in the United States. This Empire of Liberty, they believed, could set an example for the world. They believed that the republican and constitutional principles they were testing in the American experiment had applicability worldwide. They were also aware of future dangers as well as future opportunities for human fulfillment. The dangers of antirepublican principles and forces, of disunion, of external threats to the Empire of Liberty were constantly in the minds of Jefferson and Madison. Jefferson looked to educational reforms to achieve an informed citizenry and rightful and reasonable majority rule. Legal and economic reforms would defeat the forces of special privilege and prevent their dominance in the American future. An enlarged Empire of Liberty—including coequal states carved out of the western territories and prepared for republican self-government—would constitute a haven for the oppressed from other lands and a beacon for free people everywhere. Rule by the continuing—the living—majority would keep government ever responsive to the needs of the people. So would local government—including a system of wards, a concept that anticipates twentieth century participatory democracy—keep government close to the people. These ideas add up to a continual peaceful revolution to make unpopular and tyrannical government impossible.

Madison, too, worried about the dangers of disunion and of antirepublicanism from the beginning to the end of his long and fruitful life. His approach to the future, as well as to the present, was dominated by the realistic principle that "republicans . . . must be anxious . . . in defending liberty against power, and power against licentiousness."[4] His critical response to the antirepublican danger in his own lifetime constituted a set of imperatives for future leaders: Safeguard the basic civil liberties, for without freedom of religion and speech and press and assembly there can be no openness to God, no free elections, no criticism of public officials, no republican policy. Be prepared to exert bold leadership in anticipation of the antirepublican danger. Know your friends and foes, take alarm at the selfish friends as well as the scheming foes, and be ready to organize a genuinely republican party to advance truly popular and liberty-loving principles. Resist the beginning of tyranny by protesting loudly and intensely. See the untoward consequences in the wrong principles and thus avoid the dangerous consequences by denying the principles. Be careful to distinguish between a usurpation, an abuse, and an unwise use of power. Use orthodox constitutional interpretation and constitutional weapons first, but do not abandon peaceful, majoritarian recourse to the people—the ultimate source of constituent power—if such recourse beyond the existing legal order is necessary. Always keep in reserve the natural right of militant revolt in the event tyranny is continued by those in power against a majority or minority. Madison (as I noted in Chapter 7) saw clearly that the principle of unanimity (whether in the government of the Articles of Confederation or in Calhoun's doctrine of the concurrent majority) would lead to anarchy or impotence. Nullification and secession would destroy Constitution and Union.

This legacy should encourage us even if it does not address, directly, the futuristic scenarios that are called for today if we are to ensure the future. Jefferson and Madison modestly demonstrate the reality of futuristic scrutiny and projection—not just their possibility or probability.

We cannot, of course, perfectly anticipate the future and all its problems. But we can do a better job than we are now doing. Moreover, as we argued in Chapter 7, we can do a better and safer job in performing this fourth task because prophetic politics is predicated on the initial premise that there is not now, and never can be, an earthly paradise; on the second proposition of preserving the tension between what ought to be and what is (between the prophetic paradigm and the existing order, in even the best constitutional order); and on the third proposition of a continuing battle against idolatries of every kind. These premises encourage us to utilize—as we have modestly utilized—negative and positive futuristic scenarios in exploring the future. The popularity and impact upon our modern consciousness of negative scenarios such as *1984* and *Brave New World* illustrate the potentiality of such scenarios.[5] A host of other negative futuristic scenarios also illustrate the potentiality of such futuristic scrutiny and projection. Our task is to make these negative scenarios even more realistic and to utilize them to avert future dangers.

But, in addition, we need to develop more fully the few positive futuristic scenarios that have already surfaced—particularly among those whom I have called the *political futurists*—and that hold out great promise for reckoning with the future. No one should pretend that these scenarios are miraculous blueprints that futuristic political architects can flawlessly employ to build the future. Yet they do require us to face the future in a serious way. As thought experiments, they enable us to probe the future in fruitful ways. As, in these thought experiments, we logically explore future problems—ethically, empirically, and prudentially—we enhance our ability to understand the future and future courses of action. In particular, we sharpen our ability to articulate a defensible theory of transition that can realistically move us from where we are now to where we would like to be. The best of the political futurists (for example, Richard Falk) are very conscious of the need to address the problem of a feasible theory of transition, even as they might concede that their own efforts have not been universally successful or persuasive. But they have courageously made a start. Others now need to join the enterprise.

We have already touched upon some of these scenarios. One such scenario involves a more effective democratic and constitutional global order—building on the functional approach to global problems. This scenario accepts the reality of the emerging global community and the reality of political actors (despite other differences) working together to deal with common problems: for example, in combating disease, in facilitating global communications, in fighting pollution, in increasing agricultural production, in predicting the weather, and the like. A host of functional agencies are already at work in dealing with these problems. So we are dealing with more than probabilities or possibilities; we are acknowledging actualities. The task confronting the political futurists is that of moving on from these success stories to other successes in dealing with larger, more intractable global problems, such as war, economic depression, gross and persistent violations of human rights, and more difficult ecological malaise. These are the problems that go beyond the power of functional agencies to handle with success. They, too, are the problems that go beyond the present capacity of the present sovereign nation-states to handle.

Another scenario calls for exploring a variety of participatory political economies, each of which might be able, within political communities, to deal more adequately with poverty, distributive justice, and worker alienation. Again, here there are limited, isolated, success stories: for example, in Sweden, in the Israeli kibbutz, in worker management in Yugoslavia, in certain industries in Spain, the United States, or Japan. The task is to explore the fuller application of these success stories—and other even more imaginative ones—in futuristic scenarios.

Yet another futuristic scenario would, and can be expected to, explore how we can move toward a more genuine community wherein civilizing and liberating education prepares people for competent, rich, and fulfilling lives. This effort, too, is not simply possible or probable; it is an effort already under way. Again, the difficult task of the political futurist is to explore the feasibility of the effort on a wider front.

The work of the political futurists, I am arguing, has already demonstrated attention to the task of constructing positive futuristic scenarios. Their work, although limited, especially in articulating a persuasive theory of transition, at least points in the right direction. Some attempts at futuristic scrutiny and projection have already been made; we have already begun, modestly, to test the probability of such possibilities in a serious way. Farfetched scenarios we can theoretically conceive; their testing in the years ahead will demonstrate their probability.

CONCLUSION: THE PROPHETIC POLITICIAN AS CREATIVE ARTIST

Is it, however, the paradoxical case that prophetic politics is ethically necessary but politically impossible, or—if possible —highly improbable for us today, regardless of the prophetic achievements of the generation of 1776–87 and of other twentieth century political actors?[6]

My argument has been that a more prophetic politics is ethically necessary if we are to achieve civilized life, healthy growth, and creative fulfillment. I have also argued that prophetic politics, because we can conceive it, is theoretically possible.

Moreover, the reality of a more prophetic politics has been demonstrated, modestly, in history; I have used the example of 1776–87 to illustrate and underscore that modest demonstration. However, the probability—the likelihood—of a more prophetic politics, even if historically plausible, is by no means fully assured. And even if we concede its modest probability in some respects, we would have to admit that its wholesale implementation is by no means imminent. We do not know for sure how distant or near is its fuller practical realization. And we worry about the costs and consequences of such realization. We still face the creative challenge of probing the fuller probability of the possibility of a more prophetic politics.

We may be helped in this probing if we see the prophetic politician as a creative artist of religious faith and prophetic politics as a creative political art. Artistry characterizes all four distinguishing characteristics of prophetic politics. First, creative artists are guided by ideals and purposes that elevate them in their artistic conduct. Second, they must work within the world as it is—with what is given—even as they struggle to transform the given in accord with their artistic ideals. Third, they are not satisfied with the mere statement (or criticism) that their ideal does not exist, that the given is not in accord with their ideal. They must transform the given in the light of their artistic vision of imaginative possibilities. In doing so, they cannot abolish all that is given. Some things they must accept as they are. But they are capable of creative breakthroughs on a number of fronts—in imaginative vision, in penetration of reality, and, modestly, in the artistic transformation of the world. Finally, they have the capacity for continual scrutiny and analysis of even their best work. And this can lead to additional breakthroughs as they are able to carry their artistic achievements, via farfetched scenarios of things as they might be, to greater heights.

In a very real sense, then, the creative artist illustrates the four distinguishing characteristics of prophetic politics. This parallel points up the hopefulness of the probability of the possibility of prophetic politics and inspires theorists of a more prophetic politics in their sometimes lonely labors. In prophetic politics as a creative art we can take renewed confidence in our ability to move up to a higher level of politics that can more effectively ensure vital civilized life, healthy growth, and creative fulfillment for the marvelous human beings capable of the prophetic consciousness. In this way, moreover, we can have confidence in our ability to safeguard the future of the democratic revolution, a revolution involving individual realization for all peoples throughout the globe within the framework of a common good ordained by prophetic commandments. Can we, then, move up to the level of a more prophetic consciousness—and without too great a cost? Theoretically, yes. Practically, partially and modestly. The extent of that practical success is up to us.

Notes

CHAPTER 1

1. Neal Riemer, *The Revival of Democratic Theory* (New York: Appleton-Century-Crofts, 1962).

2. Neal Riemer, *James Madison* (New York: Washington Square Press, 1968); New York: Twayne, 1970).

3. Neal Riemer, *The Democratic Experiment* (Princeton, N.J.: Von Nostrand, 1967).

CHAPTER 2

1. See Isaiah Berlin, "The Question of Machiavelli," *New York Review of Books,* November 4, 1971, pp. 20–32; also to be found as "The Originality of Machiavelli," in Berlin's *Against the Current* (New York: Penguin Books, 1982), pp. 25–79. See also Martin Fleisher, ed., *Machiavelli and the Nature of Political Thought* (New York: Atheneum, 1972); and Anthony Parel, ed., *The Political Calculus: Essays on Machiavelli's Philosophy* (Toronto: University of Toronto Press, 1972).

2. See the helpful and valuable collection by De Lamar Jensen, ed., *Machiavelli: Cynic, Patriot, or Political Scientist?* (Boston: D. C. Heath, 1960). For those who have emphasized the difference between domestic and international politics, see, for example, Stanley Hoffmann, "Theory and International Relations," in *International Politics and Foreign Policy*, ed. James N. Rosenau (New York: Free Press, 1969); and David Fromkin, *The Independence of Nations* (New York: Praeger, 1981).

3. These ideas suffuse Machiavelli's political writings about the state—the state that was not yet in his day the modern nation-state.

4. Francesco de Sanctis, *Storia della letteratura italiana,* vol. 2 (Milan: Feltrinelli Editore, 1956); quoted in Jensen, *Machiavelli,* p. 23.

5. Niccolo Machiavelli, *The Prince and the Discourses* (1513; reprint ed., New York: Modern Library, 1940), chap. 24, p. 90; chap. 14, p. 53. The reference here is to *The Prince.* Subsequent references to either work will be to this edition.

6. Machiavelli, *The Prince,* chap. 15, p. 56.

See note 5, Chapter 2. Author's preferred style is to list the original date of publication immediately following the title of the work: the date following the publication information is the edition used for this text.

7. It might be argued that it is Machiavelli who, perhaps more than any other author, has helped to give the word *prudence* a bad name in the modern world. Because Machiavelli has departed from the classical view of prudence as articulated, for example, in Aristotle's *Ethics,* I have put *prudent* and *prudential* in quotation marks when using them in connection with Machiavelli. Questions as to the proper understanding of prudent statesmanship can be seen in the controversies surrounding Henry Kissinger. See, in particular, Seymour M. Hersh, *The Price of Power: Kissinger in the Nixon White House* (New York: Summit Books, 1983). Stanley Hoffman, in "The Kissinger Anti-Memoirs"—his review of Hersh's book in the *New York Times Book Review,* July 3, 1983—writes (pp. 16–17): "Mr. Nixon instinctively and Mr. Kissinger intellectually were Machiavellians—men who believed that the preservation of the state (inseparable in Machiavelli from that of the Prince) requires both ruthlessness and deceit at the expense of foreign and internal adversaries."

8. Machiavelli, *The Prince,* chap. 18, p. 64

9. Ibid., p. 66.

10. Machiavelli, *The Discourses,* chap. 41, p. 528.

11. Machiavelli, *The Prince,* chap. 17, p. 64.

12. Ibid., p. 65.

13. Ibid.

14. Ibid., chap. 7, p. 30.

15. Ibid.

16. Ibid.

17. Hans J. Morgenthau, in *Politics among Nations: The Struggle for Power and Peace,* 5th ed. (New York: Knopf, 1978), has cogently argued for these propositions. Anthony D'Amato in "The Relevance of Machiavelli to Contemporary World Politics," in Parel, *The Political Calculus,* p. 210, identifies Morgenthau, Kenneth Thompson, and George Kennan as writers who "have articulated neo-Machiavellian notions of power politics." Certainly they would agree with the strengths of Machiavellian politics identified in the passage just written in the text. However, this does not mean that they share the outlook of a Nixon or a Kissinger.

18. Frederick the Great, *Réfutation du Prince de Machiavel,* 1739 in *Oeuvres de Frédéric II, Roi de Prusse,* vol. 2 (Berlin: Chez Voss et Fils, Decker et Fils, et Chez Treuttel, 1789); translated by and cited in Jensen, *Machiavelli,* p. 7.

19. See, for example, Robert C. Johansen, *The National Interest and the Human Interest* (Princeton, N.J.: Princeton University Press, 1980).

20. See Neal Riemer, "Prophetic Politics and Foreign Policy," *International Interactions* 8 (1981): 25–39; and idem, "Watergate and Prophetic Politics," *Review of Politics* 36 (April 1974): 284–97.

21. Reinhold Niebuhr, *The Children of Light and the Children of Darkness* (New York: Scribner's, 1944).

22. See Jacques Maritain, "The End of Machiavellianism," *Review of Politics* 4 (January 1942): 1–33; in Jensen, *Machiavelli*, p. 91.

23. Ibid., p. 96.

24. G. P. Gooch, *Studies in Diplomacy and Statecraft* (New York: Logman, Green, 1942); in Jensen, *Machiavelli*, p. 89.

25. See Neal Wood's (ed.) Introduction to *Machiavelli's The Art of War* (New York: Liberty of the Liberal Arts, 1965) (revision of Ellis Farneworth's translation).

26. Gooch, *Studies*, p. 89.

27. See Neal Riemer, "Creative Breakthroughs in Politics," *Political Inquiry* 2 (1974): 1–22.

28. Gooch, *Studies*, p. 90. Compare to the point by both Maritain and Gooch about short-term triumph and long-term misfortune Stanley Hoffmann's observation: "The problem with Machiavellianism is, first, that sooner or later it invites a formidable reaction at home. Secondly, it is neither morally nor politically tenable abroad. The kind of interventionism in the domestic affairs of others represented by American policy in Chile—which was based primarily on a fear of contagion rather than direct threats to American security—may lead to short-term gain, but it only builds up deep anti-American resentments that will be increasingly difficult to control. And in its methods as well as its principles, it violates some of the key values for which the United States claims to speak in world affairs." See Hoffmann, "The Kissinger Anti-Memoirs," p. 16.

29. Pasquale Villari, *The Life and Times of Niccolo Machiavelli*, 2 vols. (London: Ernest Benn Ltd., 1919), vol. 2; in Jensen, *Machiavelli*, p. 20.

30. Berlin, "The Question of Machiavelli," pp. 20–32; and idem, "The Originality of Machiavelli," pp. 25–79.

31. See, particularly, pp. 66–79 of Berlin, "The Originality of Machiavelli."

32. Ibid., pp. 74–75.

33. Ibid., p. 76.

34. Ibid., p. 78.

35. Ibid., p. 79.

CHAPTER 3

1. Thomas Molnar, *Utopia: The Perennial Heresy* (New York: Sheed and Ward, 1967); Buckminster R. Fuller, *Utopia or Oblivion: The Prospects for Humanity* (New York: Bantam, 1969).

2. See George Kateb, *Utopia and Its Enemies* (New York: Free Press, 1963), p. 164, n. 28. Certainly, *The Republic* is a great feat of the utopian imagination. Whether Plato himself was a utopian, or whether he was *only* a uto-

pian, is another question. There can be little doubt that Plato has exerted a great influence on the utopian imagination. Francis M. Cornford, editor and translator, *The Republic of Plato* (New York: Oxford University Press, 1945). For an older edition, see Plato, *The Republic,* John L. Davis and David J. Vaughan, editors and translators (London: Macmillan, 1929).

   3. See Crane Brinton, "Utopia and Democracy," in *Utopias and Utopian Thought,* ed. Frank Manuel (Boston: Beacon Press, 1967), p. 51.

   4. Fyodor Dostoevski, *The Brothers Karamazov* (New York: Random House, Modern Library Edition, 1950), bk. 5, chap. 5.

   5. B. F. Skinner, *Walden Two* (New York: Macmillan, 1948).

   6. "The Marxist utopia today exists in a number of standard versions: a Western one—its utopian character is borderline—that is becoming ever more pragmatic and is merging with the ideal of the capitalist welfare state; Soviet Marxism, which on principle would cut itself off from its utopian origins but allow for a recrudescence of futuristic utopian speech on ceremonial occasions; Maoism, which at least at one time stressed egalitarian elements in the Marxist utopian heritage that Soviet Marxism deliberately neglected; and a dissident Marxism, which had a meteoric success in 1968, that would integrate Marx with the whole Western utopian tradition, emphasizing moral values rather than scientific socialism and at times denying the worth of the theory altogether." See Frank E. Manuel and Fritzie F. Manuel, *Utopian Thought in the Western World* (Cambridge: Harvard University Press, Belknap Press, 1979), p. 803. The literature on Marx is legion. For a brief sample, see David McLellan, *Karl Marx: His Life and Thought* (New York: Harper & Row, 1973); Isaiah Berlin, *Karl Marx: His Life and Environment* (1939) (New York: Oxford University Press, 1959); John Plamenatz, *German Marxism and Russian Communism* (London: Longman, 1954); George Lichtheim, *Marxism: An Historical and Critical Study* (New York: Praeger, 1961); Robert C. Tucker, *Philosophy and Myth in Karl Marx* (Cambridge: At the University Press, 1961); idem, *The Marxian Revolutionary Idea* (1969) (New York: Norton, 1970); Peter Gay, *The Dilemma of Democratic Socialism* (1952) (New York: Collier Books, 1962); Ralf Dahrendorf *Class Conflict in Industrial Society* (1957) (Palo Alto, Calif.: Stanford University Press, 1959); Schlomo Avineri, *The Social and Political Thought of Karl Marx* (Cambridge: At the University Press, 1968); M. C. Howard and J. E. King, *The Political Economy of Marx* (London: Longman, 1975); Leszek Kolakowski, *Main Currents of Marxism: Its Origins, Growth and Dissolution,* 3 vols. (Oxford: Oxford University Press, 1981).

   7. For a sample of Marx's adverse criticism of utopians and utopian socialists, see Robert C. Tucker, ed., *The Marx-Engels Reader* (New York: W. W. Norton, 1972). Hereinafter, all page references to the writings of Marx—or of Engels—cited here are keyed to the Tucker anthology. For example, see Marx's *For a Ruthless Criticism of Everything Existing,* pp. 7–10; Marx and

Engels, *Manifesto of the Communist Party,* pp. 359–61; Marx, *The Civil War in France,* especially p. 558; Marx, *Circular Letter to Bebel,* especially pp. 401–2; and Engels, *Socialism: Utopian and Scientific,* pp. 605–39.

8. Quoted in Martin Buber, *Paths in Utopia* (1949) (Boston: Beacon Press, 1958), p. 11. Adam Ulam in his essay, "Socialism and Utopia," in Manuel, *Utopias,* p. 116, also writes: "Socialism and utopia. These two words were once thought to be closely associated, if indeed not synonymous."

9. For the roots, development, and rich variety of utopian thought, see Manuel and Manuel, *Utopian Thought.* "Utopia is a hybrid plant, born of the crossing of a paradisaical, other-worldly belief of Judeo-Christian religion with the Hellenic myth of an ideal city on earth. The naming took place in an enclave of sixteenth-century scholars excited about the prospect of a Hellenized Christianity" (p. 15). "The conception of a heaven on earth that underlies Western utopian thought presupposes an idea of perfection in another sphere and at the same time a measure of confidence in human capacity to fashion on earth what is recognized as a transient mortal state into a simulacrum of the transcendental" (p. 17).

10. Kateb, *Utopia and Its Enemies.*

11. Ibid., p. 7.

12. Ibid., p. 8.

13. Ibid., p. 9.

14. Ibid., p. 17.

15. Although these are the values the young Marx articulated in the *Economic and Philosophical Manuscripts of 1844* (see Tucker, *The Marx-Engels Reader*), there is no reason to believe that the mature Marx abandoned his commitment to them as the core values of Communist society. I share this view with Tucker, *Philosophy and Myth*; and with Erich Fromm, *Marx's Concept of Man* (New York: Ungar, 1961).

16. Marx, *Economic and Philosophical Manuscripts of 1844,* especially the section on "Estranged Labour," pp. 56–67. For Marx, achieving the "true realm of freedom" meant emancipating people more completely from the "realm of necessity," or necessary labor. See *Capital,* vol. 3, p. 320.

17. These quotations will be found in *Manifesto of the Communist Party* (jointly authored by Marx and Engels) and in Marx's *Critique of the Gotha Program,* p. 353 and p. 388, respectively.

18. Marx's famous statement emphasizing an idyllic diversity is to be found in *The German Ideology,* pt. 1 in ibid. p. 124. For a preview of the communist society, one gets some hints from Marx, *The Civil War in France,* pt. 3, pp. 551–64.

19. F. M. Cornford, ed., *The Republic of Plato* (New York: Oxford, 1945). In pt. 2 (bk. 4), chap. 12, p. 129, Socrates declares "that when each order—tradesman, Auxiliary, Guardian—keeps to its own proper business in the commonwealth and does its own work, that is justice and what makes for a good society." His "universal principle" is "that everyone ought to perform

the one function in the community for which his nature best suited him" (p. 127). The good state is "wise, brave, temperate, and just" (p. 121). For Socrates, "the highest object of knowledge is the essential nature of the Good, from which everything that is good and right, derives its value for us" (pt. 3 [bk. 6], chap. 23, p. 215).

20. See Dostoevski, *The Brothers Karamazov*, pp. 266–68. For my own earlier treatment of this magnificent chapter, see Neal Riemer, "Some Reflections on the Grand Inquisitor and Modern Democratic Theory," *Ethics* 67 (July 1957): 249–56. A book-length study is Ellis Sandoz's *Political Apocalypse: A Study of Dostoevsky's Grand Inquisitor* (Baton Rouge: Louisiana State University Press, 1971).

21. B. F. Skinner, "Utopia and Human Behavior," in *Moral Problems in Contemporary Society*, ed. Paul Kurtz (Englewood Cliffs, N.J.: Prentice-Hall, 1969), p. 96.

22. "Some Issues Concerning the Control of Human Behavior," *Science* 124 (Nov. 30, 1956): 1059; quoted in Kateb, *Utopia and Its Enemies*, p. 145.

23. In addition to *Walden Two*, see B. F. Skinner's *Beyond Freedom and Dignity* (New York: Knopf, 1971); and idem, *About Behaviorism* (New York: Knopf, 1974).

24. Brinton, "Utopia and Democracy," emphasizes the role of an "elite" (p. 50), a "benevolent despotism" (p. 53), a "creative minority" (p. 54), and "the cultural engineer" (p. 63) in utopian thought.

25. See Marx, *Manifesto of the Communist Party*, in Tucker, *The Marx-Engels Reader*, for Marx's general position.

26. See, especially, Marx's *The German Ideology* and Preface to *A Contribution to the Critique of Political Economy*.

27. "With the change of the economic foundation the entire immense superstructure is more or less rapidly transformed." Preface to Marx's *A Contribution to the Critique of Political Economy*, p. 5. And also see p. 4: "The sum total of these relations of production constitutes the economic structure of society, the real foundation, on which rises a legal and political superstructure and to which correspond definite forms of social consciousness. The mode of production conditions the social, political, and intellectual life process in general. It is not the consciousness of men that determines their being, but, on the contrary, their social being that determines their consciousness."

28. Marx, *Critique of the Gotha Program* (1875, but published in 1891), p. 392.

29. Marx, *Capital*, vol. 1, in ibid., p. 249.

30. Ibid., pp. 250–51.

31. Ibid., Preface to the First German Edition, p. 193.

32. Marx and Engels, *Manifesto of the Communist Party*, p. 345.

33. Ibid., p. 338.

34. Ibid., p. 351.

35. Marx, *The Eighteenth Brumaire of Louis Bonaparte,* pp. 473-74: "By now stigmatising as *'socialistic'* what it had previously extolled as *'liberal,'* the bourgeoisie therefore confesses that its own interest dictates that it should be delivered from the danger of *governing in its own name*; that, in order to restore tranquility in the land, its bourgeois parliament must, first of all, be given its quietus; that in order to preserve its social power inviolate, its political power must be broken; that the private bourgeois can only continue to exploit the other classes and to enjoy undisturbed property, family, religion and order on condition that their class be condemned along with the other classes to like political nullity; that in order to save its purse, it must abandon the crown, and the sword that is to safeguard it must at the same time be hung over its own head like the sword of Damocles." Some critics see in *The Eighteenth Brumaire* Marx's anticipation of fascism.

36. Marx, *Circular Letter to Bebel,* p. 403.

37. Cornford, *The Republic of Plato.* Socrates, in fact, maintains that "both knowledge and truth are to be regarded as like the Good, but to identify either with the Good is wrong" (pt. 3 [bk. 6], chap. 23, p. 220). The "Form or essential nature of Goodness" "gives to the objects of knowledge their truth"; it "is the cause of knowledge and truth" but "beyond truth and knowledge" (p. 220). The myth, "fable," or "fiction" of the metals is in pt. 2 (bk. 3), chap. 10, pp. 106-7. Socrates is, of course, convinced that the just, and harmonious, republic rests upon knowledge—"the real as it is"—and not upon opinion or mere belief *(doxa).* In this sense there is a scientific foundation for the republic (pt. 3 [bk. 5], chap. 19, p. 186). John L. Davies and David J. Vaughan translate the key passage differently—"Science . . . has for its provence to know the nature of the existent" ([bk. 5], p. 478)—in their edition of *The Republic of Plato* (London: Macmillan, 1920), p. 193. The basic point is the same: science, or real knowledge, is to be distinguished from both ignorance and opinion.

38. The Grand Inquisitor is worried about the wrong kind of science, a science that he associates with the "confusion of free thought" and "cannibalism." There is, however, a knowledge that can produce happiness, and one would have to interpret the following basic proposition as a scientific hypothesis if not a scientific law: "There are three powers, three powers alone, able to conquer and to hold captive forever the consciences of these impotent rebels for their own happiness—these forces are miracle, mystery, and authority."

39. Skinner, *Beyond Freedom and Dignity,* p. 215. Skinner is very explicit in holding that "traditional 'knowledge' . . . must be corrected or displaced by a scientific analysis" (p. 19).

40. Marx, "Theses on Feuerbach," p. 1091.

41. See, for example, Marx and Engels', *Manifesto of the Communist Party*; Marx's *Address of the Central Committee to the Communist League,* and his *Letter to*

Bebel. David McLellan notes that "Marx persisted in his view that in Britain a peaceful transition to socialism was possible." See McLellan, *Karl Marx,* p. 44.

42. See Marx, *The Civil War in France,* pp. 526–76, and particularly pt. 3; Marx and Engels, *Manifesto of the Communist Party,* p. 352; and Marx, *The Civil War in France,* p. 557 (for the quotations in the text).

43. "Between capitalist and communist society lies the period of the revolutionary transformation of the one into the other. There corresponds to this also a political transition period in which the state can be nothing but the revolutionary dictatorship of the proletariat." See Marx, *Critique of the Gotha Program,* p. 395. Engels in his 1891 Introduction to *The Civil War in France* wrote: "Of late, the Social-Democratic philistine has once again been filled with wholesome terror at the words: Dictatorship of the Proletariat. Well and good, gentlemen, do you want to know what this dictatorship looks like? Look at the Paris Commune. That was the Dictatorship of the Proletariat"; in ibid., p. 537.

44. Marx, *The Civil War in France,* pp. 552, 554, 555, 557–58.

45. Marx and Engels, earlier, in the *Manifesto of the Communist Party,* (p. 352), saw the need "to increase the total of productive forces in the hands of the state."

46. Marx, *Critique of the Gotha Program,* pp. 368–88.

47. Among other important questions: How will the dictatorship of the proletariat function in making decisions? Will decisions be made by majority vote? In the factories? By governmental representatives? How will decisions about the common good—the public interest of the whole society—be reconciled with decisions made by local governments and by thousands of economic units?

48. See Marx, "For a Ruthless Criticism of Everything Existing," p. 8; and the criticism by Marx and Engels of the utopian socialists in the *Manifesto*; and Marx's *The Civil War in France,* p. 558.

49. Marx, *Manifesto of the Communist Party,* pp. 352–53.

50. Marx, *Critique of the Gotha Program,* p. 388.

51. Marx, *The German Ideology,* pt. 1, p. 395.

52. "Well then . . . do you agree that our scheme of a commonwealth and its constitution has not been a mere day-dream? Difficult it may be, but possible, though only on the one condition we laid down, that genuine philosophers . . . shall come into power in a state. . . . They must send out into the country all citizens who are above ten years old, take over the children, away from the present habits and manners of their parents, and bring them up in their own ways under the institutions we have described." Cornford, *The Republic of Plato,* pt. 3 (bk. 7), chap. 38, p. 262. See also pt. 2 (bk. 3), chap. 10 (on the selection of rulers and their manner of living) and pt. 2 (bk. 5), chap. 16 (on the abolition of the family for guardians). In *The Statesman* and *The*

Laws, by way of contrast to the *Republic,* there is considerable recognition by Plato of the role of prudent judgment.

53. Dostoevski, *The Brothers Karamazov,* bk. 5, chap. 5, p. 260, 262, 263, 267, 269. The universal utopian strain in the Grand Inquisitor is dramatically underscored by his emphasis on the "universal happiness of man," on "universal peace," and on "universal unity" in a "universal state" (p. 267).

54. Skinner, *Walden Two,* p. 225. As Kateb, in *Utopia and Its Enemies,* pp. 205-6, has emphasized, Frazier/Skinner is scornful of democratic politics. He advocates a "social system in which decision-making is vested in a few Planners and Managers, and in which the very idea of citizenship is missing."

55. See Fred L. Polak's rewarding study, *The Image of the Future,* 2 vols. (New York: Oceana, 1961).

56. See Paul Tillich's essay, "Critique and Justification of Utopia," in his chapter, "The Political Meaning of Utopia," in Paul Tillich, *Political Expectation* (New York: Harper & Row, 1971), pp. 168–80. Substantially the same "Critique and Justification of Utopia" is also included as a chapter in Manuel, *Utopias and Utopian Thought,* pp. 296–309. I shall here cite the essay in Manuel. The quote in my text is on p. 297 of *Utopias and Utopian Thought.*

57. Tillich, "Critique and Justification of Utopia," in Manuel, *Utopias and Utopian Thought,* p. 300.

58. Ibid., pp. 297–98.

59. Ibid., p. 298.

60. Ibid., p. 299.

61. See, especially, Erich Fromm, *Escape from Freedom* (New York: Rinehart, 1941).

62. See my argument on "The Sin of Procrustes," in Neal Riemer, *The Revival of Democratic Theory* (New York: Appleton-Century-Crofts, 1962).

63. Tillich, "Critique and Justification of Utopia," in Manuel, *Utopias and Utopian Thought,* p. 299.

64. See Reinhold Niebuhr, *The Children of Light and the Children of Darkness* (New York: Scribner's, 1944).

65. See Marx's *Contribution to the Critique of Hegel's Philosophy of Right. Introduction,* in Tucker, *The Marx-Engels Reader,* p. 22. And also: "Communism is the riddle of history solved, and it knows itself to be this solution." See Marx, *Economic and Philosophical Manuscripts of 1844,* p. 71.

66. A. J. Talmon, *The Origins of Totalitarian Democracy* (London: Secker and Warburg, 1952), p. 252.

67. Ibid., p. 254.

68. Ibid., pp. 1–2.

69. A. J. Talmon, *Political Messianism: The Romantic Phase* (London: Secker and Warburg, 1960), p. 516.

70. Norman Cohn, *The Pursuit of the Millennium: Revolutionary Millenarians and Mystical Anarchists of the Middle Ages,* rev. and enl. (New York: Oxford University Press, 1970), p. 15.

71. Norman Cohn, *The Pursuit of the Millennium* (London: Secker and Warburg, 1957), p. 307. The fuller quotation, linking medieval millenarian and modern totalitarian movements, is not found in the revised and expanded 1970 edition cited above. Did Cohn change his mind about the comparison?

72. Tillich, "Critique and Justification of Utopia," in Manuel, *Utopias and Utopian Thought*, p. 300.

73. Again, see Niehuhr's hard-hitting criticism in *The Children of Light and the Children of Darkness*; and also see, idem, *Moral Man and Immoral Society* (New York: Scribner's, 1932). For other keen critical analyses of the weaknesses of utopian thought, see Karl Popper, *The Open Society and Its Enemies* (Princeton, N.J.: Princeton University Press, 1945); Judith N. Shklar, *After Utopia: The Decline of Political Faith* (Princeton, N.J.: Princeton University Press, 1957); and idem, "The Political Theory of Utopia: From Melancholy to Nostalgia," in Manuel, *Utopias and Utopian Thought*, pp 101–15.

74. Cohn, *The Pursuit of the Millennium*, 1957, p. 310.

75. Ibid., p. 309.

76. Ibid., p. 308.

77. See, particularly, Kateb, *Utopia and Its Enemies*.

78. Tillich sees impotence as the third negative feature of utopia. He maintains that utopia's "untruth and unfruitfulness" lead "inevitably to disillusionment," that such disillusionment is an inevitable consequence of confusing the ambiguously preliminary with the unambiguously ultimate, and that disillusionment leads to fanaticism and terror. "Critique and Justification of Utopia," in Manuel, *Utopias and Utopian Thought*, p. 301.

79. See, here, John Bunzel, *Anti-Politics in America* (New York: Knopf, 1967); Maurice Cranston, ed., *The New Left* (New York: Library Press, 1971); and Bernard Crick, *In Defense of Politics*, 2d ed. (Chicago: University of Chicago Press, 1972).

80. Tillich, "Critique and Justification of Utopia," in Manuel, *Utopias and Utopian Thought*, pp. 306, 307. Tillich's position on rejecting "expectation of perfection within history" is found in his essay on "Religious Socialism," in Tillich, *Political Expectation*. This essay and others in the unit on "The Political Meaning of Utopia," pp. 125–80, should be read for the fuller understanding of Tillich's position.

CHAPTER 4

1. On constitutionalism, see Charles McIlwain, *Constitutionalism—Ancient and Modern* (1940; reprint ed., Ithaca, N.Y.: Cornell University Press, Cornell Paperbacks, 1966); Carl J. Friedrich, *Constitutional Government and Democracy*, rev. ed. (Boston: Ginn, 1950); and Alexander Hamilton, James

Madison, and John Jay, *The Federalist*, ed. Jacob E. Cooke (Cleveland, Ohio: Meridian, 1961). On the liberal democratic state, see A. D. Lindsay, *The Modern Democratic State* (London: Oxford University Press, 1943); J. Roland Pennock, *Liberal Democracy* (New York: Rinehart, 1950); Henry B. Mayo, *An Introduction to Democratic Theory* (New York: Oxford University Press, 1960); Giovanni Sartori, *Democratic Theory* (Detroit, Mich.: Wayne State University Press, 1962); Neal Riemer, *The Revival of Democratic Theory* (New York: Appleton-Century-Crofts, 1962); Carl Cohen, *Democracy* (Athens: Georgia University Press, 1971); Leslie Lipson, *The Democratic Civilization* (New York: Oxford University Press, 1964); and Karl Popper, *The Open Society and Its Enemies* (Princeton, N.J.: Princeton University Press, 1945).

2. See J. Roland Pennock, *Democratic Political Theory* (Princeton, N.J.: Princeton University Press, 1979); Robert A. Dahl, *A Preface to Democratic Theory* (Chicago: University of Chicago Press, 1956); idem, *Polyarchy: Participation and Opposition* (New Haven, Conn.: Yale University Press, 1970); and idem, *After the Revolution? Authority in a Good Society* (New Haven, Conn.: Yale University Press, 1970).

3. See Edward A. Purcell, Jr., *The Crisis of Democratic Theory* (Lexington: University of Kentucky Press, 1973).

4. See, for example, Daniel Bell, *The End of Ideology* (New York: Free Press, 1964).

5. For a sample, see Russell Kirk, *The Conservative Mind* (Chicago: Regnery, 1953); Ludwig von Mises, *Omnipotent Government* (New Haven, Conn.: Yale University Press, 1945); Friedrich Hayek, *The Road to Serfdom* (Chicago: University of Chicago Press, 1944); William F. Buckley, *Up From Liberalism* (New York: Honor Books, 1959); and Robert Nozick, *Anarchy, State, and Utopia* (New York: Basic Books, 1974).

6. For a sample, see Christian Bay, *The Structure of Freedom* (Stanford: Stanford University Press, 1958); Henry S. Kariel, *The Promise of Politics* (Englewood Cliffs, N.J.: Prentice-Hall, 1966); Peter Bachrach, *The Theory of Democratic Elitism* (Boston: Little, Brown, 1967); Robert J. Pranger, *The Eclipse of Citizenship* (New York: Holt, Rinehart and Winston, 1968); Robert Paul Wolff, Barrington Moore, Jr., and Herbert Marcuse, *A Critique of Pure Tolerance* (Boston: Beacon, 1965, p.b. reprint ed. 1969); Victor C. Ferkiss, *The Future of Technological Civilization* (New York: Braziller, 1974); C. B. Macpherson, *Democratic Theory: Essays in Retrieval* (Oxford: Oxford University Press, 1973); and idem, *The Life and Times of Liberal Democracy* (Oxford: Oxford University Press, 1977). Needless to say, these critics on the Left—as well as the critics on the Right—are by no means in agreement on all points in my rough summary in the text.

7. On the vision of constitutional politics, see Aristotle, *Politics*, Benjamin Jowett, trans. (New York: Random House, 1953); James Harrington, *The Political Writings of James Harrington*, Charles Blitzer, ed. (Indianapolis,

266 / FUTURE OF THE DEMOCRATIC REVOLUTION

Ind.: Liberal Arts Press, 1955); John Locke, *Second Treatise on Civil Government* (1690), in *Two Treatises on Constitutional Government*, edited by Peter Laslett (New York: Mentor, 1965); Hamilton, Madison, and Jay, *The Federalist*, edited by Jacob E. Cooke (Cleveland, Ohio: Meridian Press, 1961); Bernard Crick, *In Defense of Politics*, 2d ed. (Chicago: University of Chicago Press, 1972); and Neal Riemer, *The Democratic Experiment* (Princeton, N.J.: Van Nostrand, 1967). The concept of balance is prominent in the constitutional vision from Aristotle to the twentieth century American pluralists—Arthur Bentley, Pendleton Herring, David Truman, and Robert Dahl.

8. James Madison, *The Writings of James Madison*, 9 vols. (New York: G. P. Putnam's Sons, 1900-10), 5: 223 (1788) (Speech in the Virginia Ratifying Convention, 1788). For Madison's fuller views on the nature of man, and the possibilities of politics (which informs this entire paragraph), see Neal Riemer, *James Madison* (New York: Washington Square Press, 1968; New York: Twayne, 1970), particularly pp. 46-50. Although many liberal democrats—particularly those in the pluralist tradition—draw upon the Madisonian perspective, they often fail to understand Madison's fuller and bolder "republican" commitments.

9. Hamilton, Madison, and Jay, *The Federalist*, no. 10.

10. Ibid.

11. See, for example, Bernard Berelson's influential article, "Democratic Theory and Public Opinion," *Public Opinion Quarterly* 16 (Fall 1952): 313-30 (reprinted in Heinz Eulau, Samuel J. Eldersveld, and Morris Janowitz, eds., *Political Behavior* [Glencoe, Ill.: Free Press, 1956]); Joseph A. Schumpeter's equally influential *Capitalism, Socialism, and Democracy* (New York: Harper, 1942); Pendleton Herring's widely read *The Politics of Democracy* (New York: Norton, 1940); Dahl, *After the Revolution?*; idem, *Dilemmas of Pluralist Democracy: Autonomy vs. Control* (New Haven, Conn.: Yale University Press, 1982); and Pennock, *Democratic Political Theory*. For adverse criticism of "The Costs of Realism: Contemporary Restatement of Democracy," see Lane Davis's article with that title in Henry S. Kariel, ed., *Frontiers of Democratic Theory* (New York: Random House, 1970). As settling for less leads to democratic elitism, see Bachrach, *The Theory of Democratic Elitism*.

12. The tradition that leads to these conclusions can be traced from such realists in the pluralist tradition as Arthur Bentley, *The Process of Government* (1908; reprint ed., Cambridge: Harvard University Press, 1967), through Herring, *The Politics of Democracy*, to David B. Truman, *The Governmental Process* (New York: Knopf, 1951), and Robert A. Dahl. Dahl's efforts to develop a more self-critical (and more democratic and progressive) variety of pluralism can be detected in some of his later works—for example, *After the Revolution?* and *Dilemmas of Pluralist Democracy*. A recent critic has labeled this version of pluralism "Pluralism II." See John Manley, "Neopluralism: A Class Analysis of Pluralism I and Pluralism II," *American Political Science Review*

77 (June 1983): 368–83. The responses of those labeled "neopluralists"—C. E. Lindblom and Robert Dahl—are to be found on pp. 384–89 of the same issue of the *Review*. As might be expected, the term *public interest* itself may still figure in the rhetoric of liberal democrats in the pluralist tradition. "Clearly, many private organization compete and cooperate with government in determining the allocation of governmental largess. Pluralists maintain that bargaining among such organization culminates in the 'public interest.' " From Robert V. Presthus, *Men at the Top* (New York: Oxford University Press, 1964), extracted in Kariel, *Frontiers of Democratic Theory*, with quotation in text at pp. 294–95. On the slippery nature of the public interest, and on its use and abuse, see Frank J. Sorauf, "The Public Interest Reconsidered," *Journal of Politics* 19 (November 1957): 616–19; and Richard E. Flathman, *The Public Interest* (New York: Wiley, 1966). On division within the democratic camp on the reality, significance, and justification of public interest and common good, see Purcell, *The Crisis of Democratic Theory*.

13. Madison still best expresses the position summarized here. For Madison's fuller position one must go beyond his numbers in the *The Federalist*; one must, for example, also look to his essays in *The National Gazette* (*The Writings of James Madison*, vol. 6) attacking the policies of the Hamiltonian-lead Federalist Party and the Alien and Sedition Acts, and one must also examine (in vol. 9) his devastating criticism of Calhoun and his followers. For the full development of Madison's political theory, see Riemer, *James Madison*.

14. Constitutionalists still fight over the best way to achieve limited yet strong and effective government. Madison, for example, was an advocate of a strong and effective central government, yet he fought (what he held to be) the plutocratic policies of Hamilton and the Federalists and energetically opposed efforts to limit civil liberties. And, of course, constitutionalism does not necessarily require federalism or a separation of powers. Historically, the balance of social, economic, and political interests has manifested itself in a balance of governmental organs; and social, economic, and political diversity has inhibited a monopoly of social, economic, and political power—and thus the abuse of power.

15. As one moves away from a monolithic theory of political obligation (for example, obedience only to the interest of the state), one almost inevitably has to develop a more sophisticated pluralist theory of obligation and accountability. Pennock, *Liberal Democracy*, has articulated a particularly astute treatment of responsibility. See also my argument on behalf of "pluralistic and conditional obligation" in *The Revival of Democratic Theory*, pp. 135–48. In the text I have focused on the question of the government's responsibility, but the government is composed of men and women who themselves feel a number of loyalties—to the principles that sustain the state, to the principles of religion or natural law, to party, to a majority in the electorate, to powerful economic

interests, and so on. Here, again, diversity and plurality almost dictate the politics of balance and accommodation.

16. On the meaning of representation, and on the role of representatives, see Neal Riemer, ed., *The Representative: Trustee? Delegate? Partisan? Politico?* (Lexington, Mass.: D. C. Heath, 1967).

17. See Dahl, *The Preface to Democratic Theory*, on "minorities rule"; his now classic study *Who Governs?* (New Haven, Conn.: Yale University Press, 1961) for the rejection of the monolithic power elite theory; his *Pluralist Democracy in the United States* (Skokie, Ill.: Rand McNally, 1967); and his *After the Revolution?*, which underscores how the principles of competence and of economy (time) limit citizen participation. Rule by democratic elites is not, of course, the same as rule by an antidemocratic elite, although rule by democratic elites may (and in fact does) inhibit fuller, more genuine, more active citizen participation and may (and in fact does) conceal aristocratic, oligarchic, and plutocratic realities. On the reality of elite rule in American politics, see Thomas Dye and L. Harmon Ziegler, *The Irony of Democracy*, 2d ed. (New York: Duxbury, 1972).

18. See, again, Bell, *The End of Ideology*. The stress on stability, on equilibrium, on order, can be seen in the theoretical models of Talcott Parsons, David Easton, and Gabriel Almond and Sidney Verba, as well as in the guiding theory and empirical inquiries of such students as Samuel Huntington.

19. C. B. Macpherson, in *The Real World of Democracy* (Oxford: Oxford University Press, 1966), pp. 6, 39, emphasizes the prominence of the principle of choice in liberal democracy.

20. Henry S. Kariel stresses the conservative character of pluralistic politics in his *The Decline of American Pluralism* (Stanford: Stanford University Press, 1961). One of the best defenses of the politics of pluralistic balance remains Herring's *The Politics of Democracy*. See also the writing of Robert Dahl on the virtues—and the difficulties—of pluralistic balance.

21. On the strengths of the idealistic-realistic model of liberal democratic politics, see (in addition to Herring, Dahl, and Pennock) Reinhold Niebuhr, *The Children of Light and the Children of Darkness* (New York: Scribner's, 1944); and Gabriel A. Almond and Sidney Verba, *The Civic Culture* (Princeton, N.J.: Princeton University Press, 1963).

22. Fred L. Polak, *The Image of the Future*, 2 vols. (New York: Oceana, 1961) (Elsevier Scientific, 1973); Sheldon Wolin, *Politics and Vision* (Boston: Little, Brown, 1960); Henry S. Kariel, *The Promise of Politics*; Bay, *The Structure of Freedom*; Michael Harrington, *Socialism* (New York: Bantam Books, 1973); Dennis F. Thompson, *The Democratic Citizen* (London: Cambridge University Press, 1970); Robert W. Friedrichs, *A Sociology of Sociology* (1970) (New York: Free Press, 1972). See also the critics cited in Herman Belz, "New Left Reverberations in the Academy: The Antipluralist Critique of Constitutionalism," *Review of Politics* 36 (April 1974): 265–83.

23. In addition to the excellent collection in Kariel, *Frontiers of Democratic Theory*, and Belz, "New Left Reverberations," see also Charles A. McCoy and John Playford, eds., *Apolitical Politics* (New York: Crowell, 1967); Christian Bay, "Politics and Pseudopolitics: A Critical Evaluation of Some Behavioral Literature," *American Political Science Review* 59 (March 1965): 39–51; Michael Harrington, *The Other America: Poverty in the United States* (New York: Macmillan, 1962); Michael Parenti, *Democracy for the Few*, 3d ed. (New York: St. Martin's Press, 1980).

24. On the subject of creative breakthroughs, see Neal Riemer, "Creative Breakthroughs in Politics," *Political Inquiry* 2 (1974): 1–22; and idem, *Political Science: An Introduction to Politics* (New York: Harcourt Brace Jovanovich, 1983). On the need for "reconstructive ideals" that can help to preserve the tension between what ought to be and what is, see Thompson, *The Democratic Citizen*. For Madison's eloquent plea for bold and creative prudential action, see *The Federalist,*, no. 14.

25. See, again, Kariel, *Frontiers of Democratic Theory*, and Belz, "New Left Reverberations." Belz, it should be clear, is attempting to summarize, analyze, and criticize these "reverberations." He does not endorse their analysis and their call for bolder action and judgment.

26. Belz, "New Left Reverberations," explicitly warns against this temptation. Although there are problems for constitutionalism inherent in the reforms Belz identifies with the New Left—"civil disobedience as a source of political renewal," "democratization of economic organization," "a new theory of politics based upon a revival of citizenship"—I do not interpret these as destructive of constitutionalism. Belz, however, holds that civil disobedience might "more likely" lead to "an expedient people's justice than constitutional government as we have known it historically" and warns of the possible dangers of the "new politics" (pp. 271, 272–79).

CHAPTER 5

1. Among the modern political philosophers who have thoroughly appreciated the importance of the religious dimension in politics is Carl J. Friedrich. See Friedrich's *Transcendent Justice—The Religious Dimension of Constitutionalism* (Durham, N.C.: Duke University Press, 1964).

2. See A. J. Talmon, *Political Messianism: The Romantic Phase* (London: Secker and Warburg, 1960), p. 514.

3. See Neal Riemer, "Covenant and the Federal Constitution," *Publius* 10 (Fall 1980): 135–48. In the following paragraphs I have drawn extensively upon this article. This entire issue of *Publius*, edited by Daniel J. Elazar, is entitled "Covenant, Polity, and Constitutionalism."

4. On the dangers of a "mad messianism," see Talmon's *Political Messianism: The Romantic Phase*, p. 516, and also his *The Origins of Totalitarian Democracy* (London: Secker and Warburg, 1952), pp. 1–2, 252, 254. On this theme, see also Norman Cohn, *The Pursuit of the Millennium: Revolutionary Millenarians and Mystical Anarchists of the Middle Ages* (1957) rev. ed. (New York: Oxford University Press, 1970).

5. See my argument in Neal Riemer, *The Democratic Experiment* (Princeton, N.J.: Van Nostrand, 1967).

6. Carl J. Friedrich, *Limited Government: A Comparison* (Englewood Cliffs, N.J.: Prentice-Hall, 1974), p. 120. See also Friedrich's *Transcendent Justice*.

7. In this analysis I will, again, draw fully upon my article "Covenant and the Federal Constitution," pp. 136–48.

8. See Edward S. Corwin, *The "Higher Law" Background of American Constitutional Law (1928–1929)* (Ithaca, N.Y.: Cornell University Press, 1955).

9. On the relationship between prophetic standards and the religion of the American republic, see Samuel Huntington's recent book in which he cites Sidney Mead's contention that (in Mead's words) the "religion of the Republic is essentially prophetic." America's "ideals and aspirations," wrote Mead, "stand in constant judgment over the passing shenanigans of the people, reminding them of the standards by which their current practices and those of their nation are ever being judged and found wanting." For the quotation, see Samuel P. Huntington, *American Politics: The Promise of Disharmony* (Cambridge: Harvard University Press, 1981), p. 30.

10. I am indebted to the late Herman Finer for calling this quotation to my attention.

11. See also Neal Riemer, *James Madison* (New York: Washington Square Press, 1968; New York: Twayne, 1970), p. 48; idem, *The Democratic Experiment*, pp. 113, 158.

12. See also Ralph H. Gabriel, *The Course of American Democratic Thought* (New York: Ronald Press, 1940), especially pp. 22–25.

13. Ibid., pp. 19, 399 ff.

14. See Riemer, *James Madison,* pp. 25, 170.

15. See here Reinhold Niebuhr, *The Nature and Destiny of Man,* 2 vols. (1941) (New York: Scribner's, 1949), p. 143.

16. See Neal Riemer, "The Civil Religion in America and Prophetic Politics," *Drew Gateway* 44 (Fall 1973): 20–32; and idem, "Watergate and Prophetic Politics," *Review of Politics* 36 (April 1974): 284–97.

17. See Jean Jacques Rousseau, *The Social Contract*, ch. 8, pp. 106–15 in *The Social Contract and the Discourses,* translated by G. D. H. Cole (New York: Dutton, 1946). For an excellent introduction to the concept of the civil religion, see Russell E. Richey and Donald G. Jones, eds., *American Civil Religion* (New York: Harper & Row, 1974).

18. See, again, Riemer, *The Democratic Experiment*; and idem, *The Revival of Democratic Theory* (New York: Appleton-Century-Crofts, 1962). Also on the democratic strand, see A. D. Lindsay, *The Modern Democratic State* (London: Oxford University Press, 1943); and J. Roland Pennock, *Liberal Democracy: Its Merits and Prospects* (New York: Rinehart, 1950). On the concept of the least free, see Christian Bay, *The Structure of Freedom* (Stanford: Stanford University Press, 1958); and idem, *Strategies of Political Emancipation* (Notre Dame: University of Notre Dame Press, 1981). The prophetic standard under which American democracy operates is also emphasized, as I noted in n. 9, by Sidney Mead.

19. See Jacob Bronowski, *Science and Human Values* (New York: Harper Torchbook, 1959); and idem, *The Common Sense of Science* (Cambridge: Harvard University Press, 1953).

20. For the debt to Greek philosophy, see Werner Jaeger, *Paideia: The Ideals of Greek Culture*, 3 vols. (New York: Oxford University Press, 1939–44), particularly vol. 2, *In Search of the Divine Center*. For both the debt to Greek and natural law philosophy, see also George H. Sabine, *A History of Political Theory* (New York: Holt, 1937).

21. On the role of the Enlightenment, see the early work of Carl Becker, *The Heavenly City of the Eighteenth Century Philosophers* (New Haven, Conn.: Yale University Press, 1932); Alfred Cobban, *In Search of Humanity: The Role of the Enlightenment in Modern History*; Peter Gay, *The Enlightenment: An Interpretation* (New York: Knopf, 1966); and idem, *The Science of Freedom* (New York: Knopf, 1969). Ironically, the philosophes were often hostile to religion, largely, of course, because of their opposition to religious bigotry and superstition. They were not consciously fulfilling a religiously orthodox prophetic position (any more than Greek political philosophers were). Yet if the philosophes were, in a sense, modern pagans, as Gay argues, they illustrated a secular prophetic impulse. Writes Gay in *The Enlightenment*: "The men of the Enlightenment united on a vastly ambitious program, a program of secularism, humanity, cosmopolitanism, and freedom, above all, freedom in its many forms—freedom from arbitrary power, freedom of speech, freedom of trade, freedom to realize one's talents, freedom of aesthetic response, freedom, in a world, of moral man to make his own way in the world" (p. 3). Two American philosophes, Jefferson and Madison, splendidly illustrate the translation of constitutional theory into constitutional practice.

22. Mic. 4: 3; Isa. 2:4.

23. Mic. 6:8.

24. Isa. 58:7.

25. Isa. 58:6–7.

CHAPTER 6

1. Mic. 3: 3; and Isa. 10: 2. See also Amos 8: 4; and Isa. 3: 15; 10: 1–2; 59: 8–9, 14–15.

2. See Martin Buber, *The Prophetic Faith* (1949) (New York: Harper Torchbook, 1960); R. E. Clements, *Prophecy and Tradition* (Atlanta, Ga.: John Knox Press, 1975); and John Paterson, *The Goodly Fellowship of the Prophets* (New York: Scribner's, 1948); Gerhard von Rad, *The Message of the Prophets* (New York: Harper & Row, 1967).

3. This is Fred L. Polak's phrase in *The Image of the Future,* 2 vols. (New York: Oceana, 1961).

4. Here, and in the following pages exploring the four major concerns of prophetic criticism, I have drawn upon my analysis in Neal Riemer, *Political Science: An Introduction to Politics* (New York: Harcourt Brace Jovanovich, 1983), particularly chaps. 16, 17, 18, and 19.

5. A. H. Robertson, "Human Rights: A Global Assessment," in *Human Rights and American Foreign Policy*, eds. Donald P. Kommers and Gilburt D. Loescher (Notre Dame: University of Notre Dame Press, 1979), p. 7; also quoted in Riemer, *Political Science*, p. 375.

6. Quoted in Riemer, *Political Science*, p. 378.

7. Former Secretary of State Cyrus R. Vance, quoted in ibid., p. 368.

8. On the plight of the poor, see also Ruth Leger Sivard, *World Military and Social Expenditures, 1983* (Washington, D.C.: World Priorities, 1983).

9. The phrase is that of William Ophuls, quoted in Riemer, *Political Science*, p. 424. See Ophuls's *Ecology and the Politics of Scarcity* (San Francisco: Freeman, 1977).

10. There are, of course, those who are more optimistic about our ecological future. See Herman Kahn, William Brown, and Leon Martel, *The Next 200 Years* (New York: Morrow, 1976); and Julian L. Simon, *The Ultimate Resource* (Princeton, N.J.: Princeton University Press, 1981). For a more sobering assessment, see Gerald O. Barney, director, *The Global 2000 Report to the President: Entering the Twenty-First Century*, vol. 1 (Washington, D.C.: Government Printing Office, 1980).

11. This is Paul Tillich's phrase in his essay on utopia in Frank E. Manuel, ed., *Utopias and Utopian Thought* (Boston: Beacon Press, 1967), pp. 297, 298. This same essay is found in Tillich's *Political Expectation* (New York: Harper & Row, 1971).

12. No major systematic effort has yet been undertaken to develop the modern theory of prophetic criticism outlined here.

CHAPTER 7

1. In this chapter I have drawn upon a number of my earlier works. See Neal Riemer, "Creative Breakthroughs in Politics," 2 (1974): 1–22; also see

my book-length study of Madison's political philosophy in idem, *James Madison* (New York: Washington Square Press, 1968; Boston: Twayne, 1970); and finally, see my essays on Williams and Madison in idem, *The Democratic Experiment* (Princeton, N.J.: Van Nostrand, 1967).

2. For a sample of the literature on Roger Williams and the theory of religious liberty, see Samuel H. Brockunier, *The Irrepressible Democrat: Roger Williams* (New York: Ronald, 1940); James Ernest, *The Political Thought of Roger Williams* (Seattle: University of Washington Press, 1929); William Haller, *Liberty and Reformation in the Puritan Revolution* (New York: Columbia University Press, 1955); W. K. Jordan, *The Development of Toleration in England*, 4 vols. (Cambridge: Harvard University Press, 1933–40); Perry Miller, *Roger Williams: His Contribution to the American Tradition* (New York: Bobbs-Merrill, 1953); Irwin H. Polishook, *Roger Williams, John Cotton and Religious Freedom: A Controversy in New and Old England* (Englewood Cliffs, N.J.: Prentice-Hall, 1967).

3. For a sample of the literature on Madison and the theory of the extensive republic, see Irving Brant's splendid six-volume biography, *James Madison*, 6 vols. (Indianapolis, Ind.: Bobbs-Merrill, 1941–61); or the one-volume summary, in idem, *The Fourth President* (Indianapolis, Ind.: Bobbs-Merrill, 1970). Also see Ralph Ketcham, *James Madison: A Biography* (New York: Macmillan, 1971); Adrienne Koch, *Jefferson and Madison: The Great Collaboration* (New York: Knopf, 1950); Marvin Meyers, *The Mind of the Founders: Sources of the Political Thought of James Madison* (Indianapolis, Ind.: Bobbs-Merrill, 1973); Harold S. Schultz, *James Madison* (New York: Twayne, 1971), and Riemer, *James Madison*.

4. My understanding of Calhoun owes a great deal to Louis Hartz, *The Liberal Tradition in America* (New York: Harcourt Brace, 1955); and to Richard Hofstadter, *The American Political Tradition and the Men Who Made It* (New York: Knopf, 1948). I have been unimpressed by those studies that see Calhoun as a great political philosopher.

CHAPTER 8

1. My analysis in this chapter draws upon my exploration of these four areas of concern in Neal Riemer, *Political Science: An Introduction to Politics*, especially chap. 16, pp 363–64; 17, pp. 389–91; 18, pp. 415–18 and 19, pp. 439–41. From *Political Science: An Introduction to Politics*, copyright © 1983 by Harcourt Brace Jovanovich, Inc. Reprinted with permission of the publisher.

2. On the quest for peace, see Francis A. Beer, *Peace against War: The Ecology of International Violence* (San Francisco: Freeman, 1981); Richard A. Falk, *A Study of Future Worlds* (New York: Free Press, 1975); James M. Fallows, *National Defense* (New York: Random House, 1981); Harvard

Nuclear Study Group, *Living with Nuclear Weapons* (New York: Bantam, 1983); Stanley Hoffmann, *Duties beyond Borders: On the Limits and Possibilities of Ethical International Politics* (Syracuse, N.Y: Syracuse University Press, 1981); Robert C. Johansen, *The National Interest and the Human Interest* (Princeton, N.J.: Princeton University Press, 1980); Gerald Mische and Patricia Mische, *Toward a Human World Order: Beyond the National Security Straitjacket* (New York: Paulist Press, 1977); and David A. Mitrany, *A Working Peace System: An Argument for the Functional Development of International Organization*, 4th ed. (London: National Peace Council, 1946).

3. George F. Kennan, "Reflections: Two Views of the Soviet Problem," *New Yorker*, November 2, 1981, pp. 54–62. Also see idem, "A Modest Proposal," *New York Review of Books*, July 16, 1981, pp. 14, 16; also quoted in Riemer, *Political Science*, p. 360.

4. On the quest for human rights, see Richard A. Falk, *Human Rights and State Sovereignty* (New York: Holmes and Meir, 1981); Vivian Gornick and Barbara K. Moran, eds., *Woman in Sexist Society* (New York: Free Press, 1975); Natalie Kaufman Hevener, ed., *The Dynamics of Human Rights in American Foreign Policy* (New Brunswick, N.J.: Transaction Books, 1981); Donald P. Kommers and Gilburt D. Loescher, eds., *Human Rights and American Foreign Policy* (Notre Dame, Ind.: University of Notre Dame Press, 1979); Jeane J. Kirkpatrick, *Dictatorships and Double Standards: Rationalism and Reason in Politics* (New York: American Enterprise/Simon and Schuster, 1982); Paul Newburg, ed., *U.S. Foreign Policy and Human Rights* (New York: New York University Press, 1981); Jonathan Powers, *Amnesty International: The Human Rights Story* (New York: McGraw-Hill, 1981); Edward James Schuster, *Human Rights Today: Revolution or Evolution?* (New York: Philosophical Library, 1981); U.S., Department of State, *Country Reports on Human Rights Practices* (Washington, D.C.: Government Printing Office, yearly); and Vernon Van Dyke, *Human Rights, the United States, and World Community* (New York: Oxford University Press, 1970).

5. On the quest for economic well-being, see Peter L. Berger, *Pyramids of Sacrifice: Political Ethics and Social Change* (Garden City, N.Y.: Anchor Press, Doubleday, 1976); Willy Brandt, chairman, Independent Commission on International Development, *North-South: A Program for Survival* (Cambridge: MIT Press, 1980); Harrison S. Brown, *The Human Future Revisited: The World Predicament and Possible Solutions* (New York: Norton, 1978); Susan George, *How the Other Half Dies: The Real Reason for World Hunger* (New York: Ballantine Press, 1978); William Loehr and John P. Powelson, Jr., eds., *Economic Development, Poverty, and Income Distribution* (Boulder, Colo.: Westview Press, 1977); Gunnar Myrdal, *The Challenge of World Poverty* (New York: Pantheon Books, Random House, 1970); and Ruth Leger Sivard, *World Military and Social Expenditures, 1983* (Washington, D.C.: World Priorities, 1983). On proposed rich nations-poor nations ratios, see Neal Riemer, *Political Science: An Introduction to Politics*, p. 417, footnote 24.

6. On the quest for ecological balance, see Gerald O. Barney, director, *The Global 2000 Report to the President: Entering the Twenty-First Century*, vol 1 (Washington, D.C.: Government Printing Office, 1980); Paul Ehrlich and Anne Ehrlich, *Population, Resources, Environment* (San Francisco: Freeman, 1972); Victor C. Ferkiss, *The Future of Technological Civilization* (New York: Braziller, 1974); Garrett Hardin, *Exploring New Ethics for Survival* (New York: Viking, 1972); Herman Kahn, William Brown, and Leon Martel, *The Next 200 Years: A Scenario for America and the World* (New York: Morrow, 1976); William Ophuls, *Ecology and the Politics of Scarcity* (San Francisco: Freeman, 1977); David W. Orr and Marvis S. Sorros, eds., *The Global Predicament: Ecological Perspectives on World Order* (Chapel Hill: University of North Carolina Press, 1979); Dennis Pirages, *Global Ecopolitics: The New Context for International Relations* (North Scituate, Mass.: Duxbury Press, 1978); and Julian L. Simon, *The Ultimate Resource* (Princeton, N.J.: Princeton University Press, 1981).

CHAPTER 9

1. The task of continuous prophetic scrutiny and futuristic projection has been aided by a number of students. Some, in my judgment, are in the prophetic tradition; others are not. All, however, whether we agree or disagree with their perspectives, are serious students of the future. See, for example, Richard A. Falk, *A Study of Future Worlds* (New York: Free Press, 1975); Victor C. Ferkiss, *The Future of Technological Civilization* (New York: Braziller, 1974); Harvey Wheeler, *Democracy in a Revolutionary Era* (New York: Praeger, 1968); Gerald Mische and Patricia Mische, *Toward a Human World Order: Beyond the National Security Straitjacket* (New York: Paulist Press, 1977); Gene Sharp, *Exploring Nonviolent Alternatives* (Boston: Porter Sargent, 1971); idem, *The Politics of Nonviolent Action* (Boston: Porter Sargent, 1973); Kenneth Boulding, *The Meaning of the Twentieth Century* (Evanston, Ill.: Harper & Row, 1964); Andrei P. Sakharov, *Progress, Coexistence, and Intellectual Freedom* (New York: Norton, 1968); William Ophuls, *Ecology and the Politics of Scarcity* (San Francisco: Freeman, 1977); Erich Fromm, *The Revolution of Hope: Toward a Humanized Technology* (New York: Bantam Books, 1968); Warren W. Wagar, *Building the City of Man* (New York: Grossman, 1971); L. S. Stavrianos, *The Promise of the Coming Dark Age* (San Francisco: Freeman, 1976); Paul Hawken, James Ogilvy, Peter Schwartz, *Seven Tomorrows* (New York: Bantam Books, 1982); Daniel Bell, *The Coming of Post-Industrial Society* (New York: Basic Books, 1973); Herman Kahn, William Brown, and Leon Martel, *The Next 200 Years: A Scenario for America and the World* (New York: Morrow, 1976); Robert Heilbroner, *The Human Prospect: Updated and Reconsidered for the 1980s*, rev. ed. (New York: Norton, 1982); and Irving Howe, ed., *1984 Revisited: Totalitarianism in Our Century* (New York: Harper & Row, 1983). For a more

extended criticism of three political futurists (Falk, Ferkiss, and Stavrianos), see Neal Riemer, "Prophetic Politics: On the Political Philosophy of Stavrianos, Ferkiss and Falk," *Alternative Futures* 2 (Fall 1979): 66–82. They are struggling, I argue, but not with entire success, to move beyond a utopian politics to a more prophetic politics. They do not persuasively present a cogent theory of transition from present to future, and they do not address more completely the politics of the long-range future—extraordinarily difficult but necessary tasks for political futurists.

2. Here I have drawn upon chap. 20, "The Challenging Future of Political Science," of Neal Riemer, *Political Science: An Introduction to Politics*, pp. 449–51. From *Political Science: An Introduction to Politics* by Neal Riemer, copyright © 1983 by Harcourt Brace Jovanovich, Inc. Reprinted with permission of the publisher.

3. See also, for example, Louis Rene Beres, *Apocalypse: Nuclear Catastrophe in World Politics* (Chicago: University of Chicago Press, 1980).

4. For a thoughtful analysis of the past and present of totalitarianism that also sheds light on the future of totalitarianism, see Richard Lowenthal's "Beyond Totalitarianism," in Howe, *1984 Revisited*, pp. 209–67.

5. See, for example, Heilbroner, *The Human Prospect*; and also Bertram Gross, *Friendly Fascism: The New Face of Power in America* (New York: Evans, 1980).

6. See Falk, *A Study of Future Worlds*, p. 307.

7. Ibid., p. 237.

8. Ibid., p. 246.

9. Ibid.

10. Ibid., pp. 249, 248–51.

11. Ibid., pp. 324, 327, 328, 329, 333, 335.

12. See, again, Riemer, "Prophetic Politics."

CHAPTER 10

1. See Neal Riemer, *The Democratic Experiment* (Princeton, N.J.: Van Nostrand, 1967); and idem, "The Tradition of Prophetic Politics: 1776 and 1787—A Religious Model for Interpreting American Politics," *Drew Gateway* 52 (Winter 1982): 23–36.

2. These quotations are from Jefferson's *The Declaration of Independence*; letter from Jefferson to Madison, December 20, 1787, in Saul K. Padover, ed., *The Complete Jefferson* (New York: Duell, Sloan and Pearce, 1943), pp. 129–30; and Jefferson's First Inaugural Address, March 4, 1801, in Padover, *The Complete Jefferson*, p. 386.

3. Alexis de Tocqueville, *Democracy in America* (1835); ed. Phillips Bradley, 2 vols. reprint ed. (New York: Knopf, 1946), 1:7.

4. Gaillard Hunt, ed., *The Writing of James Madison*, 9 vols. (New York:

Putnam's, 1900–10), 6:85. See also chap. 6, "The Anti-Republican Danger and Democratic Politics," in Neal Riemer, *James Madison* (New York: Washington Square Press, 1968; New York: Twayne, 1970).

5. See George Orwell, *1984* (1949) (New York: New American Library, 1983); Aldous Huxley, *Brave New World* (Garden City, N.Y.: Doubleday, 1932). See also Irving Howe, ed., *1984 Revisited: Totalitarianism in Our Century* (New York: Harper & Row, 1983); and Aldous Huxley, *Brave New World Revisited* (New York: Harper, 1958).

6. My own conviction about the probability of the possibility of a more prophetic politics—rooted in a superior ethical vision, a more generous and yet more realistic understanding of political reality, and a bolder and more far-sighted sense of political becoming—has been reinforced by the words and deeds of a number of twentieth century figures. Here I single out a few of these figures. Thus, among religious writers and leaders: Abraham J. Heschel, Paul Tillich, Pope John XXIII, and Martin Luther King; among philosophers and psychologists: John Dewey, Eric Fromm, and Abraham Maslow; among social scientists: Kenneth Boulding, Gunnar Myrdal, Fred Polak, and Richard A. Falk; and among physical and biological scientists: Albert Einstein, Rene Dubos, and Harrison Brown.

Bibliography

Almond, Gabriel A., and Verba, Sidney. *The Civic Culture*. Princeton, N.J.: Princeton University Press, 1963.

Aristotle. *Politics*. Benjamin Jowett, trans. New York: Random House, 1943.

Avineri, Schlomo. *The Social and Political Thought of Karl Marx*. Cambridge: Cambridge University Press, 1968.

Bachrach, Peter. *The Theory of Democratic Elitism*. Boston: Little, Brown, 1967.

Bailyn, Bernard. *The Ideological Origin of the American Revolution*. Cambridge: Harvard University Press, Belknap Press, 1967.

Barker, Ernest. *Principles of Social and Political Theory*. Oxford: Oxford University Press, 1951.

Barney, Gerald O., director. *The Global 2000 Report to the President: Entering the Twenty-First Century*. Vol. 1. Washington, D.C.: U.S. Government Printing Office, 1980.

Bauer, Raymond A., ed. *Social Indicators*. Cambridge: MIT Press, 1966.

Bay, Christian. *The Structure of Freedom*. Stanford, Calif.: Stanford University Press, 1958.

———. "Politics and Pseudopolitics: A Critical Evaluation of Some Behavioral Literature." *American Political Science Review* 59 (March 1965): 139–51.

———. *Strategies of Political Emancipation*. Notre Dame, Ind.: University of Notre Dame Press, 1981.

Becker, Carl. *The Heavenly City of the Eighteenth Century Philosophers*. New Haven, Conn.: Yale University Press, 1932.

Beer, Francis A. *Peace against War: The Ecology of International Violence*. San Francisco: Freeman, 1981.

Bell, Daniel. *The End of Ideology*. New York: Free Press, 1964.

———. *The Coming of Post-Industrial Society*. New York: Basic Books, 1973.

Bell, Daniel, ed. *Toward the Year 2000*. Boston: Houghton Mifflin, 1968.

Belz, Herman. "New Left Reverberations in the Academy: The Anti-pluralist Critique of Constitutionalism." *Review of Politics* 36 (April 1974): 265–83.

Bentley, Arthur. *The Process of Government*. 1908. Reprint. Cambridge: Harvard University Press, 1967.

Berelson, Bernard. "Democratic Theory and Public Opinion." *Public Opinion Quarterly* 16 (Fall 1952): 313–30.

Beres, Louis René. *Apocalypse: Nuclear Catastrophe in World Politics*. Chicago: University of Chicago Press, 1980.

Berger, Peter L. *Pyramids of Sacrifice: Political Ethics and Social Change*. Garden City, N.Y.: Anchor Press, Doubleday, 1976.

Berlin, Isaiah. *Karl Marx: His Life and Environment.* 1939. New York: Oxford University Press, 1959.

———— . "The Question of Machiavelli." *New York Review of Books,* November 4, 1971, pp. 20–32.

———— . *Against the Current.* New York: Penguin Books, 1982.

Boulding, Kenneth. *The Meaning of the Twentieth Century.* Evanston, Ill.: Harper & Row, 1964.

Brandt, Willy, chairman, Independent Commission on International Development. *North-South: A Program for Survival.* Cambridge: MIT Press, 1980.

Brant, Irving. *James Madison.* 6 vols. Indianapolis, Ind.: Bobbs-Merrill, 1946–61.

———— . *The Fourth President.* Indianapolis, Ind.: Bobbs-Merrill, 1970.

Brinton, Crane. "Utopia and Democracy." In Frank M. Manuel, ed., *Utopias and Utopian Thought* (Boston: Beacon Press, 1967), pp. 50–68.

Brockunier, Samuel H. *The Irrepressible Democrat: Roger Williams.* New York: Ronald, 1940.

Bronowski, Jacob. *The Common Sense of Science.* Cambridge: Harvard University Press, 1953.

———— . *Science and Human Values.* New York: Harper Torchbook, 1959.

Brown, Harrison S. *The Challenge of Man's Future.* New York: Viking, 1954.

———— . *The Human Future Revisited: The World Predicament and Possible Solutions.* New York: Norton, 1978.

Brown, Stuart Gerry. *The First Republicans: Political Philosophy and Public Policy in the Party of Jefferson and Madison.* Syracuse, N.Y.: Syracuse University Press, 1954.

Buber, Martin. *Paths in Utopia* 1949. Boston: Beacon Press, 1958.

———— . *The Prophetic Faith* 1949. Reprint. New York: Harper Torchbook, 1960.

Buckley, William F. *Up from Liberalism.* New York: Honor Books, 1959.

Bunzel, John. *Anti-Politics in America.* New York: Knopf, 1967.

Clements, R. E. *Prophecy and Tradition.* Atlanta, Ga.: John Knox Press, 1975.

Cobban, Alfred. *In Search of Humanity: The Role of the Enlightenment in Modern History.* New York: Braziller, 1960.

Cohen, Carl. *Democracy.* Athens: Georgia University Press, 1971.

Cohn, Norman. *The Pursuit of the Millennium: Revolutionary Millenarians and Mystical Anarchists of the Middle Ages.* 1957. New York: Oxford University Press, rev. ed., 1970.

Commager, Henry Steele. *Jefferson, Nationalism, and the Enlightenment.* New York: Braziller, 1975.

Cornford, F. M., ed. *The Republic of Plato.* New York: Oxford, 1945.

Corwin, Edward S. *The "Higher Law" Background of American Constitutional Law (1928–1929).* Ithaca, N.Y.: Cornell University Press, 1955.

Cranston, Maurice, ed. *The New Left*. New York: Library Press, 1971.

Crick, Bernard. *In Defense of Politics*. 2d ed. Chicago: University of Chicago Press, 1972.

Current, Richard N. *John C. Calhoun*. New York: Washington Square Press, 1963.

Dahl, Robert A. *A Preface to Democratic Theory*. Chicago: University of Chicago Press, 1956.

_____. *Who Governs?* New Haven, Conn.: Yale University Press, 1961.

_____. *Pluralist Democracy in the United States*. Skokie, Ill.: Rand McNally, 1967.

_____. *After the Revolution? Authority in a Good Society*. New Haven, Conn.: Yale University Press, 1970.

_____. *Polyarchy: Participation and Opposition*. New Haven, Conn.: Yale University Press, 1971.

_____. *Dilemmas of Pluralist Democracy: Autonomy vs. Control*. New Haven, Conn.: Yale University Press, 1982.

Dahrendorf, Ralf. *Class Conflict in Industrial Society*. Palo Alto, Calif.: Stanford University Press. 1959.

D'Amato, Anthony. "The Relevance of Machiavelli to Contemporary World Politics." In Anthony Parel, ed., *The Political Calculus: Essays on Machiavelli's Philosophy* (Toronto: University of Toronto Press, 1972).

Davis, Lane. "The Costs of Realism: Contemporary Restatements of Democracy." *Western Political Quarterly* 17 (1964): 37–46. Reprinted in Henry Kanel, ed., *Frontiers of Democratic Theory* (New York: Random House, 1970).

de Sanctis, Francesco. *Storia della letterature italiano*. Vol. 2. Milan: Feltrinelli Editore, 1956.

Dewey, John. *A Common Faith*. New Haven, Conn.: Yale University Press, 1934.

Dostoevski, Fyodor. *The Brothers Karamazov*. New York: Random House, Modern Library Edition, 1950.

Dubos, Rene. *So Human an Animal*. New York: Scribner's, 1968.

_____. *Reason Awake*. New York: Columbia University Press, 1970.

_____. *A God Within*. New York: Scribner's, 1972.

Dye, Thomas, and Ziegler, L. Harmon. *The Irony of Democracy*. 2d ed. New York: Duxbury, 1972.

Easton, David. *The Political System*. New York: Knopf, 1963.

Ehrlich, Paul, and Ehrlich, Anne. *Population, Resources, Environment*. San Francisco: Freeman, 1972.

Elazar, Daniel J., ed. "Covenant, Polity, and Constitutionalism." *Publius* 10 (Fall 1980): 1–185.

Ernest, James. *The Political Thought of Roger Williams*. Seattle: University of Washington Press, 1929.

Etzioni, Amitai. *The Active Society*. New York: Free Press, 1968.

Eulau, Heinz; Eldersveld, Samuel J.; and Janowitz, Morris, eds. *Political Behavior*. Glencoe, Ill.: Free Press, 1956.

Falk, Richard A. *This Endangered Planet*. New York: Random House, 1971.

———. *A Study of Future Worlds*. New York: Random House, 1975

———. *Human Rights and State Sovereignty*. New York: Holmes and Meir, 1981.

Fallows, James M. *National Defense*. New York: Free Press, 1981.

Ferkiss, Victor C. *Technological Man: The Myth and the Reality*. New York: Braziller, 1969.

———. *The Future of Technological Civilization*. New York: Braziller, 1974.

———. *Futurology: Promise, Performance, Prospects*. Beverly Hills, Calif.: Sage, 1977.

Flathman, Richard E. *The Public Interest*. New York: Wiley, 1966.

Fleisher, Martin, ed. *Machiavelli and the Nature of Political Thought*. New York: Atheneum, 1972.

Fowler, Robert Booth, ed. "Religion and Politics." *Humanities in Society* 6 (Winter 1983): 1–126.

Frederick the Great. *Réfutation du Prince de Machiavel*, 1739 in *Oeuvres de Frédéric II, Roi de Prusse*. In De Lamar Jensen, ed., *Machiavelli: Cynic, Patriot, or Political Scientist?* (Boston: D. C. Heath, 1960).

Friedrich, Carl J. *Constitutional Government and Democracy*. Rev. ed. Boston: Ginn, 1950.

———. *Man and His Government*. New York: McGraw-Hill, 1963.

———. *Transcendent Justice—The Religious Dimension of Constitutionalism*. Durham, N.C.: Duke University Press, 1964.

———. *Limited Government: A Comparison*. Englewood Cliffs, N.J.: Prentice-Hall, 1974.

Friedrichs, Robert W. *The Sociology of Sociology*. New York: Free Press, 1972.

Fromkin, David. *The Independence of Nations*. New York: Praeger, 1981.

Fromm, Erich. *Escape from Freedom*. New York: Rinehart, 1941.

———. *The Sane Society*. New York: Holt, Rinehart and Winston, 1955.

———. *Marx's Concept of Man*. New York: Ungar, 1961.

———. *You Shall Be as Gods*. Greenwich, Conn.: Fawcett, 1966.

———. *The Revolution of Hope: Toward a Humanized Technology*. New York: Bantam Books, 1968.

Fuller, Buckminster R. *Utopia or Oblivion: The Prospects for Humanity*. New York: Bantam Books, 1968.

Gabor, Dennis. *Inventing the Future*. New York: Knopf, 1964.

———. *The Mature Society*. New York: Praeger, 1972.

Gabriel, Ralph H. *The Course of American Democratic Thought*. New York: Ronald Press, 1940.

Gardner, John W. *Excellence: Can We Be Equal and Excellent Too?* New York: Harper & Row, 1961.

Gay, Peter. *The Dilemma of Democratic Socialism* (1952). New York: Collier Books, 1962.

_____ . *The Enlightenment: An Interpretation*. New York: Knopf, 1966.

_____ . *The Science of Freedom*. New York: Knopf, 1969.

George, Susan. *How the Other Half Dies: The Real Reason for World Hunger*. New York: Ballantine Press, 1978.

Gooch, G. P. *Studies in Diplomacy and Statecraft*. New York: Longman, Green, 1942.

Gornick, Vivian, and Moran, Barbara K., eds. *Woman in Sexist Society*. New York: Free Press, 1975.

Gouldner, Alvin. *The Coming Crisis of Western Sociology*. New York: Basic Books, 1970.

Gross, Bertram. *Social Intelligence for America's Future*. New York: Allyn & Bacon, 1970.

_____ . *Friendly Fascism: The New Face of Power in America*. New York: Evans, 1980.

Haas, Ernest B. *Beyond the Nation-State*. Stanford, Conn.: Stanford University Press, 1968.

Haller, William. *Liberty and Reformation in the Puritan Revolution*. New York: Columbia University Press, 1955.

Hamilton, Alexander; Madison, James; and Jay, John. *The Federalist*. Edited by Jacob E. Cook. Cleveland, Ohio: Meridian, 1961.

Hanson, Paul D. *The Diversity of Scripture: A Theological Interpretation*. Philadelphia, Pa.: Fortress Press, 1982.

Hardin, Garret. *Exploring New Ethics for Survival*. New York: Viking, 1972.

Harrington, James. *The Political Writings of James Harrington*. Edited by Charles Blitzer. Indianapolis, Ind.: Liberal Arts Press, 1955.

Harrington, Michael. *The Other America: Poverty in the United States*. New York: Macmillan, 1962.

_____ . *The Accidental Century*. New York: Macmillan, 1965.

_____ . *Toward a Democratic Left*. New York: Simon and Schuster, 1967.

_____ . *Socialism*. New York: Bantam Books, 1973.

_____ . *The Twilight of Capitalism* New York: Simon and Schuster, 1976.

Hartz, Louis. *The Liberal Tradition in America*. New York: Harcourt Brace, 1955.

Harvard Nuclear Study Group. *Living with Nuclear Weapons*. New York: Bantam Books, 1983

Hawken, Paul; Ogilvy, James; and Schwartz, Peter. *Seven Tomorrows*. New York: Bantam Books, 1982.

Hayek, Friedrich. *The Road to Serfdom*. Chicago: University of Chicago Press, 1944.

Heilbroner, Robert. *The Human Prospect: Updated and Reconsidered for the 1980*. Rev. ed. New York: Norton, 1982.

Herring, Pendleton. *The Politics of Democracy*. New York: Norton, 1940.

Hersh, Seymour M. *The Price of Power: Kissinger in the Nixon White House.* New York: Summit Books, 1983.

Heschel, Abraham J. *Man Is Not Alone: A Philosophy of Religion.* Philadelphia, Pa.: Jewish Publication Society, 1951.

―――― . *God in Search of Man: A Philosophy of Judaism.* Philadelphia, Pa.: Jewish Publication Society, 1956.

―――― . *The Prophets* (1962). Reprint (2 vols.). New York: Harper & Row, Torchbook Edition, 1969–71.

Hevener, Natalie Kaufman, ed. *The Dynamics of Human Rights in American Foreign Policy.* New Brunswick, N.J.: Transaction Books, 1981.

Hoffmann, Stanley. "Theory and International Relations." In *International Politics and Foreign Policy,* edited by James N. Rosenau. New York: Free Press, 1969.

―――― . *Duties beyond Borders: On the Limits and Possibilities of Ethical International Politics.* Syracuse, N.Y.: Syracuse University Press, 1981.

―――― . "The Kissinger Anti-Memoirs," *New York Times Book Review,* July 3, 1983, pp. 1, 14–17.

Hofstadter, Richard. *The American Political Tradition and the Men Who Made It.* New York: Knopf, 1948.

Holcombe, Arthur N. *Our More Perfect Union: From Eighteenth Century Principles to Twentieth Century Practices.* Cambridge: Harvard University Press, 1950.

Howard, M. C., and King, J. E. *The Political Economy of Marx.* London: Longman, 1975.

Howe, Irving, ed. *1984 Revisited: Totalitarianism in Our Century.* New York: Harper & Row, 1983.

Hunt, Gallard, ed. *The Writings of James Madison.* 9 vols. New York: Putnam's, 1900–10.

Huntington, Samuel P. *Political Order in Changing Societies.* New Haven, Conn.: Yale University Press, 1968.

―――― . *American Politics: The Promise of Disharmony.* Cambridge: Harvard University Press, 1981.

Huxley, Aldous. *Brave New World.* Garden City, N.Y.: Doubleday, 1932.

Jaeger, Werner. *Paideia: The Ideals of Great Culture.* 3 vols. New York: Oxford University Press, 1939–44.

Jensen, De Lamar, ed. *Machiavelli: Cynic, Patriot, or Political Scientist?* Boston: D. C. Heath, 1960.

Johansen, Robert C. *The National Interest and the Human Interest.* Princeton, N.J.: Princeton University Press, 1980.

Pope John XXIII. *Pacem in Terris.* 1963. In *The Papal Encyclicals 1958–1981,* pp. 107–29. Wilmington, N.C.: McGrath, 1981.

Jordon, W. K. *The Development of Toleration in England.* 4 vols. Boston: Cambridge University Press, 1933–40.

Jouvenel, Bertrand de. *The Art of Conjecture.* New York: Basic Books, 1967.

Kahn, Herman; Brown, William; and Martel, Leon. *The Next 200 Years: A Scenario for America and the World.* New York: Morrow, 1976.

Kariel, Henry S. *The Decline of American Pluralism.* Stanford, Calif.: Stanford University Press, 1961.

———. *The Promise of Politics.* Englewood Cliffs, N.J.: Prentice-Hall, 1966.

———. *Open Systems.* Itasca, Ill.: Peacock, 1969.

Kariel, Henry S., ed. *Frontiers of Democratic Theory.* New York: Random House, 1970.

Kateb, George. *Utopia and Its Enemies.* New York: Free Press, 1963.

Kennan, George F. "A Modest Proposal." *New York Review of Books,* July 16, 1981, pp. 14, 16.

———. "Reflections: Two Views of the Soviet Problem." *New Yorker,* November 2, 1981, pp. 54–62.

———. *The Nuclear Delusion: Soviet-American Relations in the Atomic Age.* New York: Pantheon, 1983.

Ketcham, Ralph. *James Madison: A Biography.* New York: Macmillan, 1971.

King, Martin Luther, Jr. *Stride Toward Freedom.* New York: Harper, 1958.

———. *Why We Can't Wait.* New York: Harper & Row, 1964.

———. *Where Do We Go From Here: Chaos or Community?* New York: Harper & Row, 1967.

Kirk, Russell. *The Conservative Mind.* Chicago: Regnery, 1953.

Kirkpatrick, Jeane J. *Dictatorships and Double Standards: Rationalism and Reason in Politics.* New York: American Enterprise, Simon and Schuster, 1982.

Koch, Adrienne. *Jefferson and Madison: The Great Collaboration.* New York: Knopf, 1950.

Kolakowski, Leszek. *Main Currents of Marxism: Its Origins, Growth and Dissolution.* 3 vols. Oxford: Oxford University Press, 1981.

Kommers, Donald P., and Loescher, Gilburt D., eds. *Human Rights and American Foreign Policy.* Notre Dame, Ind.: University of Notre Dame Press, 1979.

Lasswell, Harold J. *The Future of Political Science.* New York: Atherton, 1963.

Lichtheim, George. *Marxism: An Historical and Critical Study.* New York: Praeger, 1961.

Lindsay, A. D. *The Modern Democratic State.* London: Oxford University Press, 1943.

Lipson, Leslie. *The Democratic Civilization.* New York: Oxford University Press, 1964.

Locke, John. *Second Treatise on Civil Government* 1690. In *Two Treatises on Constitutional Government,* edited by Peter Laslett. New York: Mentor, 1965.

Loehr, William, and Powelson, John P., Jr. *Economic Development, Poverty, and Income Distribution.* Boulder, Colo.: Westview Press, 1977.

Lowenthal, Richard. "Beyond Totalitarianism." In *1984 Revisited: Totali-*

tarianism in Our Century, edited by Irving Howe. New York: Harper & Row, 1983.

Machiavelli, Niccolo. *The Prince and the Discourses* (1513). Reprint. New York: Modern Library, 1940.

Macpherson, C. B. *The Political Theory of Possessive Individualism.* Oxford: Oxford University Press. 1962.

———. *The Real World of Democracy.* Oxford: Oxford University Press, 1966.

———. *Democratic Theory: Essays in Retrieval.* Oxford: Oxford University Press, 1973.

———. *The Life and Times of Liberal Democracy.* Oxford: Oxford University Press, 1977.

Madison, James. *The Writings of James Madison.* 9 vols. New York: G. P. Putnam's Sons, 1900-10.

Manley, John. "Neopluralism: A Class Analysis of Pluralism I and Pluralism II." *American Political Science Review* 77 (June 1983): 368-83.

Mannheim, Karl. *Ideology and Utopia* (1936). New York: Harcourt Brace, Reprint 1949, p. 6., 1968.

Manuel, Frank, ed. *Utopias and Utopian Thought.* Boston: Beacon Press, 1967.

Manuel, Frank E., and Manuel, Fritzie F. *Utopian Thought in the Western World.* Cambridge: Harvard University Press, Belknap Press, 1979.

Maritain, Jacques. "The End of Machiavellianism." *Review of Politics* 4 (January 1942): 1-33.

———. *Man and the State.* Chicago: University of Chicago Press, 1951.

Maslow, Abraham H. *Toward a Psychology of Being.* New York: Van Nostrand, 1968.

Mayo, Henry B. *An Introduction to Democratic Theory.* New York: Oxford University Press, 1960.

McCoy, Charles A., and Playford, John, eds. *Apolitical Politics.* New York: Crowell, 1967.

McIlwain, Charles H. *The American Revolution: A Constitutional Interpretation.* New York: Macmillan, 1923.

———. *The Growth of Political Thought in the West.* New York: Macmillan, 1932.

———. *Constitutionalism—Ancient and Modern* (1940). Reprint. Ithaca, N.Y.: Cornell University Press, Cornell Paperbacks, 1966.

McLellan, David. *Karl Marx: His Life and Thought.* New York: Harper & Row, 1973.

Mead, Sidney E. "The Nation with the Soul of a Church." In *American Civil Religion*, edited by Russell E. Richey and Donald G. Jones. New York: Harper & Row, 1974.

Myers, Marvin. *The Mind of the Founders: Sources of the Political Thought of James Madison.* Indianapolis, Ind.: Bobbs-Merrill, 1973.

Miller, Perry. *Roger Williams: His Contribution to the American Tradition*. Indianapolis, Ind.: Bobbs-Merrill, 1953.

Mische, Gerald, and Mische, Patricia. *Toward a Human World Order: Beyond the National Security Straitjacket*. New York: Paulist Press, 1977.

Mises, Ludwig von. *Omnipotent Government*. New Haven, Conn.: Yale University Press, 1945.

Mitrany, David. *A Working Peace System: An Argument for the Functional Development of International Organization*. 4th ed. London: National Peace Council, 1946.

Molnar, Thomas. *Utopia: The Perennial Heresy*. New York: Sheed and Ward, 1967.

Morgenthau, Hans J. *Politics among Nations: The Struggle for Power and Peace*. 5th ed. New York: Knopf, 1978.

Myrdal, Gunnar. *The Challenge of World Poverty*. New York: Pantheon Books, Random House, 1970.

Newburg, Paul, ed. *U.S. Foreign Policy and Human Rights*. New York: New York University Press, 1981.

Niebuhr, Reinhold. *Moral Man and Immoral Society*. New York: Scribner's, 1932.

_____ . *The Nature and Destiny of Man*. 2 vols. 1941. New York: Scribner's, 1 vol. ed., 1949.

_____ . *The Children of Light and the Children of Darkness*. New York: Scribner's, 1944.

_____ . *The Irony of American History*. New York: Scribner's, 1954.

Nozick, Robert. *Anarchy, State, and Utopia*. New York: Basic Books, 1974.

Ophuls, William. *Ecology and the Politics of Scarcity*. San Francisco: Freeman, 1977.

Orr, David W., and Sorros, Marvis S., eds. *The Global Predicament: Ecological Perspectives on World Order*. Chapel Hill: University of North Carolina Press, 1979.

Padover, Saul K., ed. *The Complete Jefferson*. New York: Duell, Sloan and Pearce, 1943.

Palmer, R. R. *The Age of the Democratic Revolution*. Princeton, N.J.: Princeton University Press, 1959.

Parel, Anthony, ed. *The Political Calculus: Essays on Machiavelli's Philosophy*. Toronto: University of Toronto Press, 1972.

Parenti, Michael. *Democracy for the Few*. 3d ed. New York: St. Martin's Press, 1980.

Paterson, John. *The Goodly Fellowship of the Prophets*. New York: Scribner's, 1948.

Pennock, J. Roland. *Liberal Democracy: Its Merits and Prospects*. New York: Rinehart, 1950.

_____ . *Democratic Political Theory*. Princeton, N.J.: Princeton University Press, 1979.

Peterson, Merrill D. *Thomas Jefferson and the New Nation*. New York: Oxford, 1970.

Pirages, Dennis. *Global Ecopolitics: The New Context for International Relations*. North Scituate, Mass.: Duxbury Press, 1978.

Plamenatz, John. *German Marxism and Russian Communism*. London: Logman, 1954.

Plato. *The Republic*. Edited and translated by Francis M. Cornford. New York: Oxford University Press, 1951. Edited and translated by John L. Davies and David J. Vaughan. London: Macmillan, 1929.

Polak, Fred L. *The Image of the Future*. 2 vols. New York: Oceana, 1961.

―――― . *Prognostics*. New York: Elsevier, 1971.

Polishook, Irwin H. *Roger Williams, John Cotton and Religious Freedom: A Controversy in New and Old England*. Englewood Cliffs, N.J.: Prentice-Hall, 1967.

Popper, Karl. *The Open Society and Its Enemies*. Princeton, N.J.: Princeton University Press, 1945.

Powers, Jonathan. *Amnesty International: The Human Rights Story*. New York: McGraw-Hill, 1981.

Pranger, Robert J. *Eclipse of Citizenship*. New York: Holt, Rinehart and Winston, 1968.

Presthus, Robert V. *Men at the Top*. New York: Oxford University Press, 1964.

Purcell, Edward A., Jr. *The Crisis of Democratic Theory*. Lexington: University of Kentucky Press, 1973.

Richey, Russell E., and Jones, Donald G., eds. *American Civil Religion*. New York: Harper & Row, 1974.

Riemer, Neal. "Some Reflections on the Grand Inquisitor and Modern Democratic Theory." *Ethics* 67 (July 1957): 249–56.

―――― . *The Revival of Democratic Theory*. New York: Appleton-Century-Crofts, 1962.

―――― . *The Democratic Experiment*. Princeton, N.J.: Van Nostrand, 1967.

―――― . *James Madison*. New York: Washington Square Press, 1968; New York: Twayne, 1970.

―――― . "The Civil Religion in America and Prophetic Politics." *Drew Gateway* 44 (Fall 1973): 20–32.

―――― . "Creative Breakthroughs in Politics." *Political Inquiry* 2 (1974): 1–22.

―――― . "Watergate and Prophetic Politics." *Review of Politics* 36 (April 1974): 282–97.

―――― . "Beyond Marx and Niebuhr: Toward a More Prophetic Politics." *Drew Gateway* 49 (Fall 1978): 14–27.

_____ . "Covenant as a Utopian Concept." *Drew Gateway* 50 (Winter 1979): 22–31.

_____ . "Prophetic Politics: On the Political Philosophy of Stavrianos, Ferkiss and Falk." *Alternative Futures* 2 (Fall 1979): 66–82.

_____ . "Covenant and the Federal Constitution." *Publius* 10 (Fall 1980): 135–48.

_____ . "Prophetic Politics and Foreign Policy." *International Interactions* 8 (1981): 25–39.

_____ . "The Tradition of Prophetic Politics: 1776 and 1787—A Religious Model for Interpreting American Politics." *Drew Gateway* 52 (Winter 1982): 23–36.

_____ . "The Future of the Democratic Revolution: Toward a More Prophetic Politics." *Humanities in Society* 6 (Winter 1983): 5–18.

_____ . *Political Science: An Introduction to Politics.* New York: Harcourt Brace Jovanovich, 1983.

Riemer, Neal, ed. *The Representative: Trustee? Delegate? Partisan? Politico?* Lexington, Mass.: D. C. Heath, 1967.

Robertson, A. H. "Human Rights: A Global Assessment." In *Human Rights and American Foreign Policy,* edited by Donald P. Kommers and Gilburt D. Loescher. Notre Dame, Ind.: University of Notre Dame Press, 1979.

Roelofs, H. Mark. *The Tension of Citizenship.* New York: Holt, Rinehart and Winston, 1957.

Rosenau, James N., ed. *International Politics and Foreign Policy.* New York: Free Press, 1969.

Rousseau, Jean Jacques. *The Social Contract and Discourses.* Translated by G. D. H. Cole. New York: E. P. Dutton, 1946. Ch. VIII, "Civil Religion," pp. 106–15.

Sabine, George H. *A History of Political Theory.* New York: Holt, 1937.

Sakharov, Andrei. *Progress, Coexistence, and Intellectual Freedom.* New York: Norton, 1968.

Sandoz, Ellis. *Political Apocalypse: A Study of Dostoevsky's Grand Inquisitor.* Baton Rouge: Louisiana State University Press, 1971.

Sartori, Giovanni. *Democratic Theory.* Detroit, Mich.: Wayne State University Press, 1962.

Schultz, Harold S. *James Madison.* New York: Twayne, 1971.

Schumpeter, Joseph. *Capitalism, Socialism, and Democracy.* New York: Harper, 1942.

Schuster, Edward James. *Human Rights Today: Revolution or Evolution?* New York: Philosophical Library, 1981.

Scott, R. B. Y. *The Relevance of the Prophets.* Rev. ed. New York: Macmillan, 1968.

Sharp, Gene. *Exploring Nonviolent Alternatives.* Boston: Porter Sargent, 1971.

————. *The Politics of Nonviolent Alternatives*. Boston: Porter Sargent, 1973.

Shklar, Judith N. "The Political Theory of Utopia: From Melancholy to Nostalgia." In Frank E. Manuel, ed., *Utopias and Utopian Thought* (Boston: Beacon, 1965), pp. 101–15.

————. *After Utopia: The Decline of Political Faith*. Princeton, N.J.: Princeton University Press, 1957.

Simon, Julian L. *The Ultimate Resource*. Princeton, N.J.: Princeton University Press, 1981.

Simon, Yves R. *Philosophy of Democratic Government*. Chicago: University of Chicago Press, 1951.

Sivard, Ruth Leger. *World Military and Social Expenditures, 1983*. Washington, D.C.: World Priorities, 1983.

Skinner, B. F. *Walden Two*. New York: Macmillan, 1948.

————. "Some Issues Concerning the Control of Human Behavior." *Science* 124 (November 1956): 1057–60, 1064–66.

————. "Utopia and Human Behavior." In Paul Kurtz, *Moral Problems in Contemporary Society*. Englewood Cliffs, N.J.: Prentice-Hall, 1969, pp. 96–116.

————. *Beyond Freedom and Dignity*. New York: Knopf, 1971.

————. *About Behaviorism*. New York: Knopf, 1974.

Smith, James Ward. *Theme for Reason*. Princeton, N.J.: Princeton University Press, 1957.

Somit, Al, ed. *Political Science and the Study of the Future*. Hinsdale, Ill.: Dryden, 1974.

Sorauf, Frank J. "The Public Interest Reconsidered." *Journal of Politics* 19 (November 1957): 616–19.

Sprout, Harold, and Sprout, Margaret. *Toward a Politics of the Planet Earth*. Princeton, N.J.: Van Nostrand, 1971.

Stavrianos, L. S. *The Promise of the Coming Dark Age*. San Francisco: Freeman, 1976.

Talmon, A. J. *The Origins of Totalitarian Democracy*. London: Secker and Warburg, 1952.

————. *Political Messianism: The Romantic Phase*. London: Secker and Warburg, 1960.

Teilhard de Chardin, Pierre. *The Future of Man*. London: Fontana Books, 1964.

Thompson, Dennis F. *The Democratic Citizen*. London: Cambridge University Press, 1970.

Thorsen, Thomas L. *The Logic of Democracy*. New York: Holt, 1962.

Tillich, Paul. *Political Expectation*. New York: Harper & Row, 1971.

_____ . "Critique and Justification of Utopia." In Frank E. Manuel, ed., *Utopias and Utopian Thought* (Boston: Beacon Press, 1965), pp. 296–309.

Tocqueville, Alexis de. *Democracy in America.* 1835. Edited by Phillips Bradley. 2 vols. New York: Knopf, 1946.

Toffler, Alvin, ed. *The Futurists.* New York: Random House, 1972.

Truman, David B. *The Governmental Process.* New York: Knopf, 1951.

Tucker, Robert C. *Philosophy and Myth in Karl Marx.* Cambridge: At the University Press, 1961.

_____ . *The Marxian Revolutionary Idea.* 1969. New York: Norton, 1970.

Tucker, Robert C., ed. *The Marx-Engels Reader.* New York: W. W. Norton, 1972.

Ulam, Adam. "Socialism and Utopia." In Frank E. Manuel, ed., *Utopias and Utopian Thought* (Boston: Beacon Press, 1967), pp. 116–34.

U.S., Department of State. *Country Reports on Human Rights Practices.* Washington, D.C.: Government Printing Office, yearly.

Van Dyke, Vernon. *Human Rights, the United States, and the World Community.* New York: Oxford University Press, 1970.

Villari, Pasquale. *The Life and Times of Niccolo Machiavelli.* 2 vols. London: Ernest Benn, 1919.

Vogelin, Eric. *Order and History: Israel and Revelation.* Baton Rouge: Louisiana State University Press, 1956.

Von Rad, Gerhard. *The Message of the Prophets.* New York: Harper & Row, 1967.

Wager, Warren W. *The City of Man.* Boston: Houghton Mifflin, 1963.

_____ . *Building the City of Man.* New York: Grossman, 1971.

Ward, Barbara, and Dubos, Rene. *Only One Earth.* New York: Norton, 1972.

Wheeler, Harvey. *Democracy in a Revolutionary Era.* New York: Praeger, 1968.

Wolff, Robert Paul; Moroe, Barrington, Jr.; and Marcuse, Herbert. *A Critique of Pure Tolerance.* Boston: Beacon Press, 1965, reprint ed., 1969.

Wolin, Sheldon. *Politics and Vision.* Boston: Little, Brown, 1960.

Wood, Neal, ed. *Machiavelli's The Art of War.* Revision of Ellis Farneworth's translation. New York: Library of the Liberal Arts, 1965.

Index

revolution, 7, 30, 31, 35, 36, 38,
    41, 42, 43, 44, 50, 51, 84,
    147, 150, 175, 179–80, 219,
    226, 230, 248–9
Richey, Russell, E., 270n
Riemer, Neal, 255n, 256n, 257n,
    259n, 263n, 265n, 266n,
    267n, 268n, 269n, 270n,
    271n, 272n, 273n, 274n,
    276n, 277n; and democratic
    experiment, 2; and revival
    of democratic theory, 1–4
right-wing authoritarianism, and
    economic well-being, 180
risk, 3, 117, 170, 199
Robertson, A. H., 272n
Rosenau, James N., 255n
Rousseau, Jean Jacques, 109,
    111, 141, 270n

Sabine, George H., 271n
Sakharov, Andrei P., 275n
Sandoz, Ellis, 260
Sartori, Giovanni, 265n
scarcity, 193
scenarios, 226, 249–51; authori-
    tarian, 201, 202, 202–3;
    catastrophic, 201–2; format
    for, 199–200; futuristic,
    198–210; questions, 207–10;
    status quo, 200–1; and pro-
    phetic politics, 203, 249–51;
    world order, 204, 205–9
Schultz, Harold S., 273n
Schumpeter, Joseph A., 266n
Schuster, Edward James, 274n
Schwartz, Peter, 275n
Science, 31, 36, 111–4, 193, 199,
    214, 215, 224, 226, 230,
    233, 234, 261n; as Big

Brother, 2–3; and ecology,
    187; and social scientific
    criticism, 119–35, 235–41;
    and technological fix, 127,
    128, 187, 191; and utopian
    politics, 35–40, 46, 53, 55–6
Second World, 121, 178 (*see also*
    Soviet Union)
separation of church and state,
    147
sexism, 64, 84, 85, 108, 123,
    124–5, 176, 209, 218
Sharp, Gene, 275n
Shklar, Judith N., 264n
Simon, Julian L., 272n, 275n
Sivard, Ruth Leger, 272n, 274n
Skinner, B. F., 29, 31, 34–5,
    39–40, 50, 51, 53, 56, 116,
    258n, 259n, 261n, 263n;
    and judgment, 46–7; and
    science, 39–40; utopian
    strengths, 49–50; utopian
    weaknesses, 50–1, 52, 53,
    56, 57; and vision, 34–5
Social Security Act, 138
Socialism, 30, 63, 84, 128, 181,
    190
Socrates, 259n–60n, 261n
Sorauf, Frank J., 267n
Sorros, Marvis S., 275
South Africa, 126
sovereign-state system, 20, 121–2
    (*see also* nationalism and
    nation-state)
Soviet Union, 5, 6, 30, 122, 124,
    148, 166, 171, 172, 174,
    178, 179, 183, 225
Spain, 173, 251
Stalin, Joseph, 5, 54, 62, 123
Stavrianos, L. S., 275n, 276n

About the Author

Neal Riemer is Andrew V. Stout Professor of Political Philosophy, Department of Political Science, Drew University. He received his B.A. (1943) from Clark University, and—after three years of military service in World War II—his M.A. (1947) and Ph.D. (1949) from Harvard University. Dr. Riemer's main teaching and research interests lie in the area of political theory, especially American and modern democratic theory. His books include *Political Science: An Introduction to Politics* (New York: Harcourt Brace Jovanovich, 1983); *James Madison* (New York: Washington Square Press, 1968; New York: Twayne, 1970); *The Representative: Trustee? Delegate? Partisan? Politico?* (Lexington, Mass.: D. C. Heath, 1967); *The Democratic Experiment* (Princeton, N.J.: Van Nostrand, 1967); *The Revival of Democratic Theory* (New York: Appleton-Century-Crofts, 1962); *World Affairs: Problems and Prospects* (New York: Appleton-Century-Crofts, 1957) (coauthor); and *Problems of American Government* (New York: McGraw-Hill, 1952). He is currently engaged in exploring the theme of "Political Health."